Digital HR

This book explores the impact of technology on Human Resource (HR) practices and how organisations can effectively incorporate progress in technology to improve HR processes. **Digital HR** provides a comprehensive overview of the various advancements that are transforming HR, including artificial intelligence (AI), machine learning, big data, and blockchain. It provides real-world examples, case studies, and best practices that illustrate how organisations are successfully leveraging technology to improve their HR management (HRM) processes and outcomes. This practical orientation makes the book valuable for professionals and scholars who are interested or have actionable insights to implement technologies for HR transformation and performance improvement in their organisations.

- Offers case studies, best practices, and real-world examples of successful and unsuccessful HR transformation initiatives.
- Illustrates the technological progress transforming HR, including AI, machine learning, big data, and blockchain – HR Software Solutions.
- Discusses challenges associated with adapting and implementing them in the various practices and processes of HRM.
- Studies different applications of AI and machine learning in HR, including talent acquisition, performance management, and employee engagement end-to-end technology implementation in their domain.

This book is intended for professionals, managers, and executives seeking an understanding of the impact of technology on the workforce and how they can leverage it to achieve their goals. It will also be useful for scholars and researchers interested in digital HR from the fields of computer science, business management, human resources, and HRM.

Artificial Intelligence, Machine Learning, Data Analytics and Automation for Business Management

Series Editor – Rajesh Dey, Senior Commissioning Editor, CRC Press, Taylor & Francis Group

The series presents a comprehensive exploration of how organisations strategically leverage technology to achieve their goals and maintain competitiveness in rapidly evolving industries. With contributions from experts across multiple disciplines, including computer science, business management, and data science, the series adopts an interdisciplinary approach, offering diverse perspectives and fostering cross-functional collaboration.

Predictive Analytics and Generative AI for Data-Driven Marketing Strategies
Hemachandran K, Debdutta Choudhury, Raul Villamarin Rodriguez, Jorge A. Wise, Revathi T

Digital HR: Technologies for HR Transformation and Performance Improvement
Deepa Gupta, Mukul Gupta, Balamurugan Balusamy, Rajesh Kumar Dhanaraj, and Parth Mukul Gupta

For more information about this series, please visit: https://www.routledge.com/Artificial-Intelligence-Machine-Learning-Data-Analytics-and-Automation/book-series/AIBM

Digital HR

Technologies for HR Transformation and Performance Improvement

Edited by
Deepa Gupta, Mukul Gupta,
Balamurugan Balusamy, Rajesh Kumar Dhanaraj,
and Parth Mukul Gupta

CRC Press
Taylor & Francis Group
Boca Raton London New York

CRC Press is an imprint of the
Taylor & Francis Group, an **informa** business
A CHAPMAN & HALL BOOK

Front cover image: Alexander Supertramp/ShutterStock

First edition published 2025
by CRC Press
2385 NW Executive Center Drive, Suite 320, Boca Raton FL 33431

and by CRC Press
4 Park Square, Milton Park, Abingdon, Oxon, OX14 4RN

CRC Press is an imprint of Taylor & Francis Group, LLC

ISBN: 978-1-032-61962-0 (hbk)
ISBN: 978-1-032-61964-4 (pbk)
ISBN: 978-1-032-61965-1 (ebk)

DOI: 10.1201/9781032619651

Typeset in Times
by codeMantra

Contents

Preface....vii
About the Editors....ix
List of Contributors....xi

Chapter 1 AI-Powered Metaverse: A New-Age Strategic Tool for Ushering Revolution in the HR Domain....1

Anjali Sharma, Ankita Goyal, and Ashish Kumar Sharma

Chapter 2 Unlocking the Talent Acquisition Potential: AI-Driven Recruitment Strategies....9

Deepa Gupta, Mukul Gupta, Parul Gupta, and Sudhakar Porwal

Chapter 3 Gamification and Virtual Reality for Effective Employee Training and Development....31

Swati Rai, Rakesh Kumar Yadav, and Mukul Gupta

Chapter 4 Exploring Blockchain Applications and Challenges in HR Management....45

Gagan Deep and Jyoti Verma

Chapter 5 Blockchain Smart Contracts in Human Resource Management: Application, Implementation Challenges, and Research Agenda....64

Joshy Mathew, Akansha Mer, and Farha Khan

Chapter 6 Robotics' Place in HR: Developments, Trends, and Effects....89

Shabana Azami and Deepa Gupta

Chapter 7 A Study of Ethical, Social and Legal Implications of Emerging Technologies in HRM....97

Himani Grewal, Aditi Vishnoi, Avinash Saxena, and Mukul Gupta

Chapter 8 Revolutionizing Workforce Management: The Future of HRM in the Digital Era....106

Mukul Gupta, Deepa Gupta, Nitin Agrawal, and Parth Mukul Gupta

Chapter 9 Promotion Decision Process in Private Company Using Neutrosophic Fermatean Similarity Measures................................. 128

R. Narmada Devi, Yamini Parthiban, Nagadevi Bala Nagaram, and Kala Raja Mohan

Chapter 10 Transforming Performance Management System (PMS): Influence of Digitalization.. 137

Preeti Malhotra, Deepa Gupta, and Rajesh Kumar Dhanaraj

Chapter 11 HR Process Automation: Current State and Future Directions....... 147

Rakesh Kumar Dixit, Pushpendra Pal Singh, and Balamurugan Balusamy

Chapter 12 The Intersection of Technology and Social Science: Transforming HR Functions and Shaping Futuristic Trends........... 163

Neha Aggarwal and Kriti Bhaswar Singh

Chapter 13 Building the HR Function of the Future: Technology and Beyond... 174

Deepa Gupta, Mukul Gupta, Rajesh Kumar Dhanaraj, and Parth Mukul Gupta

Chapter 14 A Comprehensive Analysis of the Literature on HR Factors for Industry 4.0 Adoption Success.. 192

Sanjana Kaushik, Deepa Gupta, and Mukul Gupta

Index...207

Preface

Human Resources (HR) has started an amazing trip of change in the modern period, when fast technology development shapes every aspect of human endeavour. The junction of HR operations with digital innovation has resulted not just in little adjustments but also in a basic transformation in how companies handle, interact with, and empower their employees. Examining the many, new technologies transforming HR practices and changing the fabric of workforce management, this book, *Digital HR: Technologies for HR Transformation and Performance Improvement*, explores these paradigm changes.

The path of creating this extensive collection has been motivated by the conviction that academics, business leaders, and HR experts have to be conversant with the dynamic junction of technology and human capital management. The chapters in this book methodically offer a thorough investigation of innovative technologies that could maximise HR procedures and improve organisational performance.

Chapter 1 opens readers to the transforming power of immersive, AI-driven virtual environments in reshaping HR strategies. Chapter 2 keeps disentangling AI-driven recruiting practices, showing how AI has transformed talent acquisition into a game-changer improving accuracy and efficiency.

Chapters 3 explores the application of interesting, interactive technology to propel significant learning opportunities, thereby promoting a culture of ongoing growth. As we move further, Chapters 4 and 5 clarify the uses and difficulties of blockchain technology, covering the exciting but complicated field of smart contracts in HR management, thereby providing an understanding of implementation tactics and future research direction.

Chapter 6's forward-looking study of changes, trends, and their impact on human resources centres robotics and its ramifications for HR procedures. Understanding the ethical, social, and legal ramifications of these developments, Chapter 7 looks at how new technologies subvert accepted wisdom and demand strong laws and strategic control.

Turning now to more general consequences, Chapter 8 sees labour management in a time marked by digital tools and approaches shaping itself. This book then explores data-driven, algorithmic decision-making in Chapter 9 using fresh approaches such as neutrosophic Fermatean similarity metrics for informed promotion decisions.

Emphasising how digitising is improving openness and objectivity, Chapter 10 shows the significant influence of digital technologies on performance management systems (PMS). Readers of Chapter 11 will have a thorough view of the present situation and future trends for HR process automation, which is now absolutely essential for organisational agility.

Chapter 12 addresses the confluence of technical and social scientific viewpoints, thereby bridging the gap between technology and human-centred practices and investigating their part in changing HR roles and future developments. Focussing on developing future, technologically driven HR services and analysing HR elements essential for the effective adoption of Industry 4.0, this book ends with strategic and scholarly evaluations in Chapters 13 and 14.

This book aims to be a vital tool for HR managers, corporate executives, academics, and students ready to grasp and use the creative techniques defining HR practices for decades to come. It provides evidence of the progress achieved and a road map for negotiating the terrain of always-changing digital HR.

May this book inspire and provide you the expertise to fully use technology in promoting HR excellence and sustainable performance enhancement as you flip the pages.

The Authors

About the Editors

Dr. Deepa Gupta is a distinguished academician with over 25 years of experience in management studies, serving as Dean at GL Bajaj Institute of Management, Greater Noida. Her expertise covers organisational development, corporate relations, and international collaborations, which are essential for advancing digital HR. Her doctoral research, global academic exposure, and role in corporate connections support her understanding of AI, ML, and digital practices in HRM. Recognised with 22 national and international awards for her contributions, she exemplifies innovation and excellence in academic leadership. She has authored books such as *HR Analytics, Rural Marketing Management.* and *Research Methodology*, published 15 patents, and contributed to over 45 research papers.

Dr. Mukul Gupta, Principal at GL Bajaj Institute of Management, has over 25 years of experience in teaching and the corporate sector. Holding a Doctorate in Consumer Behaviour, he is an active researcher in Consumer and Human Behavioural Analytics, with 12 national/international patents, over 40 research papers, and books like *HR Analytics*, *Research Methodology*, and *Rural Marketing Management.* He has led various professional development programmes and is part of multiple academic and professional bodies. His expertise in consumer behaviour provides valuable insights into user behaviour and AI-driven system interactions, while his leadership and extensive publications enhance management education, human analytics, and digital HR.

Dr. Balamurugan Balusamy, Associate Dean Student at Shiv Nadar University, Delhi-NCR, has extensive experience in engineering education, blockchain, and data sciences. With 14 years as a faculty member at global universities like VIT, he has over 200 publications in reputed journals and more than 80 authored books. He collaborates with global experts, serves on start-up advisory committees, and consults on Industrial IoT. His academic and publication record highlights the significance of technological advancements in HR, showcasing his ability to connect research with practical applications in HR and IT, particularly in blockchain and digitalisation.

Dr. Rajesh Kumar Dhanaraj, Professor at Symbiosis International (Deemed University), Pune, holds a Ph.D. in computer science from Anna University. His research focuses on machine learning, cyber-physical systems, and wireless sensor networks. A Senior IEEE Member and Expert Advisory Panel Member at Texas Instruments Inc., USA, Dr. Dhanaraj has authored/edited 25+ books, holds 21 patents, and published over 53 papers. His expertise supports advancements in computational intelligence and digital HR technologies, showcasing his influence and commitment to technological progress.

Parth Mukul Gupta, Director at Zarthcorp Tech Pvt. Ltd., Greater Noida, is an innovative entrepreneur and experienced technocrat known for his work in institution building, brand development, corporate relations, and growth strategies. He has transformed HR practices by implementing e-HR, HRIS, and predictive analytics, enhancing employee experience and performance prediction. He has coached HR professionals on using technology effectively and has driven organisational transformation across people, processes, strategy, structure, and technology.

List of Contributors

Neha Aggarwal
Central University of Jharkhand
Jharkhand, Ranchi, India

Nitin Agrawal
Semikron Danfoss
Utica, New York, USA

Shabana Azami
Department of Management
Galgotias University
Greater Noida, India

Balamurugan Balusamy
Shiv Nadar University
Greater Noida, India

Gagan Deep
Department of Management
Chitkara Business School, Chitkara University
Rajpura, Punjab, India

R. Narmada Devi
Department of Mathematics
Vel Tech Rangarajan Dr. Sagunthala R&D Institute of Science and Technology
Avadi, Chennai, Tamil Nadu, India

Rajesh Kumar Dhanaraj
Symbiosis International (Deemed University)
Pune, Maharashtra, India

Rakesh Kumar Dixit
Department of Management
G.L. Bajaj Institute of Management
Greater Noida, Uttar Pradesh, India

Ankita Goyal
Department of Management
Mody University of Science and Technology
Lakshmangarh, Rajasthan, India

Himani Grewal
Department of Management studies
Moradabad Institute of Technology
Moradabad, Uttar Pradesh, India

Deepa Gupta
Department of Management
GL Bajaj Institute of Management
Greater Noida, Uttar Pradesh, India

Mukul Gupta
Department of Management Studies
GL Bajaj Institute of Management
Greater Noida, Uttar Pradesh, India

Parth Mukul Gupta
Department of Engineering
Birla Institute of Technology & Sciences
Pilani, Rajasthan, India

Parul Gupta
Utica National Insurance Group
New Hartford, New York, USA

Sanjana Kaushik
Satyug Darshan College of Engineering & Technology
Faridabad, Haryana, India

Farha Khan
Department of Management
Graphic Era Hill University
Bhimtal, Uttarakhand, India

Preeti Malhotra
GD Goenka University
Gurugram, Haryana, India

Joshy Mathew
University of Technology & Applied Sciences
Al Musanna, Oman

Akansha Mer
Department of Commerce and Management
Banasthali Vidyapith
Tonk, Rajasthan, India

Kala Raja Mohan
Department of Mathematics
Panimalar Engineering College
Chennai, Tamil Nadu, India

Nagadevi Bala Nagaram
Department of Mathematics
Vel Tech Rangarajan Dr. Sagunthala R&D Institute of Science and Technology
Avadi, Chennai, Tamil Nadu, India

Yamini Parthiban
Department of Mathematics
Vel Tech Rangarajan Dr. Sagunthala R&D Institute of Science and Technology
Avadi, Chennai, Tamil Nadu, India

Sudhakar Porwal
Thales
Delhi, India

Swati Rai
Department of Management Studies
IFTM University
Moradabad, Uttar Pradesh, India

Avinash Saxena
Department of Management studies
Moradabad Institute of Technology
Moradabad, Uttar Pradesh, India

Anjali Sharma
Department of Law
Mody University of Science and Technology
Lakshmangarh, Rajasthan, India

Ashish Kumar Sharma
Department of Management
Mody University of Science and Technology
Lakshmangarh, Rajasthan, India

Kriti Bhaswar Singh
Central University of Jharkhand
Jharkhand, Ranchi, India

Pushpendra Pal Singh
Department of Mathematics
G.L. Bajaj Institute of Management
Greater Noida, Uttar Pradesh, India

Jyoti Verma
Department of Management
Chitkara Business School, Chitkara University
Rajpura, Punjab, India

Aditi Vishnoi
Department of Management studies
Moradabad Institute of Technology
Moradabad, Uttar Pradesh, India

Rakesh Kumar Yadav
Department of Management Studies
IFTM University
Moradabad, Uttar Pradesh, India

1 AI-Powered Metaverse
A New-Age Strategic Tool for Ushering Revolution in the HR Domain

Anjali Sharma, Ankita Goyal, and Ashish Kumar Sharma

1.1 INTRODUCTION

Today, the term "metaverse" is omnipresent and becoming more and more popular with every passing day. Almost everyone is on board with the notion once they comprehend it. Even the young children can acquire, interpret, and contextualize information with ease and efficiency that no Artificial Intelligence (AI)-powered computer can match to this day (Daugherty & Wilson, 2022). The metaverse is a dynamic, three-dimensional digital environment that enables lifelike online personal and professional encounters through the use of modern technologies such as Virtual Reality (VR), Augmented Reality (AR), and other cutting-edge technological tools.

Individuals interpret the metaverse in different ways. Some people view it as a social media playground. Others speculate that it might be used as a commercial area for clients and businesses. The best way to describe the metaverse is as an evolution of the contemporary internet—something we actively engage in as opposed to something we mostly observe. In order to broaden and integrate their applications, this is the merging of multiple digital technologies, including Bitcoin, AI, AR, VR, and others. In addition, the "enterprise metaverse" might come together to explore more opportunities than its current role as an online chat platform. The entire metaverse vision includes seamless interoperability between platforms and devices, simultaneous interaction of thousands of users, and applications beyond games. Numerous elements are part of the metaverse (Figure 1.1):

All these elements connect with each other in their own way, making our lives better and enjoyable.

1.2 EXPERIENCING THE METAVERSE

The use of virtual interactions has accelerated the epidemic; the metaverse aims to close the trade gap between the actual and virtual worlds. In the emerging fashion and retail metaverse, brands are already launching games, online events, and retail storefronts.

DOI: 10.1201/9781032619651-1

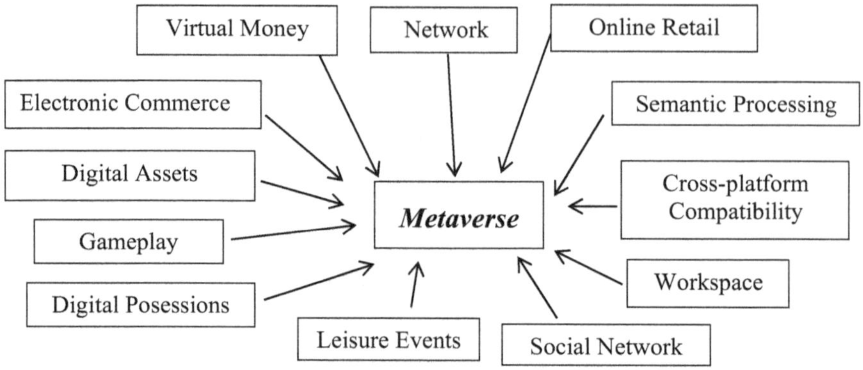

FIGURE 1.1 Elements of the metaverse.

The future metaverse will most likely be much larger. Numerous technologies, customs, standards, and monetization models will shift with the advent of 3D environments and graphics-based computers. Additionally, it can have a lasting impact. There is going to be a big generational change. Most significantly, it will impact many of the categories that, despite our long-held beliefs, have not changed as a result of the revolution brought by the internet and the mobile revolution.

Some businesses are already making use of the metaverse in their processes. Below are some real-world examples:

- Entertainment house Lil Nas X presented a virtual show on an online gaming site named Roblox during the COVID pandemic (Daire, 2020).
- As we move more and more toward virtual worlds and teamwork, commerce is changing. A McKinsey poll indicates that more than three-fourths of the users of the metaverse have bought something or the other online just to enhance their experience during online transactions. Virtual world trades are frequent, as exemplified by the purchase of V-Bucks by a Fortnight player for in-game items. In order to explore the virtual environments and Non-Fungible Tokens (NFTs), consumers can scan card packs including Quick Response (QR) codes created by the toy manufacturer L.O.L Surprise! (Value Creation in the Metaverse, 2022).
- According to reports, AR screens were used at Johns Hopkins Hospital to perform operations on actual patients, making it possible for the Neurosurgical Spine Center to do tasks more successfully than before (Witham, 2021).
- Instead of creating a paper-mâché replica of a volcano, consider having the ability to actually experience being the lava that is released into the sky. Education providers are developing resources and courses that offer one additional pedagogical tool for the teachers to teach and engage with their students. VR is being used across various industries to assist individuals in gaining knowledge and learning novel skills, including maintaining heavy vehicles and other equipment, and in certain circumstances, this leads to

a significant decrease in the training time required. Moreover, businesses may find it much more intriguing to leverage the data produced by this process when they start using AR for remote help in field operations.

Although launched a few years back, NFTs are a new investment option in the financial services sector. More research is beginning to be done in this area, and some people are asserting that NFTs can be used as collateral against loans. The usage of the metaverse cannot be ignored in developing more productive and successful procedures. Consider Bayerische Motoren Werke (BMW) as an example. The company's all-electric automobile production line functioned like a simulation for half a year. Before the final manufacturing layout was determined, one-to-one scale virtual cars had to be constructed.

1.3 THE VIRTUAL WORLD OF METAVERSE

Components like Constructive Solid Geometry (CSG), voxel, and G-Rep are now part of the metaverse design tools, offering 3D-based design processes that extend beyond the Computer-Aided Design (CAD) realm. Rather than utilizing a mouse and keyboard, architects can create 3D models by manipulating and sculpting them with haptic and kinesthetic instruments. The computer sector is seeing a number of new activities brought about by this technology, including task management, scheduling, and planning. Giants in the IT industry are competing to offer the best virtual environment experience, demonstrating how things will be displayed in the metaverse of the future. Table 1.1 indicates the main parts of which the metaverse is composed. Conversely, rendering, scenario creation, and technical techniques make up this virtual environment's operating components.

Apps and user interaction are essential to preserving the stability of the metaverse. Multimodal input/output operability interpretation requires a computational infrastructure with high performance. To maintain a high level of service, the metaverse requires a lot of network bandwidth, cyber defense, and fault-correction. There are numerous metaverse activities pertaining to development (Table 1.2). It describes how architects and designers can model metaverse elements after real-world artifacts. Here are the six main subfields that were used to construct the metaverse architecture. Each process is a tiny production system used to create the assets of this virtual area.

TABLE 1.1
The Main Parts of the Metaverse

Metaverse						
Detectors	Validation	Interpretation	Context Development	Interaction Design	Systematic Processes	Software Programs

TABLE 1.2
Metaverse Development Activities

Level	Metaverse Development Activities
1	Recognizing elements in the tangible world
2	Creating elements to simulate digital entities
3	Grouping items within collections
4	Categorizing identical items within a set
5	Associating objects with the digital environment
6	Simulating the interaction of objects within the digital environment

1.4 HUMAN-CENTRIC METAVERSE

The notion that AI research and development should be morally righteous and helpful to people is highly valued in the Human-centric AI (HAI) Human-centric AI concept. An aquatic, human-centered future social ecology is called the metaverse. The metaverse unifies virtual and actual worlds.

By using "digital clones," people can explore a virtual world without being limited by time or place, create the experience, and reap value—dramatically expanding the possibilities for human discovery. As a result, we can assume that humans are at the center of the metaverse.

One of the elements of the metaverse is absorption, indicating that its purpose is to meet people's emotional needs. If the metaverse is ever used, it will be crucial to provide users with a feeling of immersion so they can enjoy themselves, meet new people, discover new things, and get experience in the real world, just like they would in the real world. Customers will be encouraged to invest time and energy in the metaverse.

1. Human Aspects: Human-centered design (HCM) refers to a version of the metaverse that is governed by people, not by businesses. The interests of everyone are served in the metaverse, not only those of individuals or groups involved in system development. Put another way, the human-centric metaverse is one in which the promotion of human progress and happiness is viewed as the guiding principle and the realization of human worth is a prerequisite for the realization and sustainable development of the metaverse.
2. Technical Considerations: The organic synthesis of several human-centered technologies is known as HCM. The metaverse needs to develop into a location that can be explored for all time if it is to be the ultimate medium. Therefore, for the metaverse to provide a true social life, a low-latency network, and a rich sensory experience, multiple technologies are required. When the service is offered to each and everybody, the expenses must also be reduced. Operational workflows and value generation across virtual workplaces can be optimized using text mining and analytics, data visualization tools, behavioral algorithms, cognitive computing systems, and metaverse technologies (Carter, 2022).

3. Real-World Applications: The HCM application mode embraces VR but puts a lot of focus on reality. It's not an imaginary universe set apart from the real world. HCM sees the potential to create virtual environments as a tool to help people achieve many unthinkable experiences in the real world. In many real-world application scenarios involving HCM, humans are the principal body.
4. Ethical Considerations: HCM creates an ethical and responsible metaverse by fusing effective development processes, interdisciplinary approaches, and other approaches. It also leverages meaningful human control to uphold human rights and interests in areas such as ethics, human privacy, human decision-making power, and fairness in order to establish a human-centric metaverse.

1.5 METAVERSE IN HR

Even though Zoom calls still make up the majority of remote work, many businesses haven't fully embraced it. However, some businesses, mostly in the tech sector, are already making big moves toward shifting to a work style that will be defined by more authentic remote collaboration and possibly even the metaverse.

The metaverse is reshaping our workplace, and Human Resources (HR) leaders ought to be leading this change, but there could be serious consequences. HR directors need to ensure that people are taken into consideration when designing the future of work and that they have access to the resources and expertise required to make this change. Various HR practitioners believe that many theoretical and practical aspects of HR issues related to the metaverse are not covered yet (Lim, Lee, & Park, 2023).

Big computing companies are making significant investments in metaverse technologies, some of which are specifically targeted at promoting collaboration in the workplace. These companies include Apple, Microsoft, Google, and Meta (previously Facebook). Teams can work together in the same virtual environment, for example, using Microsoft's Mesh and Meta's Horizon Workrooms—both of which use VR technology—regardless of each person's actual location.

1.6 METAVERSE AT THE WORKPLACE

As the metaverse penetrates our organizations, HR can take on greater leadership and ownership roles. By integrating workplace technologies, firms can optimize employee productivity and virtual team performance by utilizing virtual avatars in immersive work environments (Zvarikova, Chug, & Hamilton, 2022). Here are three potential effects of the metaverse on HR, as well as potential future effects on our workplaces from HR.

1. **Equity in a Modern, Digital Workplace**

   A metaverse-based workspace enables the construction of a more equitable workplace. But the globalization the metaverse enables will probably draw attention to the disparities that exist now. This will present several challenges for HR professionals to overcome:

- Technophobia vs. Tech-Savviness: While many older workers would not be able to adapt to working in a metaverse, younger workers will most likely feel more at ease there.
- Bandwidth Requirements That Could Draw Attention to Inequity: A metaverse requires more internet capacity, and less-developed areas usually have fewer affordable options.
- Workplace Safety, Well-Being, and Inclusivity: The metaverse will still be a place of employment even though most interactions will occur between avatars. Businesses need to keep treating diversity, inclusion, and belonging seriously when it comes to their workforce. Therefore, HR experts will need to decide how to precisely manage harassment and other unwanted behavior in order to prevent it in this virtual setting. Determining what behavior in the metaverse qualifies as such, including those definitions in your workplace policies, and providing staff with training on it would be an acceptable starting point.

2. Establishing a Successful, Collaborative Workplace

Everyone knows that a room's layout influences how users use it. A rectangular table places the boss in the center, while a round table promotes conversation. Without the limitations of the real world, a creative, cooperative, and productive work atmosphere can be reimagined, thanks to the metaverse.

The new way of working in the metaverse may broaden the meaning of hybrid work. Thanks to this technology, workers can collaborate from a distance and engage in more sincere and organic interactions. One day, a physical office and a virtual workspace might combine.

HR departments need to set up the metaverse in their companies to increase output. With the virtual architecture of the metaverse, we can design workspaces that support teamwork, creativity, decision-making, entertainment, or any combination of these. This lets us go beyond the traditional, usually boring office environment.

HR plays a crucial role in helping companies, their departments, teams, and management figure out how best to use technology. They will be required to design new hybrid working policies and teach leaders how to lead in this new environment in order to ensure wholesome metaverse working procedures.

3. Hiring Practices Are Expected to Happen with the Metaverse

The metaverse may help HR specialists in their work. Currently, a lot of companies are testing the usage of the metaverse in hiring. For example, the Korean electronics company Samsung hosted a virtual employment fair, while the car manufacturer Hyundai used the metaverse for new hire on boarding. The UK PwC office uses technology in hiring; it created the metaverse platform Virtual Park for conducting job interviews. Similarly, Human Resources Departments may be able to use the metaverse to better integrate remote workers. Relevant training sessions may be conducted for such employees in the areas of 3D models and role-play.

The technology that can bring humanity into the metaverse era is already widely available in the market. Here are some instances of both what HR might look like in the metaverse and how it might be used in the real world:

1. Giving prospective applicants the best virtual experience possible
2. Creating a work environment that is both immersive and detached
3. A better and quicker educational experience
4. Establishing a safe and friendly work environment
5. Creating a cooperative and fruitful work atmosphere

Many recent discussions in the body of research come to the conclusion that hybrid working promotes high levels of well-being, productivity, and mental health among employees. While some labor kinds may be completed in the metaverse, not all work types can be completed there (Adhiatma, Nurhidayati, & Fachrunnisa, 2023).

1.7 CONCLUSION

People in leadership roles in Human Resources are particularly talking about the metaverse at virtual water coolers right now. Individuals want to know what it is, how it will impact HR and other areas of the business and life, and if they should believe the hype. Some people are starting to doubt the validity of this "world" created with VR in light of Meta's layoffs. The parent business of Facebook, Meta, has made significant investments in the metaverse.

A few individuals have made the link between Second Life (SL), a virtual world that attracted a lot of investors in the early 2000s, and the metaverse. SL never managed to meet the high standards set by its audience. In the current scenario, the quality of this interaction has really been enhanced in a big way by the use of VR. By extending their limbs, people wearing VR eyewear will be able to shake hands with colleagues. To have a private discussion, they can "walk" to a different area of the virtual room.

HR specialists must fully utilize metaverse in the most optimum manner to take benefit of all the resulting opportunities. However, they should be interested in it, have a healthy skepticism about it, and proceed cautiously before making a significant investment without first doing some research.

Facebook's decision to rebrand itself as Meta should indicate how the prominent business firms in the field of technology see the evolution of online communication in the future. The idea of an online metaverse—a parallel reality—is becoming more and more well-liked. The distinction between the real world and the virtual world is becoming blurred.

The study comes to the conclusion that it will take a lot of time for businesses operating in the Indian market to completely integrate metaverse because it will involve training each individual who intends to contact with the technology, including employers, employees, and executives. HR specialists must prepare them for the technologies of the metaverse and ensure that they continue to operate in the same way that they do now.

REFERENCES

Adhiatma, A., Nurhidayati, & Fachrunnisa, O. (2023). Issues and Challenges when Metaverse Replaces the Workplace. In *Conference on Complex, Intelligent, and Software Intensive Systems*, Toronto, Ontario, Canada, *176*, pp. 243–249.

Carter, D. (2022). Immersive Employee Experiences in the Metaverse: Virtual Work Environments, Augmented Analytics Tools, and Sensory and Tracking Technologies. *Psychosociological Issues in Human Resource Management, 10*(1), 35–49.

Daire, B. (2020, November 16). *Here's Roblox's Full Lil Nas X Concert.* Retrieved December 15, 2023, from https://gamerant.com/roblox-lil-nas-x-concert-replay-video/#:~:text=The%20Lil%20Nas%20X%20Roblox,X%20branded%20in%2Dgame%20items.

Daugherty, P. R., & Wilson, H. J. (2022). *Radically Human - How New Technology Is Transforming Business and Shaping Our Future.* Harvard Business Review Press.

Lim, D. H., Lee, J. Y., & Park, S. (2023). The Metaverse in the Workplace: Possibilities and Implications for Human Resource Development. *Human Resource Development Review, 23*(2), 164–198.

McKinsey & Company (2022). *Value Creation in the Metaverse.* Retrieved November 27, 2023, from https://www.mckinsey.com/~/media/mckinsey/business%20functions/marketing%20and%20sales/our%20insights/value%20creation%20in%20the%20metaverse/Value-creation-in-the-metaverse.pdf

Witham, T. (2021, February 16). Johns Hopkins Performs Its First Augmented Reality Surgeries in Patients. Retrieved November 16, 2023, from https://www.hopkinsmedicine.org/news/articles/2021/02/johns-hopkins-performs-its-first-augmented-reality-surgeries-in-patients

Zvarikova, K., Chug, J., & Hamilton, S. (2022). Virtual Human Resource Management in the Metaverse: Immersive Work Environments, Data Visualization Tools and Algorithms, and Behavioural Analytics. *Psychosociological Issues in Human Resource Management, 10*(1), 7–20.

2 Unlocking the Talent Acquisition Potential

AI-Driven Recruitment Strategies

Deepa Gupta, Mukul Gupta, Parul Gupta, and Sudhakar Porwal

2.1 INTRODUCTION: AI IN RECRUITMENT

Driven for the most part by technology, the employing system has changed fundamentally in the quick changing professional workplace of today [24]. However, key, customary employing methods now and again find it challenging to address the issues of contemporary organizations. These methodologies can be tedious, one-sided, and costly and cause failures that can hinder an organization's ability to draw and keep the best individuals [5].

Presently enters artificial intelligence (AI), revolutionizing the field of talent procurement [33]. The consolidation of AI into selection processes has begun to tackle a considerable lot of the issues related to customary recruiting techniques [6]. Organizations might assist their employing endeavors by utilizing AI, thus working on the exactness, speed, and adaptability of the interaction [8].

Through computerization/automation, one of the main ways artificial intelligence is altering employing is via robotizing routine tasks such as resume screening, interview planning, and, surprisingly, first candidate experiences; AI-fueled advances enable selection representatives to focus on additional essential exercises [10]. Through convenient and standard correspondence, this mechanization/automation brings the time down to enlist as well as upgrades the candidate experience [21].

Moreover, significant for enlisting is AI's ability to further develop independent direction [27]. Typically founded for the most part on human judgment, customary recruiting may be impacted by oblivious biases [24,25]. On the other hand, AI assesses candidates all the more unbiasedly utilizing data-driven calculations in view of a more extensive range of qualities including gifts, insight, and social fit. This ensures that recruiting choices depend on legitimacy and assists with lessening bias, thus creating a workforce/employees more fluctuated and comprehensive [24].

DOI: 10.1201/9781032619651-2

Besides, the prescient force of AI allows organizations to choose with more prominent information. AI can gauge which candidates are probably going to prevail in a certain post or remain with the association long haul by looking at past employing measurements and examples [20]. Aside from choosing the suitable faculty, this prescient review assists organizations with bringing down turnover rates, consequently saving costs connected with regular rehiring [18].

The development of AI in employing likewise denotes a change towards an up-and-comer–driven system [10]. From altered work ideas to intuitive chatbots directing competitors through the application interaction, AI-driven selecting strategies focus on giving up-and-comers customized encounters. This personalization works in the applicant's way and improves their probability of connecting with and choosing your business above others [9].

Reception of AI in recruiting presents challenges regardless of whether it has various advantages. Associations need to give close consideration to three significant worries concerning artificial intelligence-actuated predisposition, receptiveness in AI-driven decisions, and data privacy in the event that they are to use AI appropriately [5]. In any case, with the right procedure, AI might be an extraordinary device for conquering regular employing deterrents and opening new ability securing possibilities [24].

The more AI evolves, the more significant its effect on recruiting will be. Previously helping forward-looking organizations with AI-driven employing strategies, these associations are setting up a good foundation for themselves as pioneers in the vicious ability pool [11]. Adopting AI helps organizations improve their employing methods as well as assure that they attract, cooperate with, and keep the best individuals in a workforce/employees turning out to be more globalized and dynamic [21].

2.2 OVERVIEW OF TRADITIONAL RECRUITMENT CHALLENGES

Despite the fact that organizations have consistently required incredible ability, conventional employing rehearses in some cases give significant troubles. These challenges can influence recruiting techniques' overall achievement, proficiency, and viability.

a. **Time-Consuming Procedures**

   The time it takes to fill available positions is among the clearest issues with ordinary employing. Normally including a few stages, the employing system comprises work promoting, continued screening, talking, and candidate evaluation. HR specialists should give huge time and exertion at each level:

   - Manual Screening: Frequently a long and work-concentrated task is arranging hundreds or even a huge number of resumes to recognize the best candidates. Spotters need to contrast applicant capabilities and occupation rules without technology, which creates setbacks [4].
   - Arranging Meetings: Coordinating a few partners' and competitors' meetings can be strategically troublesome and as often as possible outcomes in expanded cutoff times. Managing senior positions or

concentrated ones that require input from a few colleagues makes this more troublesome [8].

- Dynamic Deferrals: The need for agreement among enlisting administrators as well as additional rounds of meetings or assessments causes the dynamic interaction to dial back following meetings. Losing top possibilities who could take offers from different associations meanwhile can follow from this deferral [5].

b. **Subjective Bias in Decision-Making**

Customary enlisting techniques are greatly impacted by human biases and abstract appraisals, which once in a while results in under-ideal work decisions:

- Oblivious Inclination: In view of things like orientation, race, age, or instructive foundation, scouts and employing authorities could accidentally lean toward up-and-comers. This bias can twist the picking system, thus restricting variety and perhaps barring truly skilled candidates [19].
- Abstract Assessment: Standard meetings ordinarily depend on emotional impressions; thus, different questioners could have fluctuating guidelines for competitor assessment. This absence of normalizing could prompt business choices dependent more upon human inclinations than on true measures and vile assessments [29].
- Social Fit versus Abilities: Now and again the emphasis on "social fit" in regular enlisting brings about employing decisions that give similarity first concern above a variety of assessments and skills. Albeit social harmoniousness is pivotal, an excess of spotlight on it can uphold consistency and smother innovativeness [10].

c. **High Prices and Ineffectiveness**

Customary employing practices can be costly and asset concentrated, consequently burdening the functional viability and spending plan of an organization:

- Publicizing Expenses: Rapidly becoming exorbitant is posting position opportunities on a few settings, including position sheets, papers, and web-based entertainment. Further heightening the monetary burden are the costs of employing organizations or talent scouts [24].
- Asset Allotment: The manual person of customary recruiting rehearses calls for huge HR. Employing supervisors and HR specialists need to commit huge opportunities to enlisting endeavors, hence disregarding other significant errands. Higher running costs could result from this inefficiency [11].
- Turnover Expenses: Terrible employing decisions welcomed on by ineffectual selecting arrangements could cause more staff turnover. Supplanting staff individuals might be costly, including rehires, onboarding, lost efficiency, and revamp [7].

Basically, regardless of whether customary recruiting rehearses have been the norm for a really long time, they present significant challenges that can think twice about the limit of an organization to draw and keep top entertainers. Managing these issues requires a change toward more goal, practical, and productive enlisting strategies spurred by AI and mechanization [13].

2.3 THE EVOLUTION OF AI IN RECRUITMENT

Throughout the course of recent years, the selecting scene has seen a tremendous change as technology assists organizations with characterizing how they draw in, survey, and gain abilities. Among the main advancements is the utilization of AI in recruitment systems, subsequently changing traditional methodologies and laying out new benchmarks for productivity, equity, and adequacy [24].

2.3.1 Development in Recruitment Technology

From fundamental worksheets and candidate global positioning frameworks (ATS), recruitment technology has been created from basic AI-driven stages that computerize and expand pretty much every feature of the selecting system. Right off the bat, recruiting was generally manual and for the most part subject to work fairs, paper advertisements, and systems administration. Work entrances achieved by the web let organizations access a bigger crowd and facilitate application entries [1].

ATS became fundamental for dealing with the surge of resumes and applications as candidate volume rose. Albeit these frameworks smoothed out competitor data capacity and recovery, their ability to fairly assess and rank applicants remained confined. This is when artificial intelligence began to show results [24].

Utilizing prescient investigation, natural language processing (NLP), and machine learning, AI-controlled selecting instruments look at huge volumes of data, spot drifts, and create data-driven proposals. By focusing on the top people, this change from manual to AI-driven recruiting has permitted organizations to oversee big quantities of uses as well as increment the nature of their representatives [2].

2.3.2 How AI Is Transforming Hiring Processes

In a few significant regards, AI is changing the recruitment cycle:

1. Sourcing and Drawing in Ability: AI-driven innovations might look through a great many web-based profiles across locales such as LinkedIn, GitHub, and online entertainment to track down uninvolved candidates that fit an organization's work standards. Through profile investigation, AI can estimate, even before a competitor applies, on the off chance that they would be a reasonable counterpart for the position [27].
2. Resume Screening and Shortlisting: Customarily, organizations would go through hours figuring out applications to track down equipped candidates. By quickly processing resumes, connecting catchphrases with sets

of expectations, and assessing applicants in view of their qualifications and experience, AI mechanizes this cycle [3]. This ensures that each candidate is decided under similar principles and assists with bringing down bias [21].

3. Candidate Commitment: AI chatbots and remote helpers might speak with competitors day in and day out, answering questions, refreshing their application progress, and in any event, setting up interviews. This keeps applicants educated and intrigued all through the employing system, thus further developing their competitor experience [21].
4. Interviewing and Appraisal: AI advances may now first be meeting up-and-comers by means of video stages and assessing their answers, manner of speaking, and even looks to decide their fit for the post [23]. Furthermore, ready to perform and dissect abilities tests, AI offers a more goal, measurably based technique for candidate assessment [20].
5. Predictive Recruiting: AI might look at past selecting data and representative execution measures to gauge which candidates are probably going to fit a specific position. This assists organizations with pursuing better informed enlisting choices, hence bringing down the turnover risk and expanding general staff creation [22].

2.3.3 Main Advantages: Scalability, Accuracy, and Speed

Counting AI into recruiting enjoys a few significant benefits:

1. Speed: AI computerizes dull tasks such as resume screening, planning, and starting possibility outreach, hence significantly slicing the chance of recruiting [23]. This allows enrolment specialists to focus on additional important errands such as making corporate marking plans and fortifying binds with top candidates [8].
2. Accuracy: AI builds candidate determination's precision by looking at gigantic volumes of data and spotting patterns that human selection representatives would disregard [9]. Greater representatives follow from work on matching between work requirements and applicant certifications [11].
3. Scalability: AI helps selecting groups to develop their exercises liberated from a related ascend in assets [9]. AI innovations can really deal with the rising responsibility whether an organization is recruiting for a solitary post or thousands, in this way ensuring that the employing system is steady and proficient all through all [10].

Hence, the rise of AI in recruiting signals a new stage in ability securing. Associations are not just expanding the productivity and adequacy of their selecting strategies but additionally delivering new potential in their staff as they continue to utilize AI-driven apparatuses and techniques. Recruitment's future is one in which human information and AI coordinate to give a more comprehensive, fair, and dynamic enlisting climate.

2.4 AI-BASED SYSTEMS FOR RECRUITMENT

By bringing progressed instruments that streamline employing, help direction, and further develop candidate encounters, AI is changing the enrolling system. Key AI advances affecting recruiting change are investigated beneath: computer vision, chatbots and remote helpers, NLP, machine learning, and prescient examination [5,19].

2.4.1 NLP

Continue Parsing and Watchword Coordinating: Current employing intensely depends on NLP, an area of AI devoted on grasping and translating human language [18,29]. Continue parsing is one of its main purposes; AI calculations consequently search and concentrate appropriate data from resumes. Scouts may quickly track down significant capacities, qualifications, and encounters fit for work models thanks to this technology [12]. NLP can actually get rid of ill-suited candidates by applying watchword matching procedures, hence ensuring that the most pertinent resumes go to the enrolling group.

Robotized Set of Working Responsibilities Creation: Mechanized set of working responsibilities age is one more significant utilization of natural language processing in employing. AI can make definite and thorough work declarations by assessing hierarchical requirements, industry patterns, and present place of employment portrayals. Alongside saving time, this computerization ensures consistency in sets of expectations for some positions. Besides, AI might suggest comprehensive and connecting with language for a pool of competitors, hence attracting a greater variety of potential [24].

2.4.2 Predictive Analyses and Machine Learning

Competitor Scoring and Positioning Calculations: Up-and-comer scoring and positioning intensely benefit from machine learning (ML), a sort of AI that allows frameworks to develop over the long run from data. To give a score or rank, these calculations evaluate people contingent upon a few measures including gifts, insight, training, and, surprisingly, delicate abilities. By assisting organizations with positioning candidates probably going to prevail in the position, this score strategy assists with limiting the time and exertion expected in screening [10].

Projecting Turnover Hazard and Applicant Achievement: Driven by machine learning, prescient examination gauges future outcomes and past straightforward competitor evaluation. AI can in this way estimate which candidates are probably going to prevail specifically in occupations and which might cause more turnover risk by analyzing past selecting data and representative execution. These acknowledge assist organizations with making more astute decisions, which improves degrees of consistency and consequences of enrolling [13,26].

2.4.3 Chatbots and Virtual Assistants

Mechanizing Beginning Up-and-Comer Cooperations: Driven by AI, chatbots and remote helpers, which computerize first competitor collaborations, have become irreplaceable instruments for this reason. From regularly providing some information about work postings to assisting competitors through the application with processing, these AI-driven applications can deal with a wide range of tasks. Chatbots free selection representatives are to focus on additional troublesome obligations, including talking and independent direction, via computerizing these dull errands [27].

Upgrading Applicant Commitment through AI-Driven Correspondence: Utilizing AI-driven correspondence advances likewise further develops competitor commitment through convenient and altered connections. Chatbots may, for instance, coordinate meetings, circle back to candidates on their application status, and even perform pre-screening interviews. Steady contact keeps candidates educated and involved, in this way upgrading their entire experience and raising the chance of effective work [19,33].

2.4.4 Computer Vision

Video Interview Examination (Non-verbal Communication, Looks): Computer Vision, an AI apparatus permitting machines to unravel visual data, is entering selecting through video interview investigation under non-verbal communication and looks. AI might assess candidates' non-verbal communication, looks, and even manner of speaking through video interview examination to accordingly gain comprehension of their certainty, genuineness, and social fit. These non-verbal signs offer a more complete evaluation by assisting one with understanding candidates past their resumes and vocal answers [6].

Use Cases in Remote Employing: Computer Vision has been particularly significant in the time of remote work. By providing enrolment specialists with a careful comprehension of up-and-comers' ways of behaving and mentalities, AI-driven video examination can assist with shutting the distance between face-to-face and remote meetings. While assessing far-off candidates for positions with serious areas of strength for requiring abilities or a certain disposition, this technology is especially useful to ensure that organizations pick individuals who will succeed in a virtual work environment [13,25].

2.5 THE AI-DRIVEN RECRUITMENT PROCESS

Counting AI into enrolling processes has changed how organizations find, survey, and instill ability. Utilizing state-of-the-art AI technology assists organizations with rearranging employing systems, lower bias, and upgrading the candidate experience by and large. This inside-and-out examination shows how AI works on a few periods of the recruiting system.

2.5.1 Automated Sourcing

Recognizing and Attracting Uninvolved Contenders: Finding and including dormant new kids on the block, individuals who could be available to the right arrangement yet are not really looking for additional opportunities, is maybe the main difficulty in joining up. To find potential individuals that fit the work principles, AI-energized obtaining systems can glance through gigantic databases, capable associations, and virtual entertainment objections. AI can figure which uninvolved up-and-comers would be enthused about new entryways by breaking down web activity, business ways, and, shockingly, virtual entertainment direct. This enables associations to contact contenders with tailored correspondences, along these lines gigantically raising responsibility rates [5,21].

Instruments and Stages Powered by AI: Obtaining AI-driven obtaining developments computerize the pursuit of qualified up-and-comers using machine learning strategies. These structures may quickly channel through a gigantic number of profiles, giving those by and large proper for the normal estimates top importance. Using AI, gadgets consolidate LinkedIn Capacity Pieces of information, Hiretual, and Entelo track down individuals' gifts, understanding, and calling desires, in this way providing scouts with a painstakingly picked pool of top prospects. AI obtaining developments save spotters a lot of time and effort through motorizing the main pursuit stage, thus enabling them to zero in on extra fundamental parts of capacity acquisition [9,27].

2.5.2 AI in Shortlisting and Screening

Redesigning Fairness and Decreasing Inclination: One of the main benefits of AI for selecting is its capacity to cut down predisposition all through the shortlisting and screening stages. Customary philosophies of resume screening are also disposed to human predispositions including unmindful tendencies for explicitly enlightening establishments, names, or past associations. Programming AI-controlled screening systems to overlook these parts and spotlight just on important affirmations, experience, and limits helps with ensuring that enormous extension data examination licenses AI to find examples and affiliations people would miss, in this way coordinating all the more obvious candidate decision [30,31].

Speeding Up the Contender Assurance Communication: By means of computerizing the essential times of joining up, AI most certainly speeds up the competitor picking process. Quickly taking a look at resumes, basic letters, and online profiles, AI structures score contenders depending upon their sensibility with the arrangement of working liabilities. While certain associations utilize perceptive assessment to expand a promising new kid on the block's show in a position, others use NLP to break out and grasp testing resumes. AI brings time down to utilize by disposing of manual screening, thus ensuring that associations can attract top capacity before rivals get it [21,25].

2.5.3 AI Talking

Coordinated Interview Frameworks Maintained by AI: Coordinated Interview Coordinated Frameworks Maintained by artificial intelligence, normalizing the requests presented and the appraisal rules used to review answers helps facilitate interview structures. This consistency guarantees fair assessment of all promising new kids on the block and game plan of the screening with the selecting objectives of the business. Through work prerequisites and prior viable utilizing,

AI structures could assist with making requests and inquiries considering these guidelines, hence cutting down the opportunity for uneven or inconsequential requests. AI could help associations with reviewing answers continuously all through the gathering, giving expedient comments and ideas for extra requests [22].

AI in Appraisal and Appraisal (Capacities Testing, Social Fit Assessment): Artificial intelligence in assessment and evaluation (social fit assessment, capacities testing, capacities testing, specific limits, decisive reasoning expertise, and social fit) are the couple of rules applicants may be overviewed on using AI-powered appraisal instruments. These instruments give objective scores and pieces of information by separating contender answers in capacities tests, coding troubles, or situational judgment assessments using machine learning estimations [19]. AI could survey candidates' convictions and exercises as per the corporate culture, thus assessing their fit into the gathering in a friendly fit assessment. This broadly comprehensive assessment framework guarantees that associations pick competitors who meet abilities as well as obliged their characteristics and culture [30,33].

2.5.4 Capacity Obtaining and Onboarding

Altered Onboarding Experiences: AI can gigantically further foster the onboarding framework by giving new delegates tailor-made experiences fit for their circumstance, learning style, and livelihood objectives. Revamped learning ways, resource ideas, and customized refreshes for basic events might be by and large made through AI-driven onboarding systems. Analyzing the establishment, limits, and tendencies of a rookie helps AI with proposing significant endeavors, mentors, and training courses so guaranteeing a predictable coordination into the business. Changed onboarding makes delegates feel appreciated and maintained all along, appropriately further developing consistency principles despite as of late added colleague productivity.

Reliable Execution Following and Improvement Ideas: AI can remain to some degree critical in capacity the chiefs even once competitors are prepared. By taking a gander at huge benchmarks such productivity, responsibility, and skill progression, AI applications can follow employees'/workers' accomplishments. These instruments can give bosses ceaseless data on the characteristics and entryways for development of their gathering, hence supporting data-driven choices on progressions, position changes, or further training. Besides, AI could give changed improvement programs depending upon market designs, execution data of a delegate, and calling goals. AI enables associations to keep top capacity and make a significantly performing workforce by engaging in constant improvement.

2.6 AI RECRUITMENT ETHICAL ISSUES

Given the rising recurrence of AI-driven employing rehearses, settling the ethical worries of applying such technology is basic. Maintaining trust in the selecting system and protecting the uprightness of business approaches rely upon AI frameworks being fair, open, and safe.

2.6.1 Bias and Fairness

Managing Artificial Intelligence-Prompted Biases: However they are intended to be impartial, AI frameworks could accidentally build up or try and disturb biases in past data. AI frameworks gain from past data; consequently any biases in the info data—like orientation, variety, or age separation—can appear in the AI's dynamic cycle. Assuming an organization's past enlisting records uncover an inclination for specific socioeconomics, for example, an AI framework instructed on that data might give competitors from those gatherings first concern, in this manner delivering one-sided results [7,10].

Looking at the datasets used to show these frameworks intently is essential to tackle AI-produced biases. Variety and portrayal of all up-and-comer bunches in training data help to diminish bias. Engineers additionally need to watch out for AI yields for signs of predisposition and adjust calculations in line. Distinguishing proof and amendment of biases could rely much upon ordinary reviews and the consideration of fairness rules.

Carrying out Fairness in AI Calculations: In artificial intelligence enlisting, fairness alludes to creating calculations that treat each candidate fairly regardless of history. Applying equity requires a multimodal procedure including:

- Algorithmic Changes: Adjusting calculations to guarantee an equivalent chance for all competitor gatherings. Strategies, for example, re-weighting, fairness constraints, and antagonistic debiasing can be applied to lessen predisposition in AI frameworks.
- Blind Recruitment: Some AI devices can anonymize competitor data, eliminating identifiers like names, orientation, or nationality to forestall oblivious inclination during beginning screening.
- Ethical Rules: Creating and complying with ethical rules for AI use in recruitment. These rules ought to stress the significance of fairness and layout techniques for taking care of predispositions in the event that they emerge.

2.6.2 Transparency and Accountability

Explaining AI Decisions to Newcomers: The seeming straightforwardness of dynamic strategies raises one of the issues with AI-driven utilization. Contenders presumably won't be aware by what implies explicit choices, for instance, being shortlisted or turned down, were picked. Nonappearance of openness in this sense could raise issues and discontent.

Associations need to guarantee that AI closes are sensible expecting they are to collect certainty. Basically, competitors should have the choice to clearly and legitimately explain how decisions roused by AI occurred. This could incorporate illustrating the AI system's actions, the data inputs considered, and how they were changed in a conclusive choice. Explainable artificial intelligence (XAI) models help to demystify AI processes consequently growing their straightforwardness to clients.

Ensuring Liability in AI-Driven Cycles: Clearly figuring out who is committed to the results of AI-driven choices is the supporting of liability in AI utilizing. Human supervision is still absolutely basic whether or not AI headways could additionally foster objectivity and adequacy. Particularly in conditions when the AI's results give off an impression of being problematic or low, associations need to set techniques for breaking down and, if important, replacing artificial intelligence decisions [7,19].

Maintaining obligation moreover infers associations should be ready to manage and fix any issues coming about as a result of AI use. This could entail constantly looking at AI execution to guarantee consistence with ethical measures and submitting question systems for up-and-comers who acknowledge they have been misleadingly dealt with [7,19].

2.6.3 Data Privacy and Security

Directing Contender Data with Care: AI-driven selecting generally depends upon data and a portion of the time calls for huge volumes of competitor data to function as it should. Regardless, the social affair, keeping, and processing of these data give serious privacy issues. Newcomer data ought to be managed with staggering thought to guarantee that essentially the normal data are collected and that these data are safely kept.

Associations need to serious solid areas for place security approaches into influence including conventional security audits, access limits, and encryption. Decreasing data maintenance is in like manner huge; candidate data should simply be saved until required and safely disposed off afterward [19].

Following Data Confirmation Plans: Data security guidelines consolidated by the General Data Security Rule (GDPR) in Europe and the California Customer Privacy Act in the US control how associations could gather and apply individual data in different areas. Noticing these rules isn't simply required authentically but also critical for saving moral AI strategies.

Associations need to guarantee their procedures for utilizing AI fit suitable data security rules. This covers getting contenders to express approval preceding social events for their data, giving clear data on how their data will be used, and permitting competitors to access, update, or delete their data. Associations should in like manner routinely overview and update their data security strategies to be as per developing guidelines [34].

2.7 USING AI THROUGHOUT YOUR RECRUITMENT STRATEGY

Counting AI into your employing plan calls for vital execution, thorough arrangement, and careful audit. Given underneath are the moves toward handling things purposefully:

2.7.1 Assessing Organizational Readiness

Breaking Down Current Recruitment Frameworks: You need to assess your present employing rehearses first prior to adding AI into your methodology. Map out the finish-to-end enlisting process first, taking note of each and every stage from obtaining candidates to onboarding. Look at the time spent, instruments applied, and the accomplishment at each level. Center particularly around issues such as exorbitant opportunity to employ, lacking candidate inclusion, or incapable screening and shortlisting. Realizing these deterrents will empower you to choose where AI can be best.

Recognizing Regions for AI Joining: Subsequent to evaluating your ongoing techniques, you ought to then find spots where artificial intelligence might be incorporated to further develop execution and productivity. AI can be particularly useful for occupations requiring quick direction, data-concentrated monotonous exercises, or ones including consistent learning [15]. Continue screening, candidate obtaining, interview booking, and, surprisingly, first competitor communication through AI-driven chatbots are a couple of such models. Ponder how AI may increment efficiency as well as lower predisposition, further develop applicant experience, and proposition data-driven bits of knowledge for better navigation [12].

2.7.2 Selecting Appropriate AI Tools

Determination of AI Recruitment Stages: Rules picking the right artificial intelligence innovations for employing requires a far-reaching consciousness of the goals and necessities of your organization. Significant boundaries to consider comprise:

- Usefulness: Guarantee the stage tends to your particular pain focuses, whether it's robotizing resume screening, further developing applicant coordinating, or improving commitment.
- Versatility: Pick an answer that can develop with your association, taking care of expanded volumes of competitors as your organization extends.
- Reconciliation: The AI apparatus ought to incorporate flawlessly with your current HR technology stack, including Candidate Global positioning frameworks (ATS) and Human Asset the Executives Frameworks (HRMS).
- Ease of Use: A stage that is not difficult to utilize will work with quicker reception by your HR group.
- Consistence: Guarantee the stage consents to applicable data assurance guidelines and has powerful safety efforts set up.

Customization versus Off-the-Rack Arrangements: Choosing AI instruments will compel you to pick between off-the-rack things and tweaking options. Customizable AI frameworks give an extraordinary level of adaptability by allowing you to fit the instrument to your own employing objectives and methodology. To apply, however, they could call for additional time and cash. On the other hand, off-the-rack arrangements could have best-practice arrangements from the get-go and are generally quicker to utilize. The choice depends on the size, spending plan, and specific requirements of your organization. Numerous organizations see that as a mixture model permitting some level of personalization inside an off-the-rack system is great [14].

2.7.3 Creating an AI-Driven Recruitment Team

Ranges of Abilities Expected for AI Coordination in HR: To effectively carry out and use AI in recruitment, your HR group necessities to foster certain ranges of abilities. This covers major areas of strength for an artificial intelligence technology and data examination as well as the ability to unravel bits of knowledge created by AI. Working with data and applying it to direct decisions shouldn't inconvenience HR specialists. Moreover, information in projecting the board and changing the executives would be vital as the AI mix ordinarily entails significant adjustments to current cycles.

Training and Advancement for HR Groups: Putting resources into training and improvement is pivotal to ensure your HR staff might take full advantage of AI arrangements. Alongside more broad instruction on the thoughts of artificial intelligence and data-driven navigation, this might incorporate authority training seminars on the most proficient method to use certain AI frameworks. Ponder allowing HR pioneers opportunities to upskill in fields such as data examination, machine learning establishments, and ethical issues in AI. Advancing a continuously learning society will empower your group to remain on the ball as AI innovations create.

2.7.4 Evaluating ROI and Success

Key Execution Markers (KPIs) for Recruitment Driven by AI: Following significant execution pointers (KPIs) reflecting both proficiency upgrades and improved results assists one with assessing the effect of artificial intelligence in enrolling. Normal KPIs include:

- Time-to-Recruit: Decrease in the normal time taken to fill a position.
- Cost-per-Recruit: Abatement in recruitment costs, taking into account both immediate and backhanded costs.
- Nature of Recruit: Improvement in the exhibition and degrees of consistency of recently added team members.
- Up-and-comer Experience: Improved fulfilment levels among competitors, as estimated by overviews and input.
- Variety Measurements: Upgrades in the variety of candidates and recruits, mirroring AI's job in lessening predisposition.

Persistent Improvement and Cycle: AI-driven enrolling is a continuous interaction requiring consistent advancement instead of a one-time application. Survey your AI devices' exhibition frequently in accordance with your KPIs and roll out required improvements [12]. Get remarks from candidates and your HR staff to find regions requiring work. As AI evolves, be prepared to iteratively work on your apparatuses and techniques to amplify the benefits. Watch creating AI patterns and advancements to ensure your recruitment plan stays serious and effective.

Keeping these rules will assist your organization with appropriately utilizing AI to increment candidate quality, smooth out recruiting systems, and lastly empower the entire capability of your endeavors on ability obtaining.

2.8 AI-DRIVEN RECRUITMENT FUTURE TRENDS

As AI continues to change numerous areas, its impact on recruiting is growingly significant. AI-driven recruiting marks an essential change in how organizations handle work the executives and ability procurement, not just a pattern. Here is a nearer perspective on what's to come in designs impacting AI-driven employing:

2.8.1 AI and the Future of Work

Arising AI Advances in Recruitment: More perplexing and concentrated technology will characterize the heading of artificial intelligence-driven employing proceeding. Profound learning models, further developed NLP, and high-level machine learning calculations are ready to change how organizations find, survey, and connect with potential candidates [12]. More exact figures of up-and-comer achievement, more prominent coordinating of sets of responsibilities with application attributes, and more modified competitor encounters will be in every way made conceivable by AI [31].

An ever-increasing number of more youthful innovations like AI-driven psychometric examination—which assesses character qualities and social fit utilizing minute language and conduct prompts—will track down use. Hence working on the recruiting system will be the reconciliation of AI with other developing innovations, including blockchain for straightforward and safe qualification approval [33].

The Job of AI in Workforce Arranging and Ability of The board: AI will assume an undeniably basic part in workforce arranging and ability of the executives. Training the executives and workforce arranging will profit from AI to an ever-increasing extent [16]. By permitting HR groups to project future ability requests relying upon corporate objectives and market patterns, prescient examination will assist with empowering more proactive enlisting arrangements. AI will likewise empower organizations to pinpoint areas of expertise deficiencies in their ongoing workforce and propose centered reskilling or redesigning programs [31].

AI-driven arrangements will give workers tailored profession ways to train the board, in this way coordinating their objectives with those of the organization. This methodology won't just further develop representative maintenance and association but in addition ensure that organizations have the right faculty prepared to confront impending hardships [23,29].

2.8.2 Human–AI Partnership in Recruitment

Offsetting AI Robotization with Human Judgment: Regardless of whether artificial intelligence gives unrivalled accuracy and effectiveness, the human part in employing is still entirely significant. While human spotters focus on creating associations, assessing social fit, and going with last enlisting decisions, the future will see a more adjusted approach by which AI handles data-driven errands such resume screening, candidate obtaining, and first assessments [17].

HR specialists will be obliged by this participation to obtain new capacities in controlling and understanding AI yields, ensuring ethical and effective use of AI advances. Key to powerful enlisting results will be the ability to mix human instinct and compassion with AI-driven experiences [19].

Upgrading HR Jobs through AI Help HR specialists will likewise be changed by artificial intelligence, becoming vital accomplices who use it to improve recruiting results. AI will empower HR experts to focus on additional essential exercises such as corporate marking, candidate experience of the executives, and variety and incorporation endeavors via computerizing dull obligations.

Whether it's deciding the ideal channels for candidate obtaining or upgrading recruitment promoting endeavors, HR experts will depend increasingly more on AI-driven measurements to direct decisions [13]. HR's future will be one of further developed abilities by which AI goes about as a powerful instrument expanding and praising human information [16].

2.8.3 Global Impact of AI in Recruitment

AI-Driven Recruitment in Various Social Settings: The impact of AI-driven employing will change contingent upon the social setting as it spreads to an ever-increasing extent. Solid accentuation on specialized development and computerized change could assist certain regions with embracing AI in selecting quickly. In others, social preferences for human contacts and relationship-based work could hinder the acknowledgment of AI strategies [18].

Associations should redo their AI-driven employing plans to fit social changes in the event that they are to flourish in an overall ability pool [27]. To ensure a consistent progress, this can entail modifying AI calculations to meet neighborhood employing rules or consolidating AI instruments with customary enlisting techniques [32].

Suggestions for Worldwide Ability Securing Strategies: AI will essentially affect worldwide ability obtaining plans as it will allow organizations to get to an assortment of ability pools all over [21]. From arranging a few languages and administrative structures to realizing nearby work market circumstances, selection representatives can successfully deal with the intricacy of global employing utilizing AI-controlled arrangements [25].

By bringing down biases and ensuring fair assessments of people from all foundations, AI will likewise allow organizations to make more comprehensive recruiting approaches. Worldwide partnerships will in this way be more fit to draw and keep top ability, subsequently advancing a more changed and imaginative workforce/employees [28].

2.9 CONCLUSION

There are both intriguing potential and testing troubles that are introduced by recruitment that is fueled by AI. AI advances that are still during the time spent creating won't just change the manners by which organizations find and draw in people, but additionally the manners by which they financially plan for and deal with their representatives as they develop. By embracing human–AI participation and thoroughly considering the overall impacts of artificial intelligence in recruiting, associations can possibly release new degrees of productivity, equity, and vital impact pertaining to their ability securing endeavors.

2.9.1 AI-Driven Recruitment System Model

2.9.1.1 System Overview

The AI-Driven Recruitment Structure is expected to include AI in each step of the utilizing framework. This will make it more capable, less uneven, and better for new kids in town. Coordinated advances will be taken to make this structure, which will integrate accommodating data for HR chiefs to use and manage AI-based selecting plans.

2.9.1.2 Structure Parts

A. Recruitment Cycle Assessment Module
- Work process Arranging Device:
  - Function: Make visual aids of current recruitment processes, from work introducing on onboarding.
  - Features: Worked on interface, process portrayal, and compromise with existing HR structures.
- Pain Centers Analyzer:
  - Function: Recognize and separate failures and bottlenecks in the continuous recruitment work process.
  - Features: Data combination from various stages, gives details in regards to handling delays, and computerized thoughts for overhauls.
- Challenge Identifier:
  - Function: Recognize key hardships like inclination, inadequacy, or nonappearance of data-driven encounters.
  - Features: Surveys and analysis variety from HR gatherings, candidate input designs, and examination of current recruitment execution.

B. Objective Definition and Estimations Module
- Objective Setting Point of communication:
  - Function: Portray clear, express targets for AI coordination.
  - Features: Objective setting designs, course of action with various leveled objectives, and following headway.
- Accomplishment Assessment Dashboard:
  - Function: Make and screen estimations for assessing AI impact.
  - Features: Steady dashboards showing estimations, for instance, time-to-utilize, cost speculation assets, and contender satisfaction scores.

C. AI Contraptions Appraisal and Decision Module
- AI Game Plans Rundown:
  - Function: Investigation and evaluate available AI mechanical assemblies.
  - Features: Detailed depictions of AI contraptions, assessment charts, and client reviews.

- Customization and Blend Coordinator:
  - Function: Choose off-the-rack versus adjusted AI courses of action and assurance blend.
  - Features: Customization decisions, joining plans, and likeness assessments with existing structures.

D. Pilot and Analysis Module

- Experiment Program Boss:
  - Function: Execute AI instruments on a more restricted size to test practicality.
  - Features: Pilot orchestrating designs, execution following, and execution checking.
- Analysis Variety System:
  - Function: Gather input from spotters and contenders.
  - Features: Surveys, analysis designs, and assessment of contribution for steady improvement.

E. Training and Collaboration Module

- Training Stage:
  - Function: Give indispensable training to HR bunches on AI gadgets.
  - Features: Online courses, online classes, and involved studios covering particular and judicious perspectives.
- Collaboration Center:
  - Function: Support composed exertion between HR specialists and AI trained professionals.
  - Features: Particular mechanical assemblies, project the board features, and data sharing resources.

F. Consistent Execution and Cycle Module

- Arranged Execution Coordinator:
  - Function: Guide the consistent joining of AI into recruitment processes.
  - Features: Stage orchestrating designs, execution following, and change rules.
- Execution Noticing and Cycle Mechanical assembly:
  - Function: Unendingly screen AI execution and make iterative updates.
  - Features: Execution examination, analysis circles, and change ideas.

G. Future-Affirmation System Module:

- Data-Driven Powerful Gadget:
  - Function: Impact AI-created encounters for key autonomous course.
  - Features: Assessment dashboards, design examination, and far-sighted assessment capacities.

- Promising New Kid in Town Experience Enhancer:
  - Function: Redo promising new kid in town correspondences and assurance a concordance between AI motorization and human touch.
  - Features: Personalization instruments, robotized correspondence work cycles, and contender responsibility estimations.
- Ethical AI Organization Framework:
  - Function: Assurance ethical use of AI and address tendencies.
  - Features: Inclination acknowledgment computations, straightforwardness instruments, and consistence plans.
- Incessant Improvement Structure:
  - Function: Remain revived with degrees of progress and search for analysis for constant overhauls.
  - Features: Update alerts, analysis arrangement instruments, and improvement following.
- Fundamental Vision Coordinator:
  - Function: Change AI recruitment approach to greater business goals and develop advancement.
  - Features: Essential plan gadgets, progression following, and business impact assessment.

2.9.1.3 Execution Plan

a. Initial Plan:
  - Deploy the Recruitment Cycle Appraisal Module.
  - Conduct an intensive evaluation of current recruitment practices.

b. Goal Setting and Device Decision:
  - Utilize the Objective Definition and Estimations Module to lay out objectives.
  - Research and select legitimate AI gadgets using the AI Instruments Evaluation and Decision Module.

c. Pilot Coordination:
  - Implement AI gadgets on a pilot premise using the Pilot and Information Module.
  - Gather analysis and make changes relying upon the circumstance.

d. Training and Consistent Rollout:
  - Provide training through the Training and Joint Exertion Module.
  - Gradually execute AI gadgets across recruitment stages using the Sluggish Execution and Accentuation Module.

e. Future-Fixing and Relentless Improvement:
  - Use the Future-Confirmation Technique Module to ensure advancing significance and suitability.
  - Regularly update and refine the system considering execution data and emerging examples (Table 2.1).

TABLE 2.1
AI-Driven Recruitment System Model

Module	Function	Features
	Recruitment Process Assessment	
Workflow mapping tool	Create visual maps of current recruitment processes	Drag-and-drop interface, process visualization, integration with HR systems
Pain points analyzer	Identify inefficiencies and bottlenecks	Data collection, process delay reports, automated improvement suggestions
Challenge identifier	Detect key challenges in recruitment	Surveys, feedback collection, analytics on recruitment performance
	Goal Definition and Metrics	
Objective setting interface	Define clear goals for AI integration	Goal-setting templates, alignment with objectives, tracking progress
Success measurement dashboard	Monitor metrics for AI impact	Real-time dashboards, metrics like time-to-hire, cost savings, candidate satisfaction
	AI Tools Evaluation and Selection	
AI solutions catalogue	Research and evaluate AI tools	Descriptions, comparison charts, user reviews
Customization and integration planner	Decide on AI solutions and ensure integration	Customization options, integration checklists, compatibility assessments
	Pilot and Feedback	
Pilot program manager	Test AI tools on a smaller scale	Pilot planning templates, tracking, performance monitoring
Feedback collection system	Gather feedback from users	Surveys, feedback forms, analysis for improvement
	Training and Collaboration	
Training platform	Provide training on AI tools	Online courses, webinars, workshops
Collaboration hub	Foster HR and AI expert collaboration	Communication tools, project management, knowledge-sharing resources
	Gradual Implementation and Iteration	
Phased implementation planner	Guide gradual AI integration	Phase planning templates, tracking, adjustment guidelines
Performance monitoring and iteration tool	Monitor AI performance and make improvements	Performance analytics, feedback loops, adjustment recommendations
	Future-Proof Strategy	
Data-driven decision-making tool	Use AI insights for strategic decisions	Analytics dashboards, trend analysis, predictive analytics
Candidate experience enhancer	Personalize interactions and balance automation with human touch	Personalization tools, automated workflows, engagement metrics
Ethical AI governance framework	Ensure ethical AI use and address biases	Bias detection, transparency tools, compliance checklists

(*Continued*)

TABLE 2.1 (*Continued*)
AI-Driven Recruitment System Model

Module	Function	Features
Continuous improvement system	Stay updated and seek feedback for improvements	Update notifications, feedback collection, improvement tracking
Strategic vision planner	Align AI strategy with business goals and foster innovation	Strategic alignment tools, innovation tracking, business impact analysis

Utilizing this Model, HR supervisors and pioneers can effectively incorporate AI into their employing techniques, subsequently coming up with a future-verification methodology further developing candidate experience, fairness, and productivity.

REFERENCES

1. Agarwal, S., & Gupta, D. (2024). Digital analytics applications for sustainable training and education. In K. Sood, P. Kalia, S. Grima, & A. Chaudhary (Eds.), *Digital Analytics Applications for Sustainable Training and Education* (p. 25). Apple Academic Press.
2. Agarwal, S., Diwedi, S., & Ghai, R. (2020). Perception of trainees towards skill development program. *International Journal of Innovative Science and Research Technology*, 5(12), 387–392. https://www.ijisrt.com.
3. Agarwal, S., Gupta, D., & Gupta, M. (2023). Impact of training method on trainees' learning and implementation on the job: A study with special reference to power sector. *AIP Conference Proceedings*, 2427(1), 020020. https://doi.org/10.1063/5.0100893
4. Agarwal, S., Gupta, D., & Gupta, M. (2023). Techno pedagogical concept with digital skills. In M. S. Manna, B. Balusamy, K. Sood, N. Chilamkurti, & I. R. George (Eds.), *Edutech Enabled Teaching* (pp. 129–152). Chapman and Hall/CRC.
5. Barocas, S., & Selbst, A. D. (2016). Big data's disparate impact. *California Law Review*, 104, 671.
6. Boden, M. A. (2016). *AI: Its Nature and Future*. Oxford University Press.
7. Bogen, M., & Rieke, A. (2018). *Help Wanted: An Examination of Hiring Algorithms, Equity, and Bias*. Upturn.
8. Brynjolfsson, E., & McAfee, A. (2017). *Machine, Platform, Crowd: Harnessing Our Digital Future*. W. W. Norton & Company.
9. Burtch, G., & Chan, J. (2019). The effects of a big data recruiting tool on human capital decisions: Evidence from field experiments. *Management Science*, 65(2), 921–940.
10. Chamorro-Premuzic, T., Akhtar, R., & Winsborough, D. (2020). The future of recruitment and selection: Integrating AI and psychology. *Journal of Work and Organizational Psychology*, 36(1), 57–65.
11. Chui, M., Manyika, J., & Miremadi, M. (2016). Where machines could replace humans—and where they can't (yet). *McKinsey Quarterly*, 7, 56–71.
12. Davenport, T. H., & Kirby, J. (2015). Beyond automation. *Harvard Business Review*, 93(6), 58–65.
13. Davenport, T. H., & Ronanki, R. (2018). Artificial intelligence for the real world. *Harvard Business Review*, 96(1), 108–116.
14. Gupta, D., & Agarwal, S. (2018). Skill development initiative-literature review. *Inspira-Journal of Modern Management and Entrepreneurship (JMME)*, 8(2), 319–322.

15. Agarwal, S., & Gupta, D. (2018). Training prospects in the power sector in India. *International Journal of Research in Engineering, IT and Social Sciences*, 8(Special Issue), 305–314.
16. Gupta, D., Gupta, M., & Rani, S. (2022). A study on training of workmen in a manufacturing organization—With reference to aluminium foundry. In A. Dvivedi, A. Sachdeva, R. Sindhwani, & R. Sahu (Eds.), *Recent Trends in Industrial and Production Engineering* (pp. 221–233). Springer, Singapore. https://doi.org/10.1007/978-981-16-3330-0_19
17. Gupta, D., Gupta, M., Tiwari, S., & Singh, N. (2021). Motivation due to fear of failure is a key contributor in maximizing workers' productivity in today's competitive arena. *International Journal of Indian Culture and Business Management*, 23(2), 193–217. https://doi.org/10.1504/IJICBM.2021.115895
18. Gupta, M., Gupta, D., & Rai, P. (2024). Exploring the impact of software as a service (SaaS) on human life. *EAI Endorsed Transactions on Internet of Things*, 10. https://doi.org/10.4108/eetiot.4821
19. Hagendorff, T. (2020). The ethics of AI ethics: An evaluation of guidelines. *Minds and Machines*, 30, 99–120.
20. He, J., & Xu, D. (2015). A state-of-the-art review of artificial intelligence applications in recruitment. *Journal of Information Technology & Software Engineering*, 5(1), 132–148. https://doi.org/10.4172/2165-7866.1000132
21. Jiang, J. (2020). How artificial intelligence is transforming the recruitment industry. *Business Horizons*, 63(5), 623–632.
22. Kumar, A., Gupta, D., Gupta, M., & Srivastava, G. (2021). India an emerging leader after pandemic: A strategy for the development of new India. *Global Journal of Enterprise Information System*, 13(1), 60–70. https://www.gjeis.com/index.php/GJEIS/article/view/629
23. Kumar, V., Gupta, M., & Gaur, S. (2023). Intrusion detection for the internet of things. In K. Kaushik, S. Dahiya, A. Bhardwaj, & Y. Maleh (Eds.), *Internet of Things and Cyber Physical Systems Security and Forensics* (1st ed., p. 183). CRC Press.
24. Lee, I. (2018). Artificial intelligence in recruitment: A critical review and research agenda. *Human Resource Management Review*, 30(1), 100–120.
25. Mehrabi, N., Morstatter, F., Saxena, N., Lerman, K., & Galstyan, A. (2021). A survey on bias and fairness in machine learning. *ACM Computing Surveys*, 54(6), 1–35.
26. Mittal, S., Srivastava, P., & Gupta, D. (2022). Emotional intelligence: Assessing its impact on financial productivity in an organization. In V. V. Rao, A. Kumaraswamy, S. Kalra, & A. Saxena (Eds.), *Computational and Experimental Methods in Mechanical Engineering* (Vol. 239, pp. 207–214). Springer, Singapore. https://doi.org/10.1007/978-981-16-2857-3_22
27. Polli, F. (2018). The future of hiring: How artificial intelligence can improve talent acquisition. *Forbes*. https://www.forbes.com/sites/forbescoachescouncil/2018/02/23/how-will-artificial-intelligence-change-the-future-of-hiring-and-recruiting/
28. Rajvanshi, P. R., Singh, T., Gupta, D., & Gupta, M. (2022). Blockchain technology for pharmaceutical drug supply chain management. In P. Singh, D. Mishra, & K. Seth (Eds.), *Transformation in Healthcare with Emerging Technologies* (1st ed., pp. 217–230). CRC Press.
29. Rani, S., Gupta, M., & Gupta, D. (2020). Artificial intelligence and personalized banking. In V. Garg & R. Agrawal (Eds.), *Transforming Management Using Artificial Intelligence Techniques* (1st ed., p. 24). CRC Press. https://doi.org/10.4324/9781003032410
30. Singh, S., & Gupta, D. (2023). Module allocation model in distributed computing system by implementing fuzzy C-means clustering technique. In R. Agrawal, P. Mitra, A. Pal, & M. Sharma Gaur (Eds.), *International Conference on IoT, Intelligent Computing and Security* (Vol. 982, pp. 145–160). Springer, Singapore. https://doi.org/10.1007/978-981-19-8136-4_14

31. Singh, S., Gupta, D., & Gupta, M. (2022). Optimized task allocation technique using mathematical fuzzy logic in heterogeneous distributed computational system. In *2022 International Conference on Computational Intelligence and Sustainable Engineering Solutions (CISES)* (pp. 37–45). IEEE. https://doi.org/10.1109/CISES54857.2022.9844410
32. Srivastava, G., & Gupta, D. (2022). Determining the relationship between job satisfaction and job burnout of the faculties of business school in Delhi. *International Journal of Indian Culture and Business Management*, 26(2), 276–286.
33. Kim, H., So, K. K. F., Shin, S., & Li, J. (2025). Artificial intelligence in hospitality and tourism: insights from industry practices, research literature, and expert opinions. Journal of Hospitality & Tourism Research, 49(2), 366–385. https://doi.org/10.1177/10963480241229235.
34. Wachter, S., Mittelstadt, B., & Floridi, L. (2017). Transparent, explainable, and accountable AI for robotics. *Science, Robotics*, 2(6), eaan6080. https://doi.org/10.1126/scirobotics.aan6080

3 Gamification and Virtual Reality for Effective Employee Training and Development

Swati Rai, Rakesh Kumar Yadav, and Mukul Gupta

3.1 INTRODUCTION

The most critical component for the success and sustainability of any organization is effective employee training and development. To meet the embryonic demands of an era where the market and the environment are continually changing, a continuous process of improving the skills, knowledge, and abilities of employees is the key to survival and success.

Employee Training refers to the process of improving an employee's knowledge, skills, and abilities in his/her current job role. It is typically short-term and focuses on enhancing job-specific skills, ensuring that employees are competent in their current tasks and can meet organizational standards. Training can cover a wide range of topics, from technical skills to soft skills such as communication and teamwork [2]. Employee training ensures that individuals possess the necessary skills to perform their job effectively. Regular training updates employees on new technologies, processes, and strategies, enhancing their productivity. With proper training, employees become more competent, efficient, and confident in their abilities, which directly impacts the company's bottom line [7].

Training and development programmes are actually a signal that the company is investing in the growth and career evolution of its staff. This makes the employees feel important and valued; they further see a path for advancement and hence are more likely to stay faithful to the organization [10].

3.2 THE ROLE OF INNOVATION IN TRAINING METHODS AND THE NEED FOR EFFECTIVE SOLUTIONS

In the rapidly evolving landscape of modern business, traditional training methods are no longer sufficient to meet the demands of today's workforce. The shift towards digital transformation, coupled with the need for continuous learning, has driven organizations to innovate in their approach to employee training. Innovative methods of training not only improve efficacy in learning but also better suit the fast-moving and dynamic nature of the current work environment. This chapter considers the

DOI: 10.1201/9781032619651-3

value of innovation in practice within a strategy of training, along with the need for efficiency in solutions that can meet the ever-changing needs of companies and their people [3].

3.2.1 Diverse Learning Needs

The workforce is more diversified than ever, with staff from every walk of life, age, and learning preference. Innovative training tools will include customized e-learning platforms or gamified training courses that best fit your particular learning style. This approach will make it possible for each and every one of the staff to be able to engage with materials that speak to them, thereby improving knowledge retention and application.

3.2.2 Complementing Technological Advancements

Technology innovation is moving at a breath-taking pace. New technologies turn industries upside down, and the workforce needs continuous updates with relevant training. Hands-on, real-world experience comes through innovative concepts such as augmented reality, Virtual Reality (VR), and artificial intelligence (AI)-driven learning, whereby these tools enable staff to learn by actually doing things, which surely must be much more effective than the previous classroom-type learning [1,19].

3.2.3 Enhanced Engagement and Motivation

Traditional training courses make employees really bored and disengaged, resulting in a loss of interest. Innovative techniques that will make the training interesting and a pleasant experience include gamification, micro learning, and interactive material. All these approaches make learning more engaging and hence enable staff members to stay driven for continuous development [11].

3.2.4 Measurability and Flexibility

The newest digital training methods will enable companies to scale up their learning programs much faster and more efficiently. Cloud-based learning management systems (LMS) enables remote access to the training material, allowing staff to learn at any time, from any location, and at their own pace, which, by the way, plays a crucial role in today's distant and hybrid work scenarios [8,9].

3.2.5 Data-Driven Insight

One of the most valuable assets for innovation in training is its capability to collect and analyse data about employee performance. Predictive analytics, AI, and machine learning enable sophisticated training systems to track progress, measure the impact on learning, and provide immediate feedback. This data-driven approach helps companies refine their training effort so that training is always aligned with organizational objectives and employee needs [4].

3.3 CREATIVE/INNOVATIVE TRAINING APPROACHES

3.3.1 Gamification

Gamification refers to the integration of training courses with game-like elements such as prizes, points, and competition. It makes learning fun, exciting, and interactive, hence increasing participation. Gamified training may motivate employees to drive healthy competition and allow them to apply their knowledge in real life [13].

3.3.2 VR

VR is the technology that would allow one to have immersive and experience-based learning. For example, this can be used to mimic unsafe situations to work in, or complex machinery for practical training of the staff without associated risks [20].

3.3.3 Micro Learning

As the name suggests, micro learning breaks down complex information into concise and easily learnable bite sized courses. This mode of learning attends to the needs of those busy working professionals who may not have the time to waste on long hours of training courses. For employees, this is ideal because it allows them to learn while on the job.

3.3.4 Adaptive Learning

AI-driven systems critically analyse the employees' pattern and style of learning. It adapts the training content by considering the knowledge level, learning pace, and learning preference of each individual employee to make sure that the content being delivered is relevant to him/her, thus optimizing his learning cycle [17,18].

3.3.5 Social Learning Platforms

Social learning provides a platform on which employees can share ideas, know-how, and problem-solving techniques among themselves. These kinds of platforms support learning by enabling the staff to teach and learn from one another, hence building up cooperation and teamwork by way of enabling a culture of continuous improvement [17].

3.4 AS INSTRUMENTS FOR INSTRUCTION, GAMIFICATION AND VR

Whenever technology begins to alter how companies do business, so too must the training strategies. Indeed, modern techniques like VR and gamification have been quite successful in employee training. Both approaches use innovative, interactive methods to engage learners, making the process more immersive, enjoyable, and effective. This article explores how Gamification and VR can be leveraged to improve training outcomes and foster a more dynamic learning environment [12].

3.4.1 Gamification in Employee Training

The application of game-design elements (like scoring points, competing with others, achieving goals, and earning rewards) in non-game contexts and learning, such as training and education, is known as Gamification. It is designed in such a manner that by harnessing into the natural human tendencies for competition, achievement, and recognition, it tends to make the learning experience more engaging and pleasant. Organizations are facing an engagement crisis. All the stakeholders of an organization, namely customers, employees, students, and citizens, struggle to meaningfully engage their precious and limited resource, *i.e.*, their time. Expectedly, these stakeholders have established protective shields to defend themselves. Few advantaged organizations are allowed to penetrate that shield, and even fewer will meaningfully engage. To go into the armour, and engross the audience, organizations need an edge. Gamification has emerged as a tactic to gain that super power, and organizations are beginning to see it as a key tool in their digital engagement strategy [6].

3.4.1.1 Key Features of Gamification in Training

a. Points and Leader Boards: Learners earn points for completing tasks, quizzes, or challenges, which are displayed on leader boards. This element promotes healthy competition and motivates participants to improve their performance.
b. Badges and Rewards: Employees receive virtual badges or rewards for accomplishing learning milestones. These achievements provide a sense of accomplishment and drive continued engagement.
c. Levels and Progression: Just like in video games, learners advance through levels as they complete training modules. This encourages progression and a sense of mastery.
d. Challenges and Quests: Big learning objectives are broken down into smaller tasks or quests, hence more absorbable and fun to learn [6].

3.4.1.2 Benefits of Serious Games in Training

a. Enhanced Engagement and Motivation: Gamification is a brilliant tool that can turn the otherwise brick-and-mortar, mundane, or dried-up components of training into an engaging experience for the learners, capable of keeping them engaged and motivated toward achieving the goals [11].
b. Higher Retention: Gamified trainings make learners more involved with the content through immediate feedback, frequent repetition of key concepts, and reinforcements, hence allowing better retention [13].
c. Personalized Learning Experience: The gamified systems can allow each learner to progress at his/her own pace and based on his/her knowledge level by customizing the learning modules as per his/her needs.
d. Improved Collaboration: Multiplayer gamified platforms improve collaboration and coordination amongst colleagues because they may have to jointly reach out for a solution to overcome a challenge.

3.4.2 VR in Training

VR in training is a form of technology that generates some sort of simulated, virtual, three-dimensional environment with which a user can interact with as if he/she were physically present within it. Particularly in practical or experiential learning, VR enables students to undergo realistic, immersive simulations during teaching [20].

3.4.2.1 Important VR Training Characteristics

a. Immersive Simulations: VR lets students engage in real-world events in a controlled, risk-free environment—such as piloting an aeroplane, operating machinery, or doing medical operations.
b. Interactive Learning: Learners of interactive learning can engage in real time with items, people, or surroundings to improve their knowledge of tasks or procedures.
c. Real-Time Feedback: In a VR training environment, students get real-time comments so they may improve approaches or fix errors throughout the simulation.
d. Customizable Environments: From the manufacturing floor to the customer service centre to emergency response scenarios, VR can realistically replicate almost any workplace.

3.4.2.2 Advantages of VR for Training

a. Enhanced Practical Learning: VR offers chances for experience learning, thereby enabling workers to practise activities that could be risky, costly, or unfeasible in the actual world.
b. Risk-Free Environment: VR is helpful in high-risk sectors like healthcare, construction, or aviation as employees can make mistakes in a virtual environment without real-world consequences.
c. Higher Retention through Immersion: Studies reveal that immersive experiences improve memory retention as students are more likely to recall first-hand what they encountered in a virtual setting.
d. Scalability and Consistency: VR training ensures that every employee experiences the same standardized training, no matter their location, ensuring uniformity in skill development.
e. Remote Access to Complex Training: Employees from anywhere in the world can engage in specialized training, reducing the costs and logistical challenges of bringing in experts or travelling to training sites (Table 3.1).

3.5 SUCCESSFUL IMPLEMENTATIONS

Several companies across different industries have successfully used **gamification** to enhance employee training, increase engagement, and boost productivity [15]. Here are some notable examples:

TABLE 3.1
Comparison of Gamification and VR in Training

Parameter	Gamification	VR
Engagement	Highly engaging through competition, rewards, and progression	Deeply engaging through immersive, real-world simulations
Learning style	Ideal for knowledge-based training, quizzes, and soft skills	Best for experiential, hands-on, and practical learning
Cost	More cost-effective, easy to integrate into digital platforms	Higher upfront costs due to specialized hardware and software
Scalability	Easily scalable for large numbers of learners across locations	Scalable but limited by access to VR equipment and infrastructure
Customization	Easily customizable with minimal technical setup	Can recreate highly specific, complex environments but requires more development time
Applications	Sales, compliance, product knowledge, customer service	Healthcare, manufacturing, construction, emergency response

3.5.1 Deloitte Leadership Academy

Deloitte needed a way to engage senior executives in leadership training programs. So it introduced gamification elements like badges, leader boards, and rewards to its online learning platform, Deloitte Leadership Academy. For finishing leadership classes and facing off against peers, participants gained points and badges.

Gamification made the learning process more fun and engaging, hence raising user involvement and participation. Users of the platform returned to finish courses in 37% more total.

3.5.2 Microsoft: Language Quality Game

For several of its software products, Microsoft had to raise the calibre of its language translations for different geographical markets. The firm developed the "Language Quality Game," which pushed staff members to assist in locating and correcting translating mistakes in Microsoft products. Workers competed to spot and fix these mistakes, gaining points and leader board recognition.

Microsoft greatly raised staff engagement and increased translating quality using gamification. The program also cut the expense of hiring outside translators.

3.5.3 Domino's Pizza: Pizza Maker Training Game

Domino's wanted to find a fun way to teach its employees how to make pies that would be of the same high standard in all of its stores. The company made the "Pizza Hero" game so that employees could learn how to make pizzas by practising online. Workers got points for how accurately they made pizzas, which helped them get faster and better at what they did.

The gamified training that Domino's employees got to make pizzas made them much more productive, which improved customer service and sped up the delivery of orders.

3.6 CHALLENGES

Implementing gamification in employee training offers many benefits, but it also comes with several challenges. Successfully integrating gamified elements requires careful planning, design, and execution to avoid pitfalls that can derail the process.

3.6.1 Misalignment with Learning Objectives

The primary goal of training is to develop skills and knowledge. If gamified elements like points, badges, and leader boards overshadow the actual learning objectives, employees may focus more on winning or scoring rather than absorbing the material. Balancing fun and educational value is a critical aspect to maintain throughout.

3.6.2 Overemphasis on Competition

Not every employee is of the same cognitive level; there are a few who consistently perform poorly. However, competition can be a strong motivator, but too much emphasis on leader boards and individual performance can demotivate such employees, leading to disengagement.

3.6.3 Diverse Learning Preferences

Not all employees respond to gamification in the same way. Some may prefer traditional learning methods, while others may be more motivated by interactive and gamified approaches. Employees with different learning styles or those unfamiliar with games may find the experience overwhelming or confusing [15].

3.6.4 Time and Resource Intensive

Developing a comprehensive and effective gamified training program requires a huge investment in terms of money as well as time. Thus it can be time-consuming and expensive especially for smaller organizations as they may find these resources difficult to allocate. It requires investment in the right technology, game design, and continuous updates to keep the content fresh and relevant.

3.6.5 Difficulty in Measuring Return on Investment (ROI)

Quantifying the impact of gamification on employee performance, engagement, and retention, especially if the results are intangible or long-term, can be a point of struggle for the organizations. Hence it can be difficult to measure the ROI of gamification in training.

3.6.6 Sustainability of Engagement

Once employees become accustomed to the gamified elements or if the challenges become repetitive over time, the novelty may wear off, leading to reduced interest and participation. Also the individuals may lose motivation. So gamification can initially boost engagement but later on may lose its effectiveness.

3.6.7 Lack of Personalization

Gamification programs that are too generic may not cater to individual learning needs. If the same experience is applied to all employees, some may feel the program is irrelevant to their role or skill level.

3.6.8 Technological Barriers

Implementing gamification often requires sophisticated technological infrastructure, such as LMS, mobile apps, or virtual platforms. Companies with out-dated systems or a lack of technical expertise may face difficulties integrating gamification into their training programs.

3.6.9 Cultural Resistance

Some employees, especially in more traditional or formal industries, may view gamification as unprofessional or trivial. This cultural resistance can prevent gamification from being accepted and effective within an organization.

3.6.10 Undue Pressure

Over-reliance on gamification can lead to ethical issues such as excessive competition, exclusion, or manipulation. Some employees may feel undue pressure to perform, while others may manipulate the system to earn rewards without genuinely learning the material.

3.6.11 Over-Complication of Design

A gamified system that is too complex or difficult to understand may overwhelm employees rather than engage them. Poorly designed gamification elements can confuse learners, making the training experience frustrating and counterproductive.

3.7 SUCCESSFUL IMPLEMENTATIONS OF VR

VR is well known for teaching hard skills and offering realistic simulations, such as for aeroplane pilots or equipment maintenance. With the rise of the metaverse, VR (which is one of several ways to enter the metaverse) is also growing more common. The PwC 2022 US Metaverse Survey found that 51% of companies are either in the process of integrating VR into strategy or have already built VR into at least one dedicated line of business. Thirty-four percent say that one of the biggest metaverse benefits they currently enjoy or foresee is "a more effective way to develop and train our people" [16].

Due to its immersive, hands-on approach, industries, from **healthcare** to **manufacturing** and **aviation**, are increasingly adopting **VR** for employee training. VR enables employees to gain valuable experience in high-stakes, real-life situations without the associated risks, improving performance and safety while reducing training costs and time.

3.7.1 Lufthansa Aviation Training: Pilot Training

Lufthansa utilizes VR to simulate both standard and emergency procedures so as to train pilots in handling complex flight situations, including emergencies, without the need for expensive flight simulators. Pilots can practise responding to in-flight issues like engine failure, turbulence, or landing gear malfunctions in a fully immersive environment.

VR training complements traditional flight simulators by providing a more cost-effective, scalable solution. Pilots gain more practice hours in realistic flight scenarios, reducing training costs and improving emergency response preparedness [14].

3.7.2 Ford: Hazardous Work Environment Training

Ford has implemented VR-based safety training programs to teach employees how to handle high-risk situations, such as working in confined spaces or with hazardous materials, and train employees in safety protocols for hazardous work environments like welding or handling dangerous chemicals.

Ford saw a 70% reduction in workplace injuries after implementing VR-based training, as employees were better equipped to deal with potentially dangerous scenarios in real-life situations.

3.7.3 Osso VR: Surgical Training

Osso VR is a VR platform used to provide hands-on training for surgeons and healthcare professionals. It offers a simulated environment where trainees can practise surgical techniques in a risk-free, controlled setting.

Surgeons using Osso VR showed a significant improvement in accuracy, speed, and procedural knowledge. By practising in the virtual environment, they were better prepared for real-life operations, reducing errors in the operating room [14].

3.8 CHALLENGES

As organizations seek to harness the immersive potential of VR for training, they often encounter various obstacles, ranging from cost and technological issues to user adaptability.

3.8.1 High Initial Costs

The upfront investment required to develop and deploy VR training can be prohibitively expensive. This includes costs for hardware (*e.g.*, VR headsets), software development, and content creation.

3.8.2 Technological Limitations

VR technology requires high-performance computing power, stable software platforms, and high-quality graphics to create immersive experiences. Any lag or poor-quality visuals can detract from the learning experience.

3.8.3 Content Development Complexity

Creating realistic simulations involves advanced 3D modelling, animation, and programming, which requires specialized skills. Therefore, developing VR training content is more difficult than conventional e-learning modules.

3.8.4 User Adoption and Resistance

Due to unfamiliarity, discomfort, or scepticism about the technology, employees may resist using VR. Some individuals may experience side effects like motion sickness or others from wearing VR headsets for extended periods.

3.8.5 Limited Customization and Flexibility

Many off-the-shelf VR training programs lack the flexibility to adapt to specific organizational needs or individual learning preferences. This can limit the relevance of the training to particular job roles or industries.

3.8.6 Space and Infrastructure Requirements

VR often requires a dedicated physical space where employees can move around freely without the risk of injury. This can be difficult to set up in smaller offices or locations where space is limited.

3.8.7 Regular Maintenance and Upgrades

VR hardware and software require regular maintenance and upgrades to stay functional and relevant. Devices can malfunction or become out-dated quickly, leading to additional costs and disruptions in the training process.

3.8.8 Limited Interpersonal Skill Development

While VR is excellent for technical training and simulations, it can struggle to effectively replicate interpersonal interactions or emotional intelligence training. This limitation affects industries where communication and human interaction are critical.

3.8.9 VR Content Creation

Organizations may lack the internal expertise to design and implement VR training that truly engages learners and achieves training goals. Even after investing in the needed tools, creating effective VR content requires a steep learning curve.

3.8.10 Data Security and Privacy Concerns

VR training may involve the collection of sensitive data, such as biometrics or personal performance metrics. Ensuring that these data are securely stored and compliant with privacy regulations can be a challenge.

3.8.11 Difficulty in Measuring Effectiveness

While traditional training methods often have established metrics for evaluating success, it can be more challenging to measure the effectiveness of VR training. Tracking tangible improvements in employee performance after VR training is not always straightforward.

3.8.12 Incompatibility with All Learning Styles

Some employees may prefer traditional, text-based, or face-to-face learning as not all employees learn best in a highly immersive, interactive environment. Some may find VR overwhelming and exciting or maybe even distracting.

3.9 INTEGRATION OF GAMIFICATION AND VR

Although there are challenges in cost, design complexity, and user adaptation still by uniting the immersive and collaborating power of VR with the motivational elements of gamification, organizations can actually generate training programs that augment employee skills, motivation, and retention. The integration of **Gamification and VR** into employee training offers a highly engaging and effective way to improve learning outcomes. Despite the various challenges discussed earlier, a well-planned strategy can lead to significant benefits across industries [5].

3.9.1 Synergies: How They Complement Each Other

- **Engagement:** While gamification keeps users engaged with tasks by adding objectives, rewards, and feedback, VR provides an immersive environment. This increases user motivation to complete training and achieve higher performance.
- **Personalization:** Gamification allows VR training to be personalized based on individual progress, skill level, and learning preferences. Adaptive difficulty levels, branching scenarios, and customized challenges make training more relevant.

- **Skill Reinforcement:** Gamification elements such as points, badges, and achievements encourage repetition and mastery of skills within the VR environment. This enhances learning by making employees return to tasks to achieve better scores or unlock higher levels.

Amongst the various other companies integrating Gamification and VR, Walmart is the one that uses the same to train its employees on customer service and managing high-pressure scenarios. The aforementioned company uses VR for employee training combined with gamification elements like points and performance feedback to simulate Black Friday shopping and other high-stress situations.

With VR providing a safe environment to practise and gamification boosting engagement, employees can gain hands-on experience in managing customer interactions and stressful situations.

3.10 CONCLUSION

For cultivating a skilled, motivated, and future-ready workforce, employee training and development are indispensable tools. They not only improve individual performance but also contribute to the overall long-term success of the organization. By prioritizing continuous learning and growth, companies create an environment where employees can thrive, innovate, and drive the business forward. In the modern workplace, investing in training and development is not just a benefit—it's a necessity for long-term sustainability and success.

In today's rapidly changing contemporary era of competition, innovation in training methods is not just a trend, rather it is a necessity. As businesses face new challenges and opportunities, innovative training solutions provide the flexibility, engagement, and efficiency needed to upskill employees and maintain a competitive edge. However, effective training solutions should be aligned with organizational goals, innovation must be balanced with practicality, and the whole process must be inclusive and measurable to ensure sustained success. Organizations can foster a culture of continuous learning by leveraging the power of innovative training, adapt to technological advancements, and equip their workforce for the future.

Both Gamification and VR represent powerful tools that cater to different learning needs and environments. **Gamification** excels in knowledge retention, motivation, and engagement for various types of training, from soft skills to compliance. **VR**, on the other hand, is a game-changer for industries that require practical, hands-on training, allowing employees to practise in real-world-like environments (Table 3.1).

The most effective training programs may use a combination of both tools to create a holistic learning environment. Although, by making learning more engaging and effective, **Gamification** and **VR** can significantly improve employee training outcomes, this comes with its own unique challenges. By understanding potential obstacles, such as misalignment with objectives, cultural resistance, or technological barriers, and implementing thoughtful solutions, organizations can reap the benefits of gamified training. Ensuring that **Gamification and VR** are aligned with learning goals, personalized to individual needs, and designed to maintain long-term engagement is key to its success in the workplace [3,7].

REFERENCES

1. Agarwal, S., & Gupta, D. (2024). Digital analytics applications for sustainable training and education. In K. Sood, P. Kalia, S. Grima, & A. Chaudhary (Eds.), *Digital Analytics Applications for Sustainable Training and Education* (p. 25). Apple Academic Press.
2. Agarwal, S., Diwedi, S., & Ghai, R. (2020). Perception of trainees towards skill development program. *International Journal of Innovative Science and Research Technology*, 5(12), 387–392.
3. Agarwal, S., Gupta, D., & Gupta, M. (2023). Impact of training method on trainees' learning and implementation on the job: A study with special reference to power sector. *AIP Conference Proceedings*, 2427(1), 020020. https://doi.org/10.1063/5.0100893
4. Agarwal, S., Gupta, D., & Gupta, M. (2023). Techno pedagogical concept with digital skills. In M. S. Manna, B. Balusamy, K. Sood, N. Chilamkurti, & I. R. George (Eds.), *Edutech Enabled Teaching* (pp. 129–152). Chapman and Hall/CRC.
5. Barrett, K. A. & Johnson, W. L. (2010). Virtual environments and serious games: Teaching cross-cultural communication skills. In W. Ritke-Jones (Ed.), *Virtual Environments for Corporate Education: Employee Learning and Solutions* (pp. 264–283). IGI Global. https://doi.org/10.4018/978-1-61520-619-3.ch015
6. Burke, B. (2014). *Gamify: How Gamification Motivates People to Do Extraordinary Things*. Bibliomotion, Inc.
7. Gary, D., & Biju, V. *Human Resource Management* (16th ed.). Pearson Education.
8. Gupta, D., & Agarwal, S. (2018). Skill development initiative-literature review. *Inspira-Journal of Modern Management and Entrepreneurship (JMME)*, 8(2), 319–322.
9. Agarwal, S., & Gupta, D. (2018). Training prospects in the power sector in India. *International Journal of Research in Engineering, IT and Social Sciences*, 8(Special Issue), 305–314.
10. Gupta, D., Gupta, M., & Rani, S. (2022). A study on training of workmen in a manufacturing organization—With reference to aluminium foundry. In A. Dvivedi, A. Sachdeva, R. Sindhwani, & R. Sahu (Eds.), *Recent Trends in Industrial and Production Engineering* (pp. 221–233). Springer. https://doi.org/10.1007/978-981-16-3330-0_19
11. Gupta, D., Gupta, M., Tiwari, S., & Singh, N. (2021). Motivation due to fear of failure is a key contributor in maximizing workers' productivity in today's competitive arena. *International Journal of Indian Culture and Business Management*, 23(2), 193–217. https://doi.org/10.1504/IJICBM.2021.115895
12. Gupta, M., Gupta, D., & Rai, P. (2024). Exploring the impact of software as a service (SaaS) on human life. *EAI Endorsed Transactions on Internet of Things*, 10. https://doi.org/10.4108/eetiot.4821
13. ELM Learning. (n.d.). Gamification in eLearning. ELM Learning. https://elmlearning.com/hub/elearning/gamification/
14. HQSoftware. (n.d.). AR/VR training use cases. Retrieved [2024], from https://hqsoftwarelab.com/blog/ar-vr-training-use-cases/
15. Continu Team. (n.d.). Gamification in training. Continu. https://www.continu.com/blog/gamification-in-training
16. Forward Networks. (2024). ROI eBook. Retrieved from https://www.forwardnetworks.com/wp-content/uploads/2024/01/ROI-eBook.pdf
17. Kumar, A., Gupta, D., Gupta, M., & Srivastava, G. (2021). India an emerging leader after pandemic: A strategy for the development of new India. *Global Journal of Enterprise Information System*, 13(1), 60–70. https://www.gjeis.com/index.php/GJEIS/article/view/629

18. Rajvanshi, P. R., Singh, T., Gupta, D., & Gupta, M. (2022). Blockchain technology for pharmaceutical drug supply chain management. In P. Singh, D. Mishra, & K. Seth (Eds.), *Transformation in Healthcare with Emerging Technologies* (1st ed., pp. 217–230). CRC Press.
19. Rani, S., Gupta, M., & Gupta, D. (2020). Artificial intelligence and personalized banking. In *Transforming Management Using Artificial Intelligence Techniques* (1st ed., p. 24). CRC Press.
20. Singh, S., & Gupta, D. (2023). Module allocation model in distributed computing system by implementing fuzzy C-means clustering technique. In R. Agrawal, P. Mitra, A. Pal, & M. Sharma Gaur (Eds.), *International Conference on IoT, Intelligent Computing and Security* (Vol. 982, pp. 145–160). Springer. https://doi.org/10.1007/978-981-19-8136-4_14

4 Exploring Blockchain Applications and Challenges in HR Management

Gagan Deep and Jyoti Verma

4.1 INTRODUCTION TO BLOCKCHAIN TECHNOLOGY

4.1.1 Explanation of Blockchain Technology and Its Fundamental Principles

The decentralized and distributed ledger technology commonly referred to as the blockchain technology has recently received much attention because of the probable applications in various fields (Nakamoto, 2008). In its essence, blockchain is an open and distributed database that chronologically stores multiple transactions while supporting transparency and the validation of multiple parties. Due to this, it will be seen that the technology in question possesses certain distinct characteristics based on a set of ideas. The absence of a central authority, or a middleman, guiding the network, which is decentralization is one of the core concepts of blockchain technology (Christidis & Devetsikiotis, 2016). This decentralized nature of Bitcoin allows for peer-to-peer transactions as well as eliminating the necessity of faith in a central entity (Tapscott & Tapscott, 2016). Two more essential principles of block chain technology include decentralization and immutability (Tapscott & Tapscott, 2016). Swan (2015) agrees that it is almost impossible to alter or manipulate the data that are involved in a particular transaction on the blockchain. The non-malleability is achieved through the application of cryptographic techniques and consensus procedures validating the information placed in the blockchain ledger (Nakamoto, 2008). The solidity of the blockchain is mostly based on consensus processes (Tapscott & Tapscott, 2016). Such protocols ensure that all network users are in agreement as to the validity of a transaction and the block's place in the chain (Christidis & Devetsikiotis, 2016). For trust and consensus in the decentralized system, a number of consensus mechanisms proposed are proof of work and proof of stake (Nakamoto, 2008; Buterin, 2014). Another concept that is achieved through the decentralized and public nature of blockchain is transparency (Swan, 2015). Each member has the capability to see all the recorded transactions in the blockchain, which helps to enhance accountability (Tapscott & Tapscott, 2016). However, other cryptographic methods that allow those users to maintain pseudo-identities and broadcast selective information can also ensure that privacy is protected (Narayanan et al., 2016).

DOI: 10.1201/9781032619651-4

4.1.2 Benefits of Blockchain in Various Industries

Due to all these benefits, blockchain is considered as a revolutionary technology that can transform numerous sectors almost in every industry. These benefits stem from the characteristic features of blockchain, such as security, risk-free, decentralization, and openness (Swan, 2015). Several industries have deemed how blockchain might establish credibility, increase effectiveness, and overhaul processes after discovering the technology. The advent of blockchain has the potential of revolutionalizing payment systems in the financial industry by making the transactions faster, safer, and cheaper (Nakamoto, 2008). Through employing the burgeoning global network of distributed and openly/more transparent ledgers, advanced and disruptive offerings such as Bitcoin—a cryptocurrency—have challenged the current financial systems (Tapscott & Tapscott, 2016). Besides, blockchain can help reduce time and cost involved in the settlement of efficient cross-border payments (Swan, 2015). Another area where the blockchain technology can be of benefit is supply chain. Blockchain has been found to have a functional utility in the supply chain where traceability, accountability, and efficiency are key issues through the transparency and immutability of the technology (Christidis & Devetsikiotis, 2016). These are ways in which blockchain can assist with logistics, put an end to counterfeiting, and provide real-time tracking of the movement of commodities (Tapscott & Tapscott, 2016). This innovative technology has the potential of improving health care in the area of interoperability and data security. The following are the numerous potential benefits as highlighted by Mettler (2016). Blockchain can enable the ease of data exchange between various stakeholders in the healthcare sector and enable secure storage of medical records, which are unprecedentedly hack-proof, and patients' unique data are more secure from third-party interference. Others include the clinical trials, pharmaceutical supply chain management, and credential verification among others (Christidis & Devetsikiotis, 2016). Blockchain has the capability of transforming the energy sector by facilitating the incorporation of renewable energy systems, playing the role of a platform for prosumers energy trading and improving the efficiency and effectiveness of managing the grid (Swan, 2015). A case in energy transactions is that blockchain can replace middlemen and smart contracts can be used to create trust (Christidis & Devetsikiotis, 2016). Besides these sectors, Tapscott and Tapscott (2016) stated that the uses of blockchain technology go beyond the mentioned sectors such as government services and facilities, real estate, intellectual property rights, and others. I am quite positive that blockchain will redesign systems and corresponding processes in many spheres incurring high costs and enhancing credibility while increasing effectiveness and minimizing fraud opportunities.

4.1.3 Relevance and Potential of Blockchain in HR Management

Blockchain is a technology that can redesign a number of industries and one of them is Human Resources (HR) management due to the main characteristics of the technology – transparency, immutability, and decentralization. One of the biggest challenges that current and future HR managers will encounter is to check candidate's credentials. Possible decentralized applications can create a safe and hack-proof way of verifying employment, record, and schooling background. Candidate verification procedures may be trustworthy and transparent using the blockchain-based platforms according to Ponomarev and Belyavskaya (2018) as it will help in reducing time as well as efforts required to conduct credential checks. Through the smart contract, the process of payroll and benefits can be operated automatically since blockchain provides a guarantee of a secure and accurate transaction. By incorporating blockchain in payroll systems, Battisti et al. (2021) argue that external data accuracy is enhanced, middlemen can be eliminated, and instant payment processing can be achieved, hence reducing costs and increasing efficiency. Candidate information is encrypted and shared through blockchain, a process that enhances the efficiency of the hiring processes. The blockchain enables one to place actual data such as references, experience, and talents; thus, it increases the chance of matching a suitable candidate and reduces the instances of fake resumes. Recruiting efficiency can also be enhanced when companies are directly in touch with job seekers using blockchain technology-based decentralized platform as pointed out by Liao et al. (2020). Ensuring data confidentiality is essential; ensuring identities of employees and their access right are well controlled. Blockchain technology in decentralized identity systems can offer workers control over their details as well as protect the information's authenticity and privacy. Conti et al. (2018) have likened blockchain-based identity management systems to the following strengths: this includes eliminating the risk of identity theft and developing a model of self-sovereign identification which will enable individuals to own their digital identities. By integrating blockchain technology, organization performance reviews can then be fair and impartial due to the maintaining of employees' performance data records. This improves equity and trust in organizations. Blockchain-based performance management systems, according to Yang et al. (2021), can produce verifiable records of accomplishments, encouraging an accountability- and transparency-focused culture.

4.2 BLOCKCHAIN APPLICATIONS IN HR MANAGEMENT

4.2.1 Recruitment and Hiring

4.2.1.1 Blockchain-Based Identity Verification and Background Checks

On this note, blockchain technology is perfect for housing and authentication of identification records because it cannot be altered. As rightly emphasized by Kshetri (2017), blockchain-based identity management may enable people to have ownership and control over their data. Since identity verification processes can also be digitized on the basis of blockchain, the immutable data of an individual can be stored on the blockchain to make the process more secure and less prone to the instances of fake identity and frauds. Blockchain technology makes self-sovereign identity possible through its functioning; people are masters of their digital identity, and they can present personal data only to the recipients they want to. Hence, there is no need for a single controlling source or mediators for identity confirmation (Rajvanshi et al., 2022a).

The following are explained by Zyskind et al. (2015) as being assured by self-sovereign identity on the blockchain: the user-centric identity management, integrity of data, and privacy. The longer and detailed background checks can be enhanced and made faster through the seamless use of blockchain-based storing and sharing of verified data. Data on the blockchain can be input and verified by the nodes or verifiers such as University and previous employers, making the record transparent. In their study, Xu et al. (2019) have offered a solution using blockchain to offer decentralized background check, a move that they posit will reduce reliance on centralized verification authorities as well as increasing efficiency. The preservation of the applicants' privacy is highly valued in blockchain-based background checks and identity verification systems. So, the usage of cryptographic methods and zero-knowledge proofs allows one to verify the required data without revealing the sensitive information. Kosba et al. (2016) have indicated that these methods ensure that only relevant information is disclosed during the verification process, and privacy of the user's information is enhanced, thus enhancing confidence. Organizations' identity systems created with the use of blockchain technologies can help people avoid the need for repeated procedures of getting the documents verified for different organizations. This increases efficiency and decreases redundancy. Blockchain-based identification solutions, as covered by Chatterjee et al. (2019), provide for safe and easy verification across several businesses while preserving data ownership and privacy as shown in Figure 4.1.

4.2.1.2 Secure and Transparent Candidate Profiles and Resumes

As earlier pointed out, the nature of blockchain means that candidate profiles submitted on the network cannot be altered without the change being reflected on the blockchain ledger. Such feature helps in having more credibility and honesty in the candidate profiles being created. When it comes to possessing candidate's information, blockchain-based platforms can provide a safe and entirely noninvaded storage to minimize the risks of fake profiles, as Ponomarev and Belyavskaya pointed out in their research in 2018. Due to the properties of blockchain that make the process of academic credentials more manageable, employers will be able to trust that the qualifications presented to them by the candidates are not fake. The records of

FIGURE 4.1 Recruitment and hiring. (Source: Author's self-generated.)

students such as their results and other academic performance indicators may be adequately safeguarded and validated through the use of the blockchain technology. Xu et al. (2017) discuss about a broad architecture of the blockchain-based system in their study where they want to make the educational certification more reliable and reduce the need of manual checking. Employment history of a candidate is considered an object of evaluation. Blockchain guarantees that the employment experience procured is accurate and transparent through creation of record of employment. The record of employment can be reported to the blockchain by the verifiers which can be other employers or professional platforms, and the record can be accurate and cannot be tampered with. Systems of job history maintained in blockchain can help to minimize the time to complete the verification processes as well as to decrease the risks associated with fake resumes, which is described by Li et al. (2019). Due to decentralized nature of the blockchain technology, the applicants may be able to retain ownership of the personal information and select which employers they would want to share it with. The participants can share the access to specific segments of their profile using private keys and smart contracts, thus ensuring the personal information's protection while providing the evaluators with the information necessary to make the evaluation. Kosba et al. (2016) look at this concept of candidate-controlled data sharing and in so doing underscore the importance of ownership and privacy of data. Hiring can also be made more efficient and effective with the use of blockchain especially on resumes and candidate profiles. Employers can save time and effort by eliminating the need for manual verification by having access to verified and reliable information. This enhances the overall effectiveness of selecting and evaluating candidates. Blockchain-based applicant profiles have the potential to streamline the hiring process and result in a more accurate assessment of qualifications, as noted by Yao et al. (2021).

4.2.1.3 Smart Contracts for Automating Hiring Processes

By leveraging the power of smart contracts, the extensive process of analysing the candidates can be done in advance and will require less effort from the employer's side. Since smart contacts are digital agreements, they can prove convenient for evaluating a candidate's qualifications and matching them to a job description using particular criteria and formulas. In the words of Fan et al. (2020), using of automation in the preliminary stages of hiring directly affects the assessment of performance probabilities of the candidates by reducing the influence of bias that may be associated with human discretion. The hiring agreements can be built for the employers and candidates through smart contracts that can facilitate honest developments that cannot be changed again. Such responsibilities, wages, and commencement dates are some of the terms and conditions which may be provided in these contracts. Smart contracts help to reduce the chance of disputes by ensuring both the parties have equal information that one cannot use against another. Xu et al. (2017) have pointed out that smart contracts provide a safe and particularly transparent environment for hiring agreements. Smart contracts allow payment procedures to be carried out and be on time, and this ensures that the workers are paid on time. Smart contracts can also enable payment upon the delivery of certain set or agreed deadlines since payment parameters can also be inputted in the smart contract. Hence, invoices and payments can be computed in an automatic way as Bhattacharya et al. (2019) have noted. This is based on the inherent attributes of blockchain that smart contracts leverage for enhancing security and trust within employment. Smart contracts reduce the risk of fraud and manipulation by the ability of all the stakeholders to see the term and conditions due to the transparency of contracts in the block chain. From the analysis of Eskandari et al. (2019), it uses the development of smart contacts in a safe and auditing way that minimizes possible risk in the recruiting processes. Smart contracts are efficient in the automation of companies' onboarding and offboarding procedures, and thus, employee transitions can be smooth (Rani et al., 2020). Smart contracts can make it easier to provide new workers with equipment, training materials, and access rights as well as to terminate access and return firm assets to departing employees by including preset procedures and actions in the contract. According to Yin et al. (2020), this automation guarantees consistency and reduces administrative overhead.

4.2.2 Employee Records and Credentials

4.2.2.1 Immutable and Tamper-Proof Storage of Employee Records

For safe custody of personnel records, there cannot be a better place than the blockchain platform since it is tamper-proof and does not allow any alteration once executed. The employment records can be made decentralized and transparent by use of blockchain technology; this is because the blockchain has the ledgers distributed. This ensures that the records cannot be manipulated or modified thereby being altered secretly. As defined by Kosba et al. (2016), blockchain-based systems result in an immutable list of transactions and a high measure of integrity and reliability.

This ensures personnel records will not be manipulated or tampered with due to the great security measures that come with the use of the blockchain. Blockchain offers uniformity, security, and validity of the employee's data since the consensus algorithms and the implementation of substantive cryptography mechanisms. As noted by Tapscott and Tapscott (2016), through the use of blockchain, there are reduced risks of illegitimate changes compared to the traditional structures in enterprise applications for safe storage of the private data of the employees. Higher levels of responsibility and openness associated with the storage of records about employees are ensured by blockchain technology's openness. Employees and all the other interested parties such as the auditors, the personnel from the human resource department, and the employees are able to check the information and ascertain that it is correct. Because record keeping is transparent, there is no need for middlemen and this makes the procedures efficient enough. Yli-Huumo et al. (2016) note because the information stored on blockchain technology is clear and can be easily traced, it can be relied on for the personnel records. Blockchain-integrated solutions provide workers with self-ownership and self-authority of their own records. It is possible to let smart contracts and private keys to give access to records while maintaining one's confidentiality, yet share essential data for HR purposes. Self-ownership of identification and data is presented by Kshetri (2017) where people are safely in charge of their own identities. It is therefore significant to note that hi-tech approaches such as blockchain facilitate the operations personnel record audits and verification processes. In blockchain, legitimacy and correctness of the information entered about the employee can be ascertained by the authorized parties expounding that there would not be a need to verify the records,

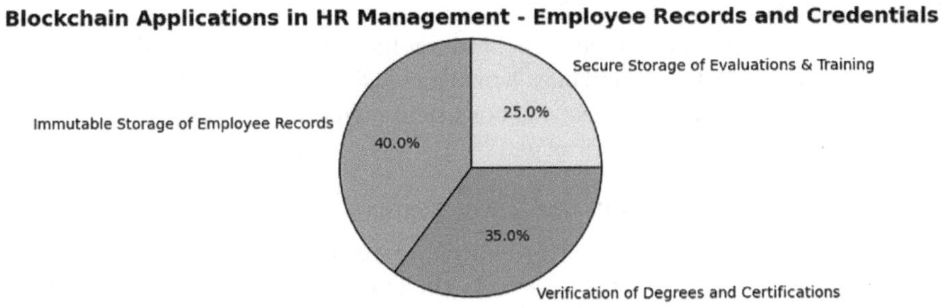

FIGURE 4.2 Employee records and credentials. (Source: Author's self-generated.)

which is time wasting and requires cross-referencing. The blockchain's decentralized and unchangeable properties minimize administrative overhead and do away with the necessity for thorough reconciliation. According to Xu et al. (2019), blockchain-based solutions simplify employee record audits and verification, increasing productivity and lowering errors as shown in Figure 4.2.

4.2.2.2 Verification of Educational Degrees and Certifications

The solution is in providing a stable and immutable record service provider and verifiable scanner for all credentials and degrees using blockchain technology. Employers, certifying authorities, and the institutions can use blockchain as a common platform to record and maintain details on the centralized and immutable database maintaining record details in a transparent manner. Similarly, Xu et al. (2017) have stressed that through application of the block chain solution, data can only be entered once; the solution engenders trust and effectively minimizes the risk of fake credentials. By using decentralized verification mechanisms offered by the blockchain, it becomes possible to validate certification as well as degrees of education in a most efficient and trustworthy manner. Some of the benefits include the following: Verifiers can easily acquire and verify the credentials without having to rely on intermediaries or conventional methods such as manual means through the implementation of smart contracts through the use of the blockchain technology and the use of cryptography. They give an example of this decentralized verification technique, which as they note is more reliable and efficient. Just as it is with self-organizing networks, blockchain-based solutions can eliminate the need for third-party verifications given that they are self-verifying systems, which may allow people to maintain ownership of their data and provide verifiers with direct access to their credentials stored in the blockchain. Molina-Markham et al. (2019) consider the concept of self-sovereign identity and verification as an individual can confirm his/her identity without third-party help. Since it provides data security and privacy features, there are no privacy concerns with regards to blockchain. Educational records that are stored on the blockchain are only accessible for any party that has the right to access them and may further be encrypted. Rong et al. (2020) has discussed how great amounts of data require protection and their methods of protecting these sensitive data by using algorithms that involve public and private keys. The dispersed nature of the block chain technologically reduces instances of hacking and unauthorized access to educational information. As a result of using blockchain technology, employers and other institutions receive more efficient credentials to accept and assess them. It's possible to share validated credentials between the different blockchain-based systems, and this eliminates redundancy, hence increasing efficiency. Blockchain-based credentialing systems enable a fast and consistent method for evaluating degrees and certifications, as noted by Becker et al. (2021).

4.2.2.3 Secure Storage of Performance Evaluations and Training Records

Employers have to ensure that performance appraisal files and training records be properly stored so that no one else except the employee can have access to those sensitive and truthful records. Blockchain technology proves to be a viable solution by providing users an immutable and secure solution to store such records. Data integrity, secrecy, and its availability only to the authorized users can be achieved through decentralized consensus methods and cryptographic methods by the help of blockchain. Zheng et al. (2017) pointed out that the prospects based on blockchain have higher security attributes and exclude the opportunities for data distortion or unauthorized access. An organization may keep vital documents such as training details and appraisals secret but at the same instance may use blockchain to ensure transparency.

4.2.3 Payroll and Compensation

4.2.3.1 Smart Contracts for Automated Payroll Processing

This technology has the potential of optimizing the delivery of payroll services to different firms through the execution of smart contracts to expedite payments for services offered while ensuring that every detail is handled with much professionalism and disclosed accordingly. Payroll rules and computations may also be executed by smart contacts through implementation of blockchain, which negates human intervention. This makes work more efficient and minimizes the risks of either embezzlement or errors being made. Based on the work of Xu et al. (2018), smart contracts enable the employees, customers, and other parties of the payroll processing services to realize self-executing and self-verifying transactions, thus ensuring that the system is dependable and impenetrable. It is important for organizations to realize that smart contracts can enhance the organization's payroll efficiency, compliance, and even the level of trust in the payment process as shown in Figure 4.3.

4.2.3.2 Transparent and Auditable Compensation Distribution

It is a critical issue for the listed companies to establish a fair and, more importantly, an auditable compensation distribution policy in place. Blockchain provides an unalterable trail of the payment process making it one of the solutions to the problem. Since compensation transactions are to be recorded in a decentralized manner with the help of blockchain, the possibilities for transparency and recording free from tampering are achieved here. This openness ensures that the company is accountable to its workers and will allow the workers verify the correctness of their pay. As observed by Jøsang et al. (2018), the principles of auditability and transparency inherent in blockchain mean that stakeholders can easily track as well as verify compensation payments, thereby enhancing the levels of transparency and confidence in the process.

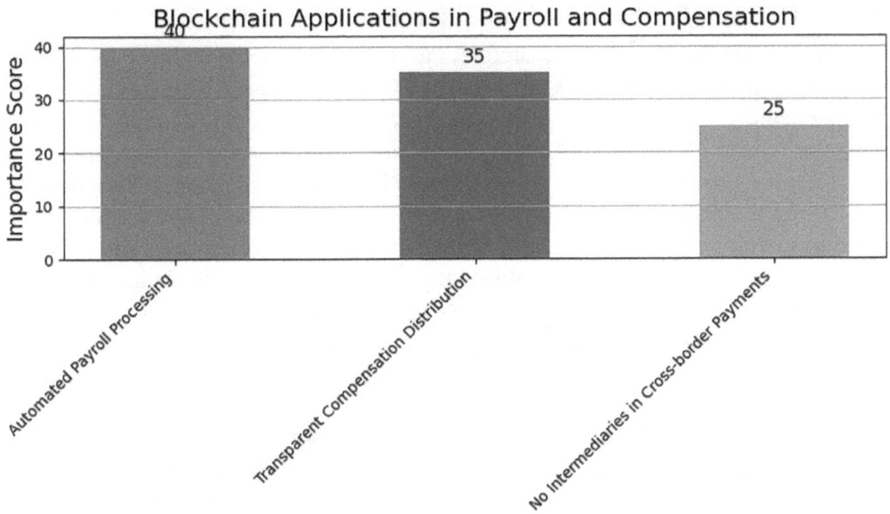

FIGURE 4.3 Payroll and compensation. (Source: Author's self-generated.)

4.2.3.3 Elimination of Intermediaries in Cross-Border Payments

The case with the application of blockchain technology is the direct transfer of payments across borders without the middleman. A number of intermediaries are often engaged in traditional cross-border payment methods, and this often results in delays, high fees, and security issues. A direct peer-to-peer transaction can be allowed by the blockchain technology without the involvement of intermediaries. In this regard, faster, cheaper, and secure cross-border payments and remittances are positively impacted, being a key highlight of the effectiveness of blockchain according to Swan (2015). It leverages the features of digital currency and smart contracts and facilitates the concepts of transparency, reduced costs, and efficient and smooth payments and transactions. This could change cross-border transactions for the better, making them easier to execute and perform.

4.2.4 Performance Management and Feedback

4.2.4.1 Transparent and Immutable Performance Tracking

An attempt at performance tracking that can be transparent and immutable is the good usage of blockchain technology. Use of blockchain enables performance monitoring solutions to provide an accurate and defensible account of the performance of an employee or an organization. The performance data are encrypted through the use of blockchain to ensure that they cannot be manipulated or be changed in any way without leaving any tracks. The systems which use blockchain ensure performance evaluation in a transparent and unalterable manner leading to accountability and confidence as postulated by Kshetri (2017). This open and verifiable method allows for the increase in objectivity of decisions or in point efficiency and reliability of performance evaluations, for example. Utilizing the blockchain technology in collecting and rating performance data makes it appealing to revolutionize performance tracking entirely.

4.2.4.2 Decentralized Feedback and Recognition Systems

Decentralized feedback and automated recognition as proposed by blockchain solutions will offer innovative thinking on fairness and openness of feedback. These systems enable PEP and P2P feedback and rewards in an unaltered and direct way due to the working of the blockchain which is decentralized and transparent. To guarantee that a record of praise or criticism is kept safely and cannot be tampered with without consensus, blockchain is used. There are two feedback and acknowledgement systems which are decentralized that benefit trust, accountability, and the trait, which make the person or employee own their achievements, which are stated by Swan et al. (2020). These technologies revolutionize the feedback and reward mechanisms because they make them more transparent, merit-based, and diverse through using blockchains.

4.2.4.3 Smart Contracts for Performance-Based Incentives

Smart contracts can be used as an effective means in order to introduce performance-based reward systems in businesses. Smart contracts enable the management and distribution of incentives depending on the performance standards set out since they operate with the help of the blockchain. This reduces the chances of bias when it comes to the computation of incentives and eliminates the need for elemental intervention. As acknowledged by Pilkington and Zeng (2017), smart contracts give visible, safe, as well as unalterable programmable bonuses. Now, smart contracts in organizations can enhance motivation and accountability for performance, align incentives with performance objectives, and improve the overall effectiveness of the performance-based incentive programs.

4.2.5 Supply Chain and Vendor Management

4.2.5.1 Verification and Monitoring of Third-Party Vendors

Due to the high risks that third parties may pose to an organization, adequate and sustainable monitoring and validation of third-party providers are mandatory. Tapscott and Tapscott (2016) opine that various vendor verification processes can be secured and made transparent through the use of blockchain and this creates a way through which businesses can check on the performance of the vendors they engage at different periods.

4.2.5.2 Tracking of Employee Benefits and Services within the Supply Chain

Any supply chain management that is to be effective needs to take a look at vendor services as well as employee benefits. Yao et al. (2019) indicated that through blockchain-based systems, companies stand to benefit from a decentralized and non-tamper-proof record of issuing and managing of employee benefits, which enables compliance with the legal requirement of equal treatment of employees all along the value chain.

4.2.5.3 Enhanced Transparency and Accountability in Vendor Relationships

In vendor relations, issues such as accountability and transparency are very crucial. Blockchain can be used to write a supply chain that can be audited and made very transparent to ensure that all vendors engaged adhere to the correct ethical and contractual standards. As Azaria et al. (2016) state that transparency is another benefit of LSPs as it enhances confidence between the contracting parties and helps in determining aspects that need to be further optimized.

4.3 CHALLENGES AND CONSIDERATIONS

4.3.1 Data Privacy and Security

4.3.1.1 Safeguarding Personal and Sensitive HR Data

One of the core responsibilities that must be met for confidentiality and preventing unwanted access is protecting private and sensitive HR data (Rajvanshi et al., 2022b). Encryption, as stated by Aljawarneh et al. (2019), protects the data while in transit and when stored helping to ensure their genuineness and security.

4.3.1.2 Ensuring Compliance with Data Protection Regulations

In order to ensure data privacy, several data protection acts have to be followed including the General Data Protection Regulation (GDPR). Bonneau et al. (2015) have opined that using blockchain technology, it will be possible to enhance compliance since the access and usage of data can be recorded in a transparent and auditable manner.

4.3.2 Adoption and Integration

4.3.2.1 Overcoming Resistance to Change and Cultural Barriers

This is because employees and stakeholders always resist changes which may warrant the implementation of new HR procedures and systems. Given this fact, these oppositions need to be covered, and by this way, cultural barriers need to be passed to ensure successful adoption. Still, other countermeasures elaborated by Armenakis and Harris (2009) such as communication, involvement of the staff, and leadership support may help to overcome the barriers to change and foster acceptance of change as an opportunity rather than a threat.

4.3.2.2 Integration Challenges with Existing HR Systems and Processes

Adopting new strategies in HR might be challenging when it comes to aligning with current systems and practices. For efficiency to grow and remain constant, there is a need to ensure that there is perfect integration and data sharing. As pointed out by Kavanagh and Thite (2018), there is a need to overcome integration challenges, to ensure a smooth transition through preparation, technical skills, and cooperation from stakeholders.

4.3.3 Scalability and Performance

4.3.3.1 Addressing Scalability Issues in Blockchain Networks

Many firms have displayed an immense level of interest towards the use of blockchain technology, and as the technology gains utilization, the challenges of scalability crop up. Sharding strategies are among the ways through which the issue of scalability can be resolved. In sharding, the blockchain network is divided into several sections or subnetworks that can work at the same time, and thus, the throughput is enhanced overall. In the research paper "Scaling Byzantine Fault Tolerant Replication to Wide Area Networks", Castro et al. (2019) present another sharding protocol which aims at maintaining the security and fault tolerance of the blockchain network while at the same time achieving high throughput and low latency. Solving the scalability issue through off-chain solutions is one of the major methods of achieving it. Off-chain transactions and activities divide tasks to be performed on the primary blockchain and other platforms to relieve the computational burden and enhance the blockchain's scalability. In Poon and Dryja's (2016) paper, "Lightning Network: Scalability of Off-Chain Instant Payments," they present the Lightning Network which is an extension built onto existing blockchains. By the application of smart contracts and payment channels, the Lightning Network supports seamless and massively individual transactions.

4.3.3.2 Ensuring Efficient Transaction Processing and Network Performance

Looking at the blockchain network then, there must be a balance between the ability of the network and the ability to process transactions. In order to complete transactions, consensus techniques are necessary in order to have the execution be as smooth as possible. The HoneyBadgerBFT algorithm is presented by Miller et al. (2016) in their paper "HoneyBadgerBFT: An algorithm that named 'A Robust, Byzantine Fault-Tolerant Consensus Algorithm.'" It also provides the ability to tolerant Byzantine faulty nodes and also provides high throughput and low latency. Due to the quick and secure processing of transactions, this algorithm is useful for those applications that require high-performance blockchain networks. Peer-to-Peer (P2P) networking protocols, therefore, serve as means of increasing performance of the network. Presented by Maymounkov and Mazieres (2002) in their research paper "Kademlia," the Kademlia protocol introduces decentralized peer discovery as well as network routing within a Peer-to-Peer Information System making use of the XOR Metric which appears in the paper "An Evaluation of an Extended XOR Metric for a Peer-to-Peer Information System." Since they reduce network latency and essay message routing, Peer-to-Peer protocols like Kademlia are likely to enhance performance.

4.3.4 Legal and Regulatory Frameworks

4.3.4.1 Legal Implications of Using Blockchain in HR Management

It is also important to understand how exactly HR management could benefit from the blockchain in several ways such as security, data integrity, and openness. Its execution does however also raise legal concerns, which need special attention. Two of these are data privacy and compliance to relevant data protection laws and acts. In the study article entitled: "Blockchain Technology and GDPR Compliance," Conti et al. (2018), the authors aim at exploring how well blockchain consones with the GDPR, of the European Union. They emphasize the need of implementing the organizational and technical measures, such as proper permission of data accessibility and pseudonymization solutions, in order to ensure GDPR compliance when adopting blockchain in the HR systems. To address the legal considerations, there are the ways of managing of digital identities and authentication in the HR procedures. The identity management solutions with reference to blockchain solutions can be a tool that will help to simplify the procedures and lower the fraud. Yet laws concerning the digital identities are still relevant. In their article, Blockchain and Digital Identity, Azaria et al. (2016) discuss the legal and legal challenges of identity systems which are based on blockchain. They draw attention to the necessity of legislative frameworks that deal with problems including responsibility, identity theft, and user permission.

4.3.4.2 Navigating Regulatory Requirements and Frameworks

The legal aspect is most essential when implementing the blockchain for enhancing the HR management since potential restrictions have to be considered. Considering the global applicability of the blockchain, understanding the regulatory landscape around the globe becomes imperative. Chohan et al. (2019) in their paper "Regulation of Blockchain and Cryptocurrency Around the World" provide an overview of how various countries have approached the regulation of the blockchain technology and cryptocurrencies. They emphasize that an increasing focus should be paid to consumer protection laws, rules and regulations of jurisdictions, and AML requirements when designing blockchain-based HR management systems. Additionally, when relying on the blockchain approach to HR procedures, it is essential to follow the rules of employment. Smart contracts are automated contracts uploaded on a blockchain that could always be utilized when doing employee payroll and employment contract. However, legal issues such as contract formation, enforceability, legal concept, and labour laws should not be ignored. The legal issues surrounding smart contracts and possible solutions are examined by Werbach and Cornell (2018) in their work "Smart Contracts." This describes how legal systems need to form part of a smart contract system that is based on blockchain to ensure accountability, fairness, and adherence to the law as shown in Figure 4.4.

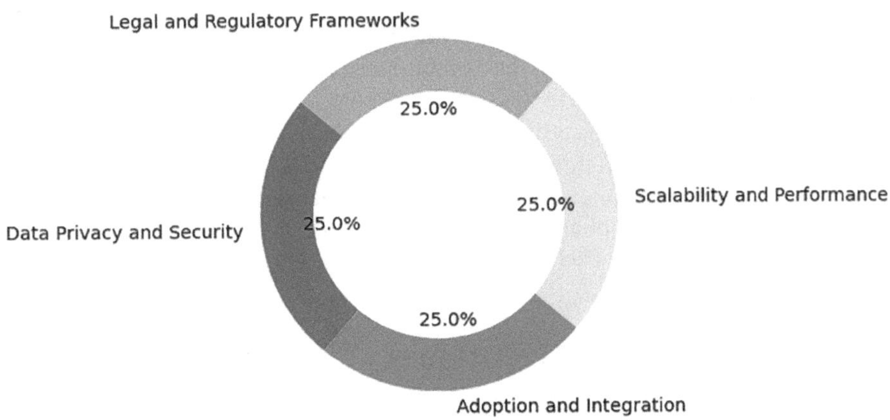

FIGURE 4.4 Challenges and considerations related to blockchain applications. (Source: Author's self-generated.)

4.4 CASE STUDIES AND REAL-WORLD EXAMPLES

4.4.1 Highlighting Successful Implementations of Blockchain in HR Management

Upwork: Lack of proper reputation systems and effective ID check are other issues with Upwork, an international marketplace for freelancers which implemented blockchain solutions. To mitigate fraud cases, improve user trust and optimize the overall efficiency of the HR functions, decentralized reputation systems and the use of the blockchain identity profiles provided the most significant value for Upwork in the context of Zhou and colleagues' (2019) framework. Bitnation: For instance, based on the blockchain technology, a decentralized governance known as Bitnation came up with World Citizenship ID which is a blockchain-based HR. Through this, people could create other digital profiles that could be confirmed and kept safe from employer raids, their working experience, and education. The adoption of blockchain enabled the employment process to be done in a faster way with accurateness of the data of the candidates (Ichikawa et al., 2018).

4.4.2 Discussing the Benefits and Lessons Learned from These Case Studies

The blocks are fixed and only authorized individuals have access to them which makes blockchain application in HR administration an excellent way of eliminating intermediaries and ensuring the data collected are accurate and secure. Blockchain has this capability of decentralizing the information and as a result protecting sensitive HR data while avoiding any form of unwanted access (Zhou et al., 2019). The adoption of blockchain in HR management has been known to have the capacity to perform several operations more swiftly than they would normally be done; these include operations such as payroll operations and identity check and credential authentication among others. Through the new form of trust-based transactions and the removal of intermediaries, companies and institutes can obtain cost reduction and operative improvement (Ichikawa et al., 2018). Transparency is offered with the use of blockchain HR solutions that present an unchangeable, joint database that can only be accessed by authorized users. In the same context, Zhou et al. (2019) observed that transparency helps stakeholders to be confident enough, hence eliminating behaviours such as fraud or manipulation. Still, these case studies demonstrate some challenges and considerations to have in mind when implementing the blockchain technology in human resource management, beside their benefits. These include scaling concerns, data privacy regulation compliance, and management of the translation from old legacy systems to intelligent blockchain solutions (Ichikawa et al., 2018).

4.5 FUTURE TRENDS AND OUTLOOK

4.5.1 Potential Future Applications of Blockchain in HR Management

1. Credential Verification and Skills Validation: Recourse to blockchain technology makes it possible to create a portable and unalterable list of

approved credentials and skills. Employers can thus swiftly and effortlessly scrutinize and validate a candidate's qualifications by keeping his/her achievements, certification, and education records on the blockchain (Ichikawa et al., 2018).
2. Payroll and Benefits Management: Payroll process can be ensured to be precise and open by using smart contracts based on the blockchain technology. The money disbursement can be programmed to be done in smart contracts depending on certain parameters such as HR policies or even timeline conditions. Application of it increases efficiency and reduces office work load (Bhardwaj et al., 2019).
3. Employee Performance and Feedback: Blockchain can enable effective, safe, and more transparent systems in employee performance management. It is advisable for organizations to adopt decentralized feedback system where feedback information is stored on the blockchain to enhance credibility of the feedback information, therefore enhancing performance (Bouras et al., 2020).

4.5.2 Challenges and Opportunities for Further Exploration

1. Scalability and Integration: The integration of the blockchain technology into the human resource management poses several challenges especially on the aspect of scalability. This means that the blockchain network has to grow to accommodate the added strain as more participants come into the network as well as the increasing transactions. To this end, scholars and industry players are exploring several scalability approaches such as sharding and off-chain solutions (Swan, 2015).
2. Data Privacy and Compliance: Privacy becomes a concern when using blockchain especially in the light of the recently passed laws on data protection such as that of the European Union's GDPR. In this regard, further studies and innovations should be focused on striking a fine line between data protection in blockchain and blockchain transparency by introducing such tools as zero-knowledge proofs and decentralized identity management systems (Conti et al., 2018).
3. Interoperability and Standards: Further advancement in blockchain will require the formulation of common interfaces to enable mutual compatibility and integration with modern human resource applications. To boost the cross-system connectivity and translate the heterarchical structure towards blockchain networks and applications, attempts are being made to establish reference architectures and specifications (Tapscott and Tapscott, 2017).
4. Adoption and Organizational Readiness: While blockchain technology has significant potential, the HR management should be ready to implement it—it will require efforts. In order to have effective business adoption, it is therefore necessary to make investments on the employees through training, increase awareness on the benefits and limitations of blockchain technology, and increase partnerships with technology providers (Ichikawa et al., 2018).

4.6 CONCLUSION

4.6.1 Recap of Key Points Discussed in the Chapter

As Zhou et al. (2019) explained that blockchain technology increases the security, transparency, and reliability of data through decentralization and immutability in the HR procedures. Among the examples, the credential validation and the HR platform of a company called Bitnation are using the blockchain for these functions (Zhou et al., 2019), and Upwork has been implementing the use of blockchain for identity check and reputation management in the platform (Ichikawa et al., 2018). Sunter efficiency, cost reduction, data accuracy, and heightened transparency are some of the benefits that blockchain presents to the process of HR administration (Ichikawa et al., 2018; Bhardwaj et al., 2019). In order for blockchain technology to be utilized in HR administration, certain challenges on the scalability of the technology, data privacy, integration of multiple perspectives and blocks, and bodies preparing for the technology must be addressed (Swan, 2015; Conti et al., 2018).

4.6.2 Emphasize the Transformative Potential of Blockchain in HR Management

It is important to emphasize that blockchain technology has the potential to revolutionalize key aspects of HR management such as payroll, performance evaluation, and credentials verification, among other payroll processing procedures. One of the major advantages of using the blockchain is that it gets rid of the middle men, has a better data protection, and increases the level of stakeholders' trust. Blockchain can help organizations enhance efficiency, reduce bureaucracy, and enhance the overall perception of the HR department from both the business side and the employees (Gupta et al., 2024).

4.6.3 Closing Thoughts on the Future of Blockchain in HR

To a great extent, the utilization of blockchain in the sphere of HR administration appears to have a promising outlook. Such uses, which are still theoretically explored based on the capabilities of blockchain technology, define the further development of blockchain technology in HR: automation of payroll, verification of credentials, performance reviews, and more. However, they include problems such as scalability, data protection, and adoption readiness, which require further research, development of better technology, and strong collaboration between the regulatory authorities and stakeholders. Taking into consideration legal and regulatory constraints, identification of the need for the interoperability standards that have to be set, and ensuring the compatibility of the existing HR systems are all critical.

REFERENCES

Aljawarneh, S., Al-Kabi, M. N., Alhawarat, A., & Alsmadi, I. (2019). Data security in cloud computing: A systematic review and open research challenges. *Journal of Cloud Computing*, 8(1), 1–28.

Armenakis, A. A., & Harris, S. G. (2009). Reflections: Our journey in organizational change research and practice. *Journal of Change Management*, 9(2), 127–142.

Azaria, A., Ekblaw, A., Vieira, T., & Lippman, A. (2016). Blockchain and digital identity. In *Proceedings of the 2016 ACM Workshop on Blockchain, Cryptocurrencies and Contracts* (pp. 55–60), Vienna, Austria.

Azaria, A., Ekblaw, A., Vieira, T., & Lippman, A. (2016). Medrec: Using blockchain for medical data access and permission management. In *Proceedings of the 2nd International Conference on Open and Big Data (OBD)* (pp. 25–30), Vienna, Austria. IEEE.

Battisti, F., De Benedittis, A., & Mattioli, A. (2021). Smart payroll: Decentralized payroll systems exploiting blockchain. *Future Generation Computer Systems*, 115, 296–303.

Becker, C., Eichler, M., Fabian, B., Hladik, D., & Weber, B. (2021). Blockchain in education: A systematic review of the literature. *Computers & Education*, 166, 104173.

Bhardwaj, S., Jain, P., & Jain, S. (2019). Blockchain in human resources: Payroll and benefits management. In *2019 4th International Conference on Internet of Things: Smart Innovation and Usages (IoT-SIU)* (pp. 1–4), Vienna, Austria.

Bhattacharya, S., Kumar, V., & Kundu, A. (2019). Intelligent blockchain-based hiring process for cybersecurity professionals. *Journal of Network and Computer Applications*, 126, 161–176.

Bonneau , J., Miller, A., Clark, J., Narayanan, A., Kroll, J. A., & Felten, E. W. (2015). Sok: Research perspectives and challenges for bitcoin and cryptocurrencies. In *IEEE Symposium on Security and Privacy* (pp. 104–121). IEEE.

Bouras, A., Spais, G., & Paspallis, N. (2020). Blockchain in human resources: A systematic literature review. In *2020 IEEE 44th International Computers, Software & Applications Conference (COMPSAC)* (Vol. 2, pp. 12–17), Madrid, Spain.

Buterin, V. (2014). A next-generation smart contract and decentralized application platform. In *Ethereum White Paper* (pp. 1–32).

Castro, M., Liskov, B., & Rodrigues, R. (2019). Scaling byzantine fault tolerant replication to wide area networks. In *Proceedings of the 2019 ACM Symposium on Principles of Distributed Computing* (pp. 3–12), Toronto, Ontario, Canada.

Chatterjee, S., Park, J., & Esposito, C. (2019). Decentralized, self-sovereign and blockchain-based identity management systems. *Future Generation Computer Systems*, 97, 532–539.

Chohan, U. W., Sancak, B. C., & Sungur, O. (2019). Regulation of blockchain and cryptocurrency around the world. In *Proceedings of the 52nd Hawaii International Conference on System Sciences* (pp. 4081–4090), Maui, Hawaii, USA.

Christidis, K., & Devetsikiotis, M. (2016). Blockchains and smart contracts for the internet of things. *IEEE Access*, 4, 2292–2303.

Conti, M., Dragoni, N., & Spognardi, A. (2018). Blockchain-based decentralized management of demand response programs in smart energy grids. *Future Generation Computer Systems*, 86, 641–653.

Conti, M., Kumar, E. V. P., Lal, C., Ruj, S., & Samanthula, B. K. (2018). Blockchain *Technology and GDPR Compliance*. In *2018 IEEE International Conference on Big Data (Big Data)* (pp. 3159–3168), Seattle, Washington, USA.

Eskandari, S., Zhong, H., Xu, W., & Fu, X. (2019). A smart contract approach for improving hiring process transparency and efficiency. *Future Generation Computer Systems*, 97, 554–563.

Fan, Y., Huang, J., Xu, C., Li, C., & Jin, H. (2020). Automating hiring decisions in the IT industry: A smart contract-based approach. *IEEE Access*, 8, 188871–188880.

Gupta, D., Gupta, M., & Gupta, P. M. (2024). *HR Analytics: The Future of HR* (p. 404), PHI Learning, New Delhi, India.

Ichikawa, D., Pan, J., Dinh, T. N., & Wang, Q. (2018). A decentralized HR platform based on blockchain technology. In *2018 IEEE International Conference on Services Computing (SCC)* (pp. 329–336), San Francisco, California, USA.

Jøsang, A., Fridgeirsdottir, K. R., & Alkhaldi, N. (2018). An audit system for the fair distribution of access rights in a blockchain-based voting system. In *Proceedings of the 2018 IEEE International Conference on Industrial Engineering and Engineering Management (IEEM)* (pp. 815–819), Bangkok, Thailand.

Kavanagh, M. J., & Thite, M. (2018). *Human Resource Information Systems: Basics, Applications, and Future Directions*. SAGE Publications.

Kosba, A., Miller, A., Shi, E., Wen, Z., & Papamanthou, C. (2016). Hawk: The blockchain model of cryptography and privacy-preserving smart contracts. In *Proceedings of the 2016 ACM SIGSAC Conference on Computer and Communications Security* (pp. 839–851), Hofburg Palace in Vienna.

Kshetri, N. (2017). Can blockchain strengthen the internet of things? *IT Professional*, 19(4), 68–72.

Li, X., Wei, Y., Liu, Q., & Wang, H. (2019). Blockchain-based secure and transparent employment history verification. *IEEE Transactions on Engineering Management*, 66(1), 147–159.

Liao, C., Chen, M., Yen, N. Y., & Su, C. J. (2020). Decentralized blockchain-based platform for direct interaction between employers and job seekers. *IEEE Transactions on Engineering Management*, 68(2), 595–604.

Maymounkov, P., & Mazieres, D. (2002). Kademlia: A peer-to-peer information system based on the XOR metric. In *Proceedings of the 1st International Workshop on Peer-to-Peer Systems* (pp. 53–65), Cambridge, MA, USA.

Mettler, M. (2016). Blockchain technology in healthcare: The revolution starts here. In *Proceedings of the 2016 IEEE 18th International Conference on e-Health Networking, Applications, and Services (Healthcom)* (pp. 1–3), Munich, Germany.

Miller, A., Xia, Y., Croman, K., & Shi, E. (2016). HoneyBadgerBFT: A robust, byzantine fault-tolerant consensus algorithm. In *Proceedings of the 2016 ACM SIGSAC Conference on Computer and Communications Security* (pp. 31–42), Vienna, Austria.

Molina-Markham, A., Akella, A., Huang, C., Wagner, D., & Sadeh, N. (2019). Privacy for all: Ensuring fair and equitable privacy protections. *Proceedings on Privacy Enhancing Technologies*, 2019(4), 54–74.

Nakamoto, S. (2008). Bitcoin: A Peer-to-Peer Electronic Cash System. Retrieved from https://bitcoin.org/bitcoin.pdf

Narayanan, A., Bonneau, J., Felten, E., Miller, A., & Goldfeder, S. (2016). *Bitcoin and Cryptocurrency Technologies: A Comprehensive Introduction*. Princeton University Press.

Pilkington, M., & Zeng, Y. (2017). Blockchain technology in the insurance sector. In David Lee and Robert Deng (Eds.), *Handbook of Blockchain, Digital Finance, and Inclusion, Volume 1: Cryptocurrency, FinTech, InsurTech, and Regulation* (pp. 439–459). Academic Press.

Ponomarev, A., & Belyavskaya, E. (2018). Blockchain-based platform for higher education admissions: Concept and prototype. *Journal of Information Systems Education*, 29(2), 88–97.

Poon, J., & Dryja, T. (2016). The Lightning Network: Scalable Off-Chain Instant Payments. Retrieved from https://lightning.network/lightning-network-paper.pdf

Rajvanshi, P. R., Singh, T., Gupta, D., & Gupta, M. (2022a). Blockchain technology for pharmaceutical drug supply chain management. In Pushpa Singh, Divya Mishra, & Kirti Seth (Eds.), *Transformation in Healthcare with Emerging Technologies* (pp. 217–229). CRC Press.

Rajvanshi, P. R., Singh, T., Gupta, D., & Gupta, M. (2022b). Cybersecurity and data privacy in the insurance market. In K. Sood, B. Balusamy, S. Grima, & P. Marano (Eds.), *Big Data Analytics in the Insurance Market* (pp. 1–20). Emerald Publishing Limited. https://doi.org/10.1108/978-1-80262-637-720221001

Rani, S., Gupta, M., & Gupta, D. (2020). Artificial intelligence and personalized banking. In Vikas Garg & Rashmi Agrawal (Eds.), *Transforming Management using Artificial Intelligence Techniques* (1st ed., pp. 105–128). CRC Press. https://doi.10.1201/9781003032410-8

Rong, C., Wang, L., Li, Z., Huang, Q., & Liao, X. (2020). A privacy-preserving credit scoring scheme based on consortium blockchain. *IEEE Transactions on Information Forensics and Security*, 16, 2540–2555.

Swan, M. (2015). *Blockchain: Blueprint for a New Economy*. O'Reilly Media.

Swan, M., Rejeb, A., & Gammelgaard, J. (2020). Blockchain-based feedback and recognition systems: A systematic literature review. *Business Process Management Journal*, 26(5), 1307–1338.

Tapscott, D., & Tapscott, A. (2016). *Blockchain Revolution: How the Technology Behind Bitcoin Is Changing Money, Business, and the World.* Penguin.

Tapscott, D., & Tapscott, A. (2017). *Blockchain Revolution: How the Technology Behind Bitcoin and Other Cryptocurrencies Is Changing the World.* Penguin.

Werbach, K., & Cornell, C. (2018). Smart contracts: Bridging the gap between expectations and legal reality.*The Journal of Institutional and Theoretical Economics*, 174(1), 82–111.

Xu, L., Weber, I., Staples, M., & Zhu, L. (2019). A taxonomy of blockchain-based systems for supply chain management. *ACM Computing Surveys*, 52(3), 56.

Xu, L., Weber, I., Staples, M., Zhu, L., Bosch, J., Bass, L., & Pautasso, C. (2019). A taxonomy of blockchain-based systems for architecture design. *IEEE Software*, 36(6), 44–53.

Yang, Y., Tian, J., Li, X., Yang, Z., & Feng, D. D. (2021). Blockchain-based performance evaluation system for privacy-aware and accountable performance management. *IEEE Transactions on Engineering Management*, 68(3), 851–861.

Yao, Q., Sheng, Q. Z., Ngu, A. H., & Zhang, W. (2021). Blockchain-based trustworthy assessment of candidate qualifications for smart hiring. *IEEE Transactions on Engineering Management*, 68(2), 605–615.

Yin, D., Xu, X., Li, C., Chen, W., & Li, X. (2020). Smart contract-based onboarding process optimization in human resources. *Concurrency and Computation: Practice and Experience*, 32(18), e6009.

Yli-Huumo, J., Ko, D., Choi, S., Park, S., & Smolander, K. (2016). Where is current research on blockchain technology?—A systematic review. *PloS One*, 11(10), e0163477.

Zheng, Z., Xie, S., Dai, H.- N., Chen, X., & Wang, H. (2017). An overview of blockchain technology: Architecture, consensus, and future trends. In *IEEE International Congress on Big Data* (pp. 557–564), Honolulu, Hawaii, USA.

Zhou, Q., Zhang, P., Lyu, C., Liu, X., & Luo, X. (2019). Research on blockchain technology application in human resource management. In *2019 IEEE International Conference on Industrial Engineering and Engineering Management (IEEM)* (pp. 998–1002), Macao, China.

Zyskind, G., Nathan, O., & Pentland, A. (2015). Decentralizing privacy: Using blockchain to protect personal data. In *2015 IEEE Security and Privacy Workshops* (pp. 180–184), San Jose, California, USA.

5 Blockchain Smart Contracts in Human Resource Management

Application, Implementation Challenges, and Research Agenda

Joshy Mathew, Akansha Mer, and Farha Khan

5.1 INTRODUCTION

Blockchain technology is an emerging and disruptive technical innovation that has revolutionized various industries by introducing decentralized and transparent ledger systems.

The distinguishing characteristic of the blockchain ledger is its immutability, which guarantees that each record or transaction, once recorded, stays unchangeable and impenetrable. This innate ability is used to build a system that securely stores employee credentials, certifications, and work histories. These records are included in an unbreakable information chain that ensures the legitimacy of a person's credentials when they are added to the blockchain. According to Koncheva et al. (2019), a blockchain-based Smart Contract is a transparent and reliable source to verify hires' qualifications by employers. Hence, it simplifies the selection process and reduces the possibility of recruiting someone with false credentials, which helps the HR department to tackle their long struggled problem.

The most significant use case of Blockchain is Smart Contracts. It is simply a self-executing computer protocol (or code) on a blockchain that performs operations whenever the terms of pre-defined conditions are met (Mishunin, 2023). Trust, transparency, speed, accuracy, security, and efficiency are significant advantages of this emerging robust technology. Therefore, this technology is highly recommended in various domains of business. The traditional contract mechanism can be replaced with this innovative self-executing contract based on a blockchain platform that can revolutionize HRM and provide an efficient, cost-effective system for HRM. The automation feature of Smart Contracts will upgrade the HRM process and reduce risk in its operations. This will also improve efficiency in various activities, such as recruitment, selection, payroll, etc.

 DOI: 10.1201/9781032619651-5

When a pre-set criterion is met, the contracts that are stored within a network of interconnected blocks and are autonomously executed. The pre-defined conditions such as disbursement of salary or renewal of contract are initiated automatically. Therefore, this framework is recommended as well-suited for processes within Human Resources management, where agreements about confidentiality, employment, and other legal records are involved. Furthermore, these contractual arrangements can enhance transparency and security within the Human Resources domain. The terms and conditions in a Smart Contract can be accessed instantly by all stakeholders involved in it. It ensures openness and reduces the possibility of disagreement or misunderstanding. The inherent nature of blockchain ensures that the terms and conditions in the contract remain unmodifiable (Hosking, 2023). Smart contracts allow organizations to dispense with the necessity of legal representation, allowing them to engage in contractual obligations with clients and employees directly. These obligations are secure and self-enforcing, their credibility stemming from the underlying cryptographic foundations.

5.2 SMART CONTRACT

Smart Contracts are digital agreements encompassing intricate coded instructions designed to carry out pre-defined tasks (McGimpsey, 2023). Once the parties reach a consensus on the rules and set them into motion, the code ensures that each action adheres to those guidelines. This automated precision differentiates smart contracts from conventional agreements. The term "Smart Contract" was introduced in the 1990s by visionary computer scientist Nick Szabo. He envisioned a world where certain agreements could be self-executing, reducing the need for intermediaries or trust in the counterparty. With the emergence of Blockchain Technology, his vision has materialized, and contracts have undergone a digital upgrade.

Present-day blockchain technology has transformed this concept into a practical reality. Contracts are no longer solely documented and signed; they are now computerized, automated, and self-executing, signifying a significant advancement in managing agreements in the era of digitalization. McGimpsey (2023) and Grace Garnett (2023) discuss the steps in Smart Contracts implementation.

5.3 IMPLEMENTATION OF A SMART CONTRACT INVOLVES THE FOLLOWING STEPS

a. An accord serves as the initial stage in establishing a Smart Contract. The entities involved in the intention to engage in a transaction or exchange of goods or services must agree regarding the arrangement's terms and conditions. Additionally, consensus must be reached on the operational aspects of the Smart Contract, including the pre-requisites for its execution and the possibility of automated implementation.
b. To construct a Smart Contract, the stipulations outlined in the accord are translated into a programming language. Consequently, the Smart Contract adheres to the same regulations and ramifications as a conventional legal contract.

c. The subsequent step involves the deployment of the Smart Contract onto a blockchain. Like any other cryptographic transaction, the Smart Contract is disseminated across the blockchain, and its code is stored in the transaction's data field. Once transactions are validated, the smart contract will be active in blockchain and become immutable record.
d. A Smart Contract operates by diligently within the blockchain and actively verifies any source for specific condition or triggers which are pre-established. These triggers encompass a wide range of digitally verifiable conditions, such as fulfilment of a designated date, the initiation of a payment, receipt of a monthly invoice, and various other verifiable situations.
e. Once the specified conditions are satisfied, a Smart Contract will activate. Due to its automation feature, the specified Smart Contract can handle activities such as dispersing salaries to employees or making rent payments.
f. Any execution of the Smart Contract is immediately recorded on the blockchain. Every action carried out by the smart contract is verified by the blockchain system, logs as a transaction, and stores as the finalized Smart Contract in the blockchain. These details of the smart contract can be accessed and reviewed by anyone at any given time.

Smart contracts in Blockchain are considered as elegant due to their automation feature. It means that they operate independently, where intermediaries like banks or lawyers are not required. Instead, it relies on pre-defined conditions embedded within the smart contract, ensuring trust and that all parties involved receive what was promised, thereby improving the transparency and trustworthiness of Human Resource Management (HRM) processes.

Even though blockchain technology is generally associated with cryptocurrencies, its influence extends beyond finance. Studies conducted by Steenholt et al. have highlighted the potential of blockchain technology in revolutionizing HRM through advanced verification and authentication of employee credentials. HR industry can be highly professional with trust and transparency by embracing this emerging technology. The in-built feature, especially immutability, can revolutionize HRM processes.

HRM uses blockchain technology in the form of smart contracts through which this department's efficiency can be highly improved. According to PwC (2017), blockchain is a unique and ideal platform for HR contracts that can self-execute and self-enforce. Decentralization is another feature of this technology that helps HR to keep away intermediaries and other human interferences. This shift can enhance the performance of human resource departments where time-consuming and resource-intensive activities are at high (Taherdoost, 2023).

For instance, an HR department is responsible for dispersing the performance bonuses of a large number of workforces. When every employee fulfils their performance requirement, it could be the number of working hours, or achieving targets, the Smart Contract executes automatically and makes payment instantly. Any possibilities of mistakes, miscommunications, or conflicts can be eliminated, and administrative procedures can be streamlined by leveraging this technology. When workers receive their just compensation on time and with accuracy, the company builds trust and employee satisfaction. This chapter intends to discuss the current state of the art of blockchain-based Smart Contracts in HRM, their applications, and implementation challenges. By studying both applications and challenges, researchers and HR professionals can make well-informed decisions about implementing this innovative technology.

5.4 RESEARCH METHODOLOGY

The study is based on secondary sources of data. The researchers have referred to research papers and magazines such as *Forbes* and *Harvard Business Review*. Furthermore, reports from renowned organizations such as McKinsey, KPMG, Deloitte, PwC, etc. have been referred.

In compliance with Tranfield et al. (2003) and Crossan and Apaydin (2010), a thorough literature review was carried out to find research themes and chances to carry out studies on blockchain technology in HRM. A clear and repeatable technique was used in a systematic manner to improve the overall quality of the evaluation (Crossan & Apaydin, 2010). The primary topics were identified, and the current research was critically examined, synthesized, and mapped as part of a comprehensive literature review process. All publications published until March 2024 for systematic review papers were considered.

The keywords used in the study are Blockchain Smart Contracts, Blockchain and HRM, application, challenges, recruitment and selection, diversity & inclusion, industrial relation & labour laws, employee engagement & retention, and remote work.

5.5 APPLICATION OF SMART CONTRACTS IN HRM

This emerging technology can revolutionize various HRM functions, such as payroll management, recruitment, training and development, identity verification, and contract management, by enabling secure, tamper-proof, and automated Smart Contracts on the blockchain.

5.5.1 Recruitment and Selection

The HR department can automate and digitalize the recruitment and selection process, from posting job vacancies to finalizing employment agreements. Traditional paper-based contracts can be replaced with transparent and immutable digital contracts.

5.5.1.1 Transparency, Fairness, and Trust

This emerging new contract system supports HRM in posting job advertisements, identifying appropriate applications, and evaluating them, which ensures that the right candidates only will be involved in the selection process (Neiheiser et al., 2019). Lack of transparency and trust are the two significant challenges in the recruitment process. The decentralized nature of smart contracts ensures transparency and fairness during the candidate selection process (Neiheiser et al., 2020). This study (Lauslahti et al., 2017) highlights the role of game theory principles in encouraging engagement from reviewers and applicants to increase the efficiency of the selection process. Third party interventions are not possible and ensure reliability by using smart contracts in recruitment and selection processes. It can establish binding rights and obligations for all parties involved. A candidate selection is complete with an agreement signing stage. This agreement between two parties can be successfully executed with expediating Smart Contracts that ensure trustworthiness, openness, and equity.

The study by Chong Tai et al. (2020) shed light on how the hiring system based on blockchain technology ensures transparency and reliability. A Smart contract plays a significant role in maintaining the mutually agreed terms between companies and candidates and prevents any unauthorized changes. A sense of trust is instilled in the recruitment process throughout if there is high transparency. Once agreements are established in a Smart Contract, it is unalterable and serves as the history of the hiring process. Any breach of the agreement can be identified easily and ensure protection by secure and resistant to manipulation feature of this technology.

5.5.1.2 Ensures Hiring the Right Person for the Right Job

Hiring the right candidate for the right job is a significant challenge for the HR department in many business organizations. Candidates' pre-screening is very important to identify the right job seeker for the position available. This challenge can be successfully addressed by utilizing Blockchain Digital Ledger Technology. This ensures not only verifying candidates' identity but also identifying career related information as well. The study by Dhanala and Radha (2020) emphasized the role of this technology in verifying candidates' information starting from schools, colleges, universities, previous workplaces, and law enforcement to authenticate the candidate details. The veracity and correctness of the job seekers' information can be verified by leveraging this innovative technology. Once candidates' information is confirmed, the system will save the data using the transaction hash value in the block. The values recorded in a block act as a code, which is immutable. For hiring purposes the employers can access these data from the blockchain. Recruiters can then access these data from the blockchain. This information about job seekers helps them in the verification process and enhances security by reducing the chances of misleading candidate information, leading to selection of the right candidates for job vacancies available.

To ensure the accuracy of the information provided by the candidates not only their work history but also the official documents like PAN and Aadhar cards can be verified by using Blockchain technology. It can highly minimize the risk of hiring individuals with irrelevant credentials (Mallick et al., 2022).

5.5.1.3 Reduces Cost of Hiring

Affordability and the selection process can be highly improved by leveraging Blockchain technology. It helps companies not only in tracking the source of candidates but also in enabling them to invest in agencies and optimize their advertising spend. This robust technology reduces the cost of selection and recruitment processes and improves the efficiency of the recruitment teams. Documentation of candidates' information and ensuring the security and confidentiality are professionally addressed by implementing blockchain technology in HRM.

According to Chong Tai et al. (2020), Smart Contracts can lower the administrative expenses related to hiring by doing away with mediators and paper records. The study further highlighted how smart contracts streamline and automate several functions of the hiring process, including notifications, written exams, interviews, and document management. This increases efficiency, streamlines the procedure, and requires less manual labour, reducing cost.

5.5.1.4 Enhanced Transaction Speed

Blockchain technology presents opportunities in the recruitment space, such as enhanced transaction speed and reliability, decreased expenses and repetitive labour, and the possibility of a long-term competitive edge for businesses (Kişi, 2022).

A study by Chong Tai et al. (2020) suggests a Smart Contract-based recruitment system to ensure dependability and prevent arbitrary changes to recruiting criteria. With Blockchain Technology, the system is intended to uphold the Smart Contract between hiring organizations and job seekers, immediately alerting candidates to any modifications to the job posting.

Example of application of blockchain in recruitment: A study by Zielinski (2021) in the Society for Human Resource Management (SHRM) describes how Velocity Network Foundation (VNF) uses blockchain technology in the recruitment and selection process. A non-profit membership organization, VNF is home to the top workforce-tech and ed-tech companies and solution providers. Its goal is to create the next-generation data utility layer that supports the world's labour market. Employing Blockchain Technology, they assist individuals, businesses, and academic institutions by facilitating the sharing of professional records around the global market. Blockchain technology has the potential not only to decrease the likelihood of fraudulent resumes but also to expedite the process of verifying applicant credentials such as job history, certifications, and degrees. By assessing reliable and authenticated credentials stored on a blockchain, recruiters can easily verify candidates' details instead of depending on the candidates to disclose their work history, job titles, skills, and education in their resumes or self-attestation. Candidates' academic qualifications can be validated by accessing their digital wallet instead of contacting the colleges or universities for their qualification verification by the recruiters.

5.5.2 Diversity, Gender Equality, and Inclusion

This technology is a powerful tool for promoting diversity and inclusion in the workplace. Diversity and inclusion is another challenge for many organizations; they face problems in terms of tracking the progress of diversity and inclusion programs post their implementation. Using Blockchain technology, organizations can support diversity initiatives by maintaining employee data such as records of demographics, job performance, and training history securely and transparently. The transparency feature of this technology ensures maintaining data integrity which can help the HRM to oversee and control employee behaviours (Hughes et al., 2019). The research by Gupta et al. discussed about a gap in how men and women are treated equally in terms of pay and career advancement within information systems. Adopting Blockchain technology in HRM, organizations effectively instigate a heightened sense of gender equality among workers and ameliorate the contentment levels of females.

5.5.2.1 Equitable and Inclusive Recruitment Process

Blockchain, Smart Contracts and metaverse are the emerging technologies that transform the workplace and add value. Technologies can address the issue of diversity, equity, and inclusion (Mer, 2023). One of our day's critical challenges is giving everyone an equal opportunity in the organization. Blockchain technology in HR gives individuals greater control over their careers and offers businesses a reliable and effective way to validate employees' talents. Companies looking for employees with specific skill sets can use the data provided by blockchain networks. Because it allows for a more equitable and inclusive recruiting process that is focused on proven skills, this will probably lead to more diverse applicant pools (Aggelen & Vedvik, 2022).

The impact of unconscious bias is a significant challenge for a hiring manager in the recruitment process to select the right candidate for the right job. *Unconscious bias* is the opinions shaped by a person's particular exposure to a complicated mixture of social, cultural, and economic events. Therefore, creating trust and credibility is complex in identifying candidates with the right skills and experiences. The study by Torvekar (2021) highlights how blockchain technology can eliminate unconscious bias in recruitment. The blockchain-based solution will ensure proper and accurate qualification, experience, and credential verification of the candidates, ultimately eliminating any unconscious bias in the recruitment process. Blockchain-powered hiring platforms can also provide verifiable assessments. Companies can evaluate candidates by having them complete coding tests that closely resemble the tasks they will be performing in the role. This test helps the candidates to evaluate their skills and cultural fit required for the job.

A study by Obu et al. (2023) focused on leveraging technology to establish an inclusive hiring process based on merit rather than personal attributes, thus significantly reducing biases and discriminatory practices in the workplace. Every candidate in the organization is assigned an identity on the blockchain-based employment platform to make sure proper assessment of their performance, effectively eliminating the prejudices. Biases mitigation and elimination of discrimination against any candidate can be addressed properly by leveraging this innovative technology.

Employees' transactions are recoded in Blockchain's shared ledger which is useful for tracking and verification of their identification to confirm its authenticity and uniqueness. This feature of blockchain technology will create a history of an employee's journey, which provides a comprehensive report about every employees and reduces the chances of hiring and promotion choices stemming from incomplete data. With Blockchain Technology, verifiable identity management becomes achievable, giving individuals control over their personal information and reducing identity-based discrimination.

5.5.2.2 Transparent Data Management and Decision-Making for Diversity and Inclusion

Martín (2021) explores how blockchain technology can help address inequality. This widespread global problem is evident in forms, including hierarchy related to caste, gender gaps, economic disparities, and political inequities. With contracts, it becomes more accessible and more transparent to establish parameters for measuring gender biases in a work setting. As a result, social adherence can be independently verified on the blockchain. Social compliance can, therefore, be independently confirmed on the blockchain. It is always possible to identify the underlying reason or systemic design flaw of gender discrimination. The focus of blockchain is on systemic design errors that are easily fixed right away.

A report by CV VC, a blockchain venture capital firm (CVVC, 2023), highlights how blockchain can foster equality and diversity through blockchain-based decentralized autonomous organization (DAO) (a legal structure where token owners run and make decisions for the organization). Employees-focused DAOs comprise employees' features such as demographics, geography, personality, performance, culture, etc. Such initiatives can increase equity and diversity in the organization and promote inclusion by implementing their goals through community meetups and conferences. Along similar lines, ET HR World (Gupta, 2023) discusses how blockchain technology allows HR to store and validate tax records, immigration papers, and work visas securely, streamlining cross-border procedures. Smart contracts are efficient in streamlining the onboarding process and ensuring a great experience for new hires.

According to Di Vaio et al. (2023), blockchain technology plays great a role in advancing gender equality and inclusion initiatives within companies. The transparency in data management solutions offered by blockchain technology supports gender equality and inclusion efforts. Organizations can ensure gender parity by incorporating blockchain technology into tech-focused governance frameworks. The gender gap can be effectively addressed by providing equal access to opportunities and information. The study further discusses how this new technology can reduce biases by providing proof of transactions, ensuring data integrity without the possibility of alterations. Utilizing this technology, the transactions are verified by a distributed network of participants that reduces the possibility of biases by centralized authorities. Smart Contracts become autonomous when pre-decided conditions are triggered, which certainly minimizes human biases in decision-making.

Frąckiewicz (2023) explores how blockchain technology can help reduce bias and inequality in the field of Human Resources. This technology is well-known for its inherent security. It is free from any kind of alteration or tampering. The HR system can ensure fairness and elimination of discrimination by leveraging this technology. All HR transactions can be documented on the Blockchain, which will serve as a proof for the decision-making process. Prejudices can be effectively addressed with the help of this emerging technology in the organization. Blockchain can detect any instances where a decision-maker or management shows favouritism towards employees based on gender or ethnicity. Therefore, such information can be used to implement measures to address such issues to ensure an equitable advancement process.

The study further shows that this emerging technology has the potential to anonymize personal data, certainly lowering the possibility of prejudice or discrimination throughout the recruiting process. Conventional hiring practices rely on resumes and private information, which may unintentionally induce bias. Businesses can securely store candidate data decentralized on blockchain so that only authorized staff can access it. In this manner, recruiting decisions can only be made based on credentials and abilities, not personal traits. Implementing smart contracts can automate human resources procedures, such as performance reviews and compensation disbursements, thereby mitigating bias and guaranteeing equity.

An article published in Forbes (Bastian, 2021) describes the potential of NFT (Non-Fungible tokens) impacted diversion, equity, and inclusion. An NFT is a blockchain-based digital asset representing unique assets like art, sounds, movies, digital content, and more. The features of these tokens include crypto graphical verifiability, scarcity or uniqueness, and ease of transferability. The report further discusses how neuro-diverse artists benefit from this technology. ARTXV is the first NFT collective for artists who identify as neuro-divergent, exhibiting the potential of neurodiversity via artwork. ARTXV aims to accelerate the financial independence of neuro-divergent artists. This forum offers a fantastic platform for people with a variety of neurodiversity, including synaesthesia, autism, and ADHD (Attention-Deficit/Hyperactivity Disorder), which directly and positively impact their work and allow them to create art from a completely new, distinctive perspective on the world.

5.5.3 Employee Engagement and Retention

Active involvement and longevity of employees significantly impact maintaining a conducive and efficient work atmosphere. Employee engagement offers numerous benefits to the firm, including a lower likelihood of employee attrition and improved organizational citizenship (Mer, 2022; Mer et al., 2023). Long-term commitment and successful organizational contributions are more likely from satisfied and engaged employees.

Blockchain technology may affect staff retention and engagement. However, compared to other HR sectors, the direct application of blockchain in these areas could not be as widespread. The innate characteristics of blockchain technology have the potential to enhance employee engagement and retention. Before implementing blockchain solutions for employee engagement and retention, organizations should carefully analyse the unique needs of their staff and the nature of their business.

The blockchain framework facilitates information sharing between managers and employees to develop and enhance the quality of the workforce. Employees' performance data are the key source for their career growth; these are generated by identifying and evaluating their skills, knowledge, and attitude. Blockchain plays a significant role in supporting HRM in enhancing employees' skills, knowledge, and attitude. This technology allows managers to track employee performance data to support career growth goals by identifying and evaluating employee skills, fostering stakeholder communication and defining competency standards for team members (Nurhasanah et al., 2020). A reward system is the best encouragement for retaining employees with the organization for a duration. A study by 2COMS Consulting Pvt. Ltd. (2023) discusses how BCT can boost employee retention rates. Employees Smart Contract will record all the incentives and other rewards paid out to the particular person until the term of the contract. Hosking (2023) also discusses blockchain-based reward systems that offer bonuses or incentives to employees who achieve pre-defined goals or milestones. Even this technology offers fair and transparent performance reviews of employees. HRM can use blockchain technology to record performance data, management feedback, and peer opinions, ensuring that assessments are fair, transparent, and based on reliable facts.

The eXo platform is a project management and team collaboration tool that offers clients a way to handle projects, teams, and tasks in one place. According to Mazour (2023), the eXo platform stands out by introducing a blockchain-based solution to enhance employee engagement and retention. Workplace disengagement is a crucial issue for HRM which can be effectively addressed by leveraging eXo as the rewards system. It is built with a gamification engine which can track interactions and reward points. The Kudos system in this platform allows colleagues to show appreciation towards each other through acknowledgement tokens, fostering a culture of celebration and recognition.

According to Yi et al. (2020), blockchain technology has the potential to revolutionize HRM. A transparent and reliable performance evaluation and reward system can significantly improve employees' engagement and retention. Smart Contracts are a key component to incentivize employees based on predetermined criteria and promote fairness and motivation. This technology ensures increased engagement of employees by giving them control over their data privacy and security, which leads to higher satisfaction levels. Blockchain technology has the ability to transform employee recognition through a system that enables monitoring and authentication of employee achievements. This platform will record and acknowledge employees' achievements, fostering a culture that values appreciation and motivation.

Employee engagement is increased when successes are recognized through digital badging. Badges can have a significant societal impact because they allow employees to communicate their achievements authentically and comprehensively. In order to confirm who issued, who earned, and what needs to be completed for the employee to complete the journey, digital badges have embedded metadata secured by blockchain technology (Chresomales, 2021).

According to a study by Club (2021), blockchain technology can positively impact employee engagement in HRM. According to Dena Ali Al Mansoori, Etisalat UAE's chief human resources officer, integrating blockchain technology in HR guarantees that employee data remain within their jurisdiction, ensuring its safety and enabling accessibility at all times and from any location. Etisalat offers its employees the privilege of lifelong entry to HR documents and complete data storage protection within the United Arab Emirates. They no longer need hard copies, and there is no longer a delay between ranking confirmation and results distribution thanks to their ability to fully automate reward and recognition certificates.

The study by Consultancy-me.com (2022) discusses using blockchain synthetic equity tokens for employee engagement and retention. "Synthetic equity is a persuasive alternative to traditional rewards for exceptional performance. It stresses the growth of the company's value to the price of their synthetic equity tokens and serves as a vehicle for capital accumulation". This system can engage the employees at a higher level and be used as a means for incentivization and retention. Productivity increases with engagement, and in order to achieve breakthrough performance and the targeted levels of innovation, engagement needs to be driven by a far stronger feeling of purpose and participation.

Blockchain technology in the human resource market provides an unprecedented chance to develop a more engaged and efficient staff. The study by Zhao et al. (2023) proposes a blockchain-based token incentive mechanism to reward stakeholders in the construction, leading to a quantifiable and incentivized system. Implementing blockchain technology in this process allows for the practical execution of tokenization, enabling employees to be acknowledged and rewarded for their contributions towards sustainable practices. The utilization of this incentive mechanism significantly influences the level of employee involvement within the organization.

The study by Král et al. (2022) highlights the potential of blockchain-based metaverse platforms to create engaging work experiences. Blockchain technology can enhance the various aspects of employee engagement and retention within virtual work environments. Implementing remote sensing tools alongside metaverse technologies contributes to establishing immersive work environments that effectively augment employee engagement.

An article published in HRcloud (Cloud, n.d.) discusses how technology affects an organization's success. Many studies now centre on how it affects employee engagement. Highly engaged employees push themselves to complete tasks without supervision, which fosters teamwork, job satisfaction, and productivity. Virtual rewards are becoming increasingly popular because they can keep employees—remote or in-house—extremely motivated. Examples include personalized gift cards, online subscriptions, and virtual courses. Employee engagement requires a digital incentive system that recognizes and compensates workers in real-time, particularly in the post-pandemic period when many workers are remote. Using digital reward systems and implementing technology can increase employee retention and foster a great work environment.

5.5.4 Industrial Relation and Labour Laws

Blockchain technology has become a legal novelty, enhancing transparency in legal transactions. Electronic registrations are widely accepted in many legal realms, and labour law must respond to these practices. Currently, only individual legal initiatives are in place to implement specific types of electronic documents, such as electronic versions of workbooks and electronic versions of pension payments. Countries like Russia, Italy, Slovenia, Estonia, and Spain have implemented electronic systems to manage employment-related data. These systems automatically send data to the Ministry of Labour and the Social Insurance Fund (Koncheva et al., 2019).

However, there are cautions in introducing legal regulations that allow electronic documents. Remote workers, regulated by legal procedures, increasingly use digital communication, electronic documentation, and digital signatures. Despite the widespread adoption of digital environments, labour law still needs to extend these rules to all types of contracts.

Digitalization is an inevitable factor for any organization's growth, and it is an ongoing process. This process plays a significant role in an employment relationship which results in standardization, workload management, and worker monitoring, particularly for low-skilled employees in sectors and countries with limited digital facilities. The shift towards digitalization could hasten the decline of traditional industrial relations bodies, pose challenges in representing new categories of non-traditional workers, and worsen regulatory gaps. However, it also allows unions to broaden their constituencies and jurisdictions (Gasparri & Tassinari, 2020).

5.5.4.1 Work Agreements

Blockchain technology and smart contracts are revolutionizing how work agreements are established and managed, paving the way for significant changes in the industry. This technology is a decentralized, peer-to-peer network for recording transactions using a distributed database. It resolves the confidence in a single entity problem by allowing multiple nodes to maintain a ledger of past transactions securely. Bitcoin, launched in 2008, introduced blockchain as a distributed infrastructure platform. Other blockchain-based systems, like Hyperledger Fabric and Ethereum, have also been suggested. Smart contracts, a cutting-edge technology, can automatically enforce legally binding agreements, reduce risk, and lower service and administration costs (Taherdoost, 2023).

Temporary work contracts play a crucial role in the global social and economic context due to increased global competition, slow economic expansion, and increased unemployment rates. The technological innovations ease the spread of atypical contract agreements, often marked by an absence of job security, uncertainty, meagre salaries, restricted opportunities for advancement, inadequate vocational education, and diminished access to social welfare schemes (Pinna & Ibba, 2018).

In a study by Shojaei et al. (2020), it was said that smart contracts, a computer program with if/then structures, can improve the working environment by reducing disputes caused by contract ambiguity, late payments, and underperforming work. This system offers clarity and enforceability, resulting in smoother contract execution and reduced disputes.

A study by Adel et al. (2022) delves into the technical aspects of smart contracts. It was said that Smart contracts are blockchain executable codes that distribute digital assets between parties. They are executed every fifteen seconds by Ethereum network peers and require verification by at least two users. BCHRM contracts, written in Solidity programming language, provide functionalities such as securely sharing employees' records and organization data, negotiating data-sharing agreements, and regulating employee behaviour. They also prevent breaches, forgery, and imitation, ensure data access, and handle HRM data with trust and transparency

Smart contracts utilize blockchain technology to automate work agreements, ensuring adherence to terms like hours, wages, and benefits, aligning with industrial relations goals. They provide transparency, efficiency, and enforceability in the digital era.

5.5.4.2 Dispute Resolution

To reduce contract problems, companies can maximize clause clarity and use simple language while drafting them. Rectification of human errors and elimination of manual interfacing and misinterpretation of contractual clauses can be properly addressed with automation in contract management. Smart contracts are basically software applications or transaction protocols that will automate the implementation process and monitor record-keeping activities according to the terms defined in the contract. They have promising benefits for construction projects, such as reducing exchange and transaction expenses, obtaining real-time cost data, ensuring clear communication, minimizing human involvement, and guaranteeing secure transactions. However due to existing barriers, the implementation of innovative contract solutions in the construction sector has not reached desired levels. Identifying and assessing these hindrances can bring about more effective solutions that ease the integration of smart contracts so that the possibility of successful application of Smart Contracts is well (Budayan & Okudan, 2023). Smart contract dispute resolution presents both challenges and opportunities. Traditional mechanisms may struggle, but new on-chain and off-chain mechanisms offer potential. Adopting best practices and involving experts can navigate disputes. One of the main benefits of deploying smart contracts is the increased efficiency and reliability of business transactions. Conventional dispute resolution methods may neutralize the efficiency achieved during transitional contractual performance (Pachahara & Maheshwari, 2022). Smart contracts and blockchain-distributed ledgers can greatly enhance litigation and speed up the conclusion of complicated cases. They can also be included in contracts for building or other anticipatory conflicts. ADR or litigation-related legal advice may be impacted by algorithmic discovery; however smart contracts have the ability to protect sensitive information. Blockchain and AI together will speed up the resolution of disputes, lower the expense of litigation, and bring clarity to complicated cases (Barnett & Treleaven, 2017). Smart contracts can reduce opportunistic behaviour and enforce performance by eliminating human discretion and using incentives from game theory models. They offer secure, cost-effective transactions across borders and limited dispute resolution processes (Howell & Potgieter, 2021). Even though they were first introduced through Bitcoin and other cryptocurrencies, smart contracts are now seen as the future of online dispute resolution and, in general, the future of the legal system. In essence, smart contracts are computer programs set up on a blockchain. They are unique in that they are self-enforcing and self-performing. This is explained by the code's immutability, which means that it cannot be changed by default and ensures that the agreement's provisions will be carried out (Kirkwood & Chaisse, 2023).

Lessons learned will shape the future of dispute resolution (Ray, 2023). Smart contracts can include mechanisms for dispute resolution, automating the resolution process based on pre-defined rules. This can streamline conflict resolution and reduce the burden on traditional legal systems.

5.6 BLOCKCHAIN IN THE MANAGEMENT OF EMPLOYEES AND FACTORY WORKERS

Organizations need to integrate Information Technology (IT) with HRM systems to effectively navigate the opportunities and challenges brought forth by Industry 4.0, or the Fourth Industrial Revolution. For these systems to succeed, an impartial, effective, transparent, and safe atmosphere must be established. With its foundation in distributed digital ledgers, blockchain technology is a key enabler in achieving these goals (Onik et al., 2018). Time-consuming HR activities can be managed in better ways by implementing this emerging technology. Blockchain is very useful in managing and monitoring part-time employees working hours and their compensation. Looking ahead, this technology can potentially document individuals' career paths, offering employers and HR managers fast and reliable insights into candidates' accomplishments (Jenkins, 2023). Corporations relying on labour for profits must balance domestic and international labour laws with worker well-being.

The global pandemic has increased dependence on manual labourers in factories. The in-built features of blockchain technology such as transparency, immutability, and accessibility make it an ideal resource for corporate accountability. It can benefit workers in various fields and corporate ladders.

Legislation should include language for employees to protect and expand labour rights globally (Basile, 2020). Blockchain technology makes it possible to swiftly and legally compliantly record employment contracts with complete protection of the rights of the employer and employee. Smart contracts are permanently stored on the blockchain and are always visible to the appropriate authorities for observation and compliance checks (Pinna & Ibba, 2018). Levi Strauss & Co is partnering with New America, ConsenSys, and Harvard TH Chan School of Public Health to develop a blockchain-based worker well-being system. The system, based on the SHINE Health and Well-being Index, will provide a workforce-wide view of factory conditions and individual health. The US State Department, the Levi Strauss Foundation, and ConsenSys support the US$800,000 collaboration. The blockchain worker well-being survey will be tested in three factories in Mexico (Wright, 2019).

5.6.1 Challenges and Considerations in Blockchain in IR

a. Legal Recognition

Despite the potential advantages, the legal recognition of smart contracts within labour laws is a continuously evolving area. It is important that adoption of Smart Contracts should adhere to existing legal frameworks and be recognized as valid agreements. The challenge of enforcing smart contracts in the industry is substantial due to their lack of recognition across all jurisdictions.

Smart contracts are considered as electronic contracts but in some places it is not recognized under existing contract laws. The absence of legal assurance in blockchain technology also affects their enforceability, as the effectiveness of the code relies on its developer, potentially making them unenforceable if incorrect (Agapiou, 2023).

The GDPR prohibits automated personal data processing from significantly impacting individuals' lives. Smart contracts can be used if Article 22(2) and Article 22(3) are met and human intervention is allowed. However, this may require distancing from the original motivations of automated processing and human intervention. The GDPR can set innovation incentives to ensure that automated data processing benefits are combined with effective protection of fundamental rights, ensuring that the benefits of automated execution are balanced with real-world requirements.

b. Privacy Concerns

Lack of data protection and privacy laws is the legal challenge associated with implementing smart contracts. The blockchain network is the basis of Smart contracts which makes them vulnerable to unauthorized access and breaches. The European Union's stringent GDPR laws can result in a significant impact on privacy concerns (Khan & Mer, 2023). Even though transparency is a strength of blockchain this can pose challenges regarding privacy; particularly when dealing with sensitive employee information, maintaining a balance between transparency and data protection is essential.

Smart contracts and data protection legislation are not incompatible, but understanding the latter is crucial to avoid violating the legislation. Public blockchains present challenges in EU data protection law, especially in B2C contexts. One solution is to use permissioned blockchains for B2C contracts, establishing the controller's identity through contract. A private permissioned blockchain network is more convenient and secure for implementing GDPR regulation than a public blockchain network. Avoiding the use of personal data on the blockchain is another strategy, especially in B2B smart contracts between legal persons. Accountability is a concern, with increased administrative sanctions and strengthened supervisory authority powers. Defining the roles of different actors in smart contracts using blockchains requires careful analysis (Voss, 2021). Blockchain smart contracts could revolutionize industrial relations and labour laws by automating processes, ensuring transparency, and enhancing compliance. However, challenges like legal recognition and privacy must be addressed for widespread adoption.

5.7 BLOCKCHAIN TECHNOLOGY FOR MANAGING REMOTE WORKERS

In recent years, remote work has grown at an unparalleled rate. Its widespread use, spurred by the COVID-19 epidemic, has made it indispensable (Mer & Virdi, 2023; Mer & Srivastava, 2023) in various sectors. Companies have embraced remote work because of its cost-effectiveness, flexibility, and access to talent worldwide. Transparent, safe, and efficient systems are more critical than ever as remote work becomes the new standard. It is impossible to overestimate the importance of smart contracts in the context of managing remote labour. In today's globalized and technologically savvy society, remote work is becoming more and more common, but it also presents a unique set of obstacles. The characteristics of remote labour may be difficult for traditional contract administration systems to adjust to, which could result in problems including delayed payments, a lack of transparency, and challenges in executing contracts (Taherdoost, 2023).

5.7.1 Remote Work: The Legal Environment and Electronic Documentation

A paradigm shift towards remote work is occurring in the workforce, and it is critical to examine the legal issues surrounding these new work arrangements and the critical role that electronic documentation plays in this context. Because more people are choosing to work remotely, current labour rules are being re-evaluated to reflect better the digital character of modern businesses (Haque, 2023).

The legal environment surrounding remote employment is complex and includes employee rights, data privacy, and contract enforcement concerns. Conventional legal frameworks need help adjusting to the peculiarities of remote work because they were frequently created for in-person work situations. In this case, using electronic documentation becomes essential to enabling smooth collaboration, communication, and contract negotiations (Kashyap & Gupta, 2023).

When employee data are entered into the blockchain, the HRM system starts the verification process. When every record is time-stamped and connected to the one before it, an unchangeable chain of records is created. Even for temporary employees, smart contracts automatically verify these data against predetermined standards, lowering the possibility of fraudulent claims and speeding up the onboarding process (Král et al., 2022).

In addition to authentication, blockchain's HRM system gives workers—including temporary workers—access to a personal cabinet and a reputation system. A fair assessment of an employee's accomplishments and contributions is produced over time by the reputation system, which compiles performance data to create an unchangeable, transparent record for both temporary and permanent staff. Employees, especially temporary staff, may safely manage their data with the personal cabinet, which fosters a sense of privacy and ownership (Hrrkoin, 2023).

The influence of blockchain on data security is one of the major benefits of HRM, especially for temporary workers. The decentralized and unchangeable characteristics of blockchain guarantee the protection of employee data, encompassing temporary personnel, against unapproved access and alteration. This not only complies with data protection laws but also gives all employees peace of mind about the privacy of their personal data (Gupta, 2023).

Blockchain technology offers numerous benefits in remote work management, including transparent compensation, and streamlined HR operations. As technology evolves, its applications in remote work management will expand.

5.7.2 Case Studies and Implementation

Gitcoin Grants: Blockchain smart contracts are used by the open-source project platform Gitcoin Grants to handle distant work contributions and guarantee immediate payment for qualified projects. Gitcoin is a distributed Ethereum-based Smart Contract network that allows job hunters, open-source contributors, and repo maintainers to collaborate, earn income, and create a globalized network (Owocki, 2022).

Upwork and Freelance platform: Freelance marketplaces such as Upwork can use blockchain smart contracts to automate the preparation and performance of work agreements, guaranteeing freelancers timely and equitable payment. Millions of people now have the opportunity to pursue freelance professions, work remotely, and take advantage of flexible schedules thanks to the gig economy, which has completely changed the way we work. Anyone with assets and skills can now find work, thanks to sites like Upwork, Uber, and Airbnb. But as the gig economy has expanded, it has also encountered certain difficulties (Bron, 2023).

Businesses may actually use blockchain to make international payments through reputable cryptocurrency platforms, doing away with the monthly headache of handling recurrent pay. Since currency rates and other fees can be very expensive, using blockchain to automate and manage HR and recruitment processes is undoubtedly more cost-effective. This procedure will cut expenses overall and eliminate the need for outside assistance. Actually, the procedure will get more transparent and efficient. All information will already be on file, and candidates who work remotely will be able to view any deductions that may have occurred. Consequently, there would be no requirement to submit supporting documentation and proofs individually (The Hummer, 2023).

Remote work has become so popular during the COVID-19 pandemic, and it has been accelerated in various industries, featuring flexibility, global talent access, and cost-effectiveness. As the new normal, efficient, secure, and transparent systems are crucial. LaborX is a blockchain-based platform that aims to bridge the gap between remote work and traditional employment. It facilitates trust, transparency, and efficient payments between employers and freelancers. LaborX uses blockchain's trust-building capabilities to address concerns about payment security and project delivery. It also offers global accessibility, allowing freelancers and employers to connect without geographical limitations. Additionally, LaborX offers multi-currency support, allowing freelancers to receive payments in various cryptocurrencies like Bitcoin and Ethereum. This innovative platform is ideal for freelancers and employers seeking top talent in the global gig economy (Damilola, 2023).

The COVID-19 pandemic resulted in a rapid increase in remote work and online education practices, generally known as work-from-home and schooling-from-home, respectively in many nations, including Indonesia. Utilizing various online platforms such as Zoom, Microsoft Teams, Skype, Google Classroom, ClassDojo, and WhatsApp has introduced specific vulnerabilities, notably Zoom bombing and heightened instances of cyber-attacks. In response to these challenges, blockchain technology has been put forth as a framework for facilitating communication among Internet of Things (IoT) devices. Blockchain can provide secure and scalable communication facilities for inter-device connections, enhancing adaptability for devices engaged in multiple connections. Integrating Blockchain into certificate services or digital identity systems can reduce the risks associated with compromised certificates, address Man-in-the-Middle threats, and streamline synchronization processes with primary servers. The study delineates the development of an IoT simulation model in NS3 and a Key-Based Authentication Architecture tailored for IoT devices utilizing Blockchain, demonstrating a secure work-from-home environment underpinned by blockchain technology and simulation (AprianI et al., 2020).

A study by Kral et al. (2022) offered a comprehensive evaluation of blockchain-enabled metaverse platforms related to digital skill development, remote working tools, and employee engagement and retention. According to their research, immersive work environments, operational workflows, and virtual training are set up by remote sensing tools and metaverse technologies. Their contribution to the literature is the clarification that digital avatars, functioning as remote workers, utilize data management tools, simulation modelling techniques, and voice and gesture detection technologies in networked, extended immersive virtual worlds.

Blockchain solutions enable instant payments to freelancers and gig workers without any intermediaries or outsourcing. Widely acknowledged cryptocurrencies can be used for payment for international remote workers and transactions on a blockchain are executed immediately. Employers can reach workers without bank accounts and maintain an unchangeable record for auditing and regulatory purposes (Wiles, 2019).

In the modern workplace, borderless hiring is the norm rather than the exception. 58% of companies already use borderless IT talent, according to Gartner. Paying employees on time and appropriately is one of the biggest issues as remote labour becomes more common. Payroll records can be safely kept on a blockchain using blockchain technology, guaranteeing accurate and timely wage delivery. Payroll procedures can be automated via smart contracts, self-executing blockchain code that lowers administrative overhead and error risk. Transparency and confidence are raised when workers have instant access to payroll data. This minimizes operational complexity and increases processing times by doing away with the requirement to pay third parties to handle reconciliations (Gupta, 2023).

Freelancers and gig workers usually experience delays in receiving payment as their work and invoices undergo manual verification. Adoption of blockchain technology can streamline this process by implementing smart contracts, enabling prompt and automated payment for these workers. Both the employer and the employee can specify the conditions under which compensation is earned with a smart contract. Pay will be disbursed immediately after the smart contract is satisfied and those requirements are fulfilled. For instance, it is possible to create a smart contract that will distribute funds to an independent truck driver as soon as the load he is transporting reaches its destination without incident. It can shield companies from false invoices in addition to assisting contractors in automatically getting paid. As the scope of distant workers increases, leading to expansion of the gig economy, businesses will become more appealing to gig and freelancers. Over time, this will become increasingly significant because an organization can draw competent employees from around the world that will determine how big or small it grows (Fincher, 2021).

5.8 CHALLENGES IN USING SMART CONTRACTS IN HRM

Even though Smart Contract technology has the potential to function as a significant disruptor in the field of HRM, it has yet to be widely adopted and accepted. The primary reason is the irreversible features of blockchain that make it impossible to correct any wrong information or transaction. Lack of technical expertise among HR professionals and lack of standardization and regulation in the blockchain industry are the other challenges (Arora, 2021).

As an emerging technology, Smart Contracts need to undergo many trial-and-error processes. Creating awareness, training and equipping HR professionals, budgeting, and technical know-how are the pre-requisites to adopting blockchain Smart Contracts in any business organization. Blockchain-enabled Smart Contracts are expected to change the HRM landscape as technology develops and regulatory environments change.

The study by Zheng et al. (2020) classifies the Smart Contracts challenges such as:

a. Creation Challenges: The first step in implementing a Smart Contract is creating a contract. Stakeholders are required to write their contracts and implement them on different blockchain systems. Smart Contracts built on blockchains are non-modifiable once implemented, as blockchains are inherently unchangeable.

b. Deployment Challenges: After contract creation, Smart Contracts will be implemented on blockchain platforms. However, to prevent any problems, Smart Contracts must be thoroughly examined. In order to minimize potential losses brought on by malevolent actions like frauds and attacks, Smart Contract authors should be knowledgeable about the contract's interaction patterns.
c. Execution Challenges: Smart Contracts functions based on real-world data. An oracle appears in a Smart Contract as an agent that locates and authenticates real-time events and transmits these data to the Smart Contract. So, the question of how to identify a reliable oracle arises. Smart Contracts are executed one after another; once the current contract is fulfilled, a miner will execute another one.
d. Completion Challenges: Transactional privacy and security are the other concerns. Therefore, organizations need to develop a privacy-preserving mechanism. Sometimes, malicious attacks by scammers are also a potential challenge to Smart Contracts.

Salah et al. highlight the anticipated adoption challenges of blockchain technology in HRM. As per this study, the significant challenges include

- regulatory and legal concerns,
- resistance to change,
- lack of awareness and understanding of this innovative technology, and
- the need for collaboration and standardization among stakeholders.

The most significant challenge for Smart Contract implementation is the inflexibility of Smart Contracts (Tai, 2019). Unforeseen events or changes in agreements cannot be addressed appropriately, which can be problematic when attempting to provide justifications for contract violations.

The study by Anaam and colleagues in 2023 provides a summary of the challenges encountered in the implementation of blockchain technology in the field of HRM.

Scalability: The performance of blockchain technology can be negatively affected as the size grows with every transaction.

Interoperability: Integration of this robust technology with an existing system or technologies will not be an easy task and time consuming due to differences in protocols and standards.

Legal and Regulatory Concerns: Legal and regulatory challenges vary from country to country which require a standardized protocol.

Energy Consumption: Another major challenge is high processing power, and energy consumption. This leads to sustainability and environmental challenges.

Data Security and Privacy: Blockchain technology is very intricate even though it provides transparency, data security, and privacy.

With regard to HRM, no well-established frameworks are available. This absence of a well-defined framework is a key factor contributing to the reluctance to embrace blockchain-based Smart Contract technology by many companies. Regulatory issues, other related laws and protocols, complexity, high implementation cost, etc. are the other significant factors. The uncertainty surrounding regulations and the complexity are the barriers to adoption of BCT-based Smart Contracts in HRM.

5.9 SCOPE FOR FUTURE RESEARCH WORK

Research on how diversity, equity, and inclusion can be impacted by blockchain smart contracts is still in its nascent stage. Further studies be conducted on how blockchain smart contracts can lead to diversity, equity, and inclusion in context of providing equal employee benefits to employees regardless of their background, gender, etc. The role of Blockchain to facilitate inclusive decision-making can be taken forward by researchers. Third, the significance of Blockchain in fostering industrial relations and proving to be a boon in labour laws can be studied. There are several sectors such as manufacturing, construction, etc. where diversity is less. Finally, how blockchain can facilitate diversity, equity, and inclusion in sectors such as manufacturing, construction, etc., where diversity is less.

5.10 CONCLUSION

Blockchain Technology, widely known for its connection to cryptocurrencies, is quickly moving outside the financial industry. A study by Steenholt et al. (2023) has shed light on the amazing potential of blockchain technology in the field of HRM to improve the authentication and verification of employee credentials. With the help of this cutting-edge technology, the HR industry will enter a new era of trust and transparency by utilizing blockchain's inherent qualities, especially its immutability.

REFERENCES

2COMS Consulting Pvt. Ltd. (2023, February 22). Blockchain could turn HR on its head: How might HR change with blockchain. https://www.linkedin.com/pulse/blockchain-could-turn-hr-its-head-how-might-change-2coms/

Adel, H., ElBakary, M., ElDahshan, K., & Salah, D. (2022). BC-HRM: A blockchain-based human resource management system utilizing smart contracts. In Awan, I., Benbernou, S., Younas, M., Aleksy, M. (eds) *The International Conference on Deep Learning, Big Data and Blockchain (Deep-BDB 2021). Deep-BDB 2021. Lecture Notes in Networks and Systems*, vol 309. Springer, Cham. https://doi.org/10.1007/978-3-030-84337-3_8

Agapiou, A. (2023). Overcoming the legal barriers to the implementation of smart contracts in the construction industry: The emergence of a practice and research agenda. *Buildings*, 13(3), 594. MDPI AG. Retrieved from https://dx doi.org/10.3390/buildings13030594

Aggelen, J. V., & Vedvik, A. J. (2022, February). A new era of recruiting promises to democratize the hiring process and boost inclusion and diversity. https://humancapital.aon.com/. https://humancapital.aon.com/insights/articles/2022/a-new-era-of-recruiting-promises-to-democratize-the-hiring-process-and-boost-inclusion-and-diversity

Aishwarya, N. (2018). Potential impact of blockchain on HR and people management. *Journal of Emerging Technologies and Innovative Research (JETIR)*, 5(9), 127. https://www.jetir.org/papers/JETIRA006284.pdf

Anaam, E. A., Ghazal, T. M., Haw, S., Alzoubi, H. M., Alshurideh, M., & Mamun, A. A. (2023). Utilization of blockchain technology in human resource management. In *2023 IEEE 2nd International Conference on AI in Cybersecurity (ICAIC)*. Houston, TX. https://doi.org/10.1109/icaic57335.2023.10044181

Apriani, M., Rousstia, D., Rifai, F. A., Harwahyu, R., & Sari, R. F. (2020). Implementation of secure work from home system based on blockchain using NS3 simulation. In *2020 7th International Conference on Electrical Engineering, Computer Sciences and Informatics (EECSI)* (pp. 54–59). Yogyakarta, Indonesia. https://doi.org/10.23919/EECSI50503.2020.9251877.

Arora, R. (2021). Blockchain technology in human resource management. www.linkedin.com. https://www.linkedin.com/pulse/blockchain-technology-human-resources-raghav-arora/

Barnett, J., & Treleaven, P. (2017, November 9). Algorithmic dispute resolution—The automation of professional dispute resolution using AI and blockchain technologies. *The Computer Journal Advance Access*. https://doi.org/10.1093/comjnl/bxx103

Basile, M. (2020). Blockchain for factory workers: a study of Levi's worker well-being program. *Blockchain Law*, 4. Retrieved from https://digitalcommons.law.ggu.edu/blockchain_law/4

Bastian, R. (2021, October 24). The diversity, equity and inclusion potential of NFTs. *Forbes*. https://www.forbes.com/sites/rebekahbastian/2021/10/24/the-diversity-equity-and-inclusion-potential-of-nfts/

Bron, D. (2023, May 1). The gig economy 2.0: how decentralized platforms are empowering freelancers and shifting the balance of power. Redefining Frameworks for 4IR Startups & Creatives. https://www.linkedin.com/pulse/gig-economy-20-how-decentralized-platforms-empowering-bron-/

Budayan, C., & Okudan, O. (2023). Assessment of barriers to the implementation of smart contracts in construction projects—Evidence from Turkey. *Buildings*, 13(8), 2084. MDPI AG. Retrieved from https://dx.doi.org/10.3390/buildings13082084

Chong Tai, P., Ki Suk, H., & Tae Young, L. (2020). Smart contract based personnel recruitment system in block chain. https://typeset.io/papers/smart-contract-based-personnel-recruitment-system-in-block-c9bz5mfj6r

Chresomales, P. (2021, October 13). Putting digital badges on blockchain. *Training*. https://trainingmag.com/putting-digital-badges-on-blockchain/

Cloud, H. (n.d.). 7 ways technology can drive higher employee engagement | HR Cloud. https://www.hrcloud.com/blog/7-ways-technology-can-drive-higher-employee-engagement

Consultancy-me.com. (2022, May 6). Synthetic equity tokenizes employee rewards on the blockchain. Consultancy_me.com. https://www.consultancy-me.com/news/4972/synthetic-equity-tokenizes-employee-rewards-on-the-blockchain

Crossan, M.M. & Apaydin, M. (2010). A multi-dimensional framework of organizational innovation: A systematic review of the literature. *Journal of Management Studies*, 47, 1154–1191.

CVVC. (2023, November 17). Blockchain: A technology with social impact. https://www.cvvc.com/blogs/blockchain-a-technology-with-social-impact

Damilola, F. (2023, September 5). Blockchain innovations meet remote work: LaborX's vision for the future. *Medium*. Retrieved from https://medium.com/@fabiyijeremiah123/blockchain-innovations-meet-remote-work-laborxs-vision-for-the-future-3dc59cef23b

Dhanala, N. S., & Radha, D. (2020). Implementation and testing of a blockchain based recruitment management system. In *2020 5th International Conference on Communication and Electronics Systems (ICCES)*. Coimbatore. https://doi.org/10.1109/icces48766.2020.9138093

Di Vaio, A., Hassan, R., & Palladino, R. (2023). Blockchain technology and gender equality: A systematic literature review. *International Journal of Information Management*, 68, 102517. https://doi.org/10.1016/j.ijinfomgt.2022.102517

Fincher, M. (2021, December 16). 5 Ways blockchain technology can revolutionize human resource management. *Trust My Paper*. Retrieved from https://spiceworks.com/hr/hr-compliance/articles/5-ways-blockchain-technology-can-revolutionize-human-resource-management/

Frąckiewicz, M. (2023, November 23). The role of blockchain in reducing bias and discrimination in HR. *TS2 SPACE*. https://ts2.space/en/the-role-of-blockchain-in-reducing-bias-and-discrimination-in-hr/#gsc.tab=0

Gasparri, S., & Tassinari, A. (2020). 'Smart' industrial relations in the making? Insights from analysis of union responses to digitalization in Italy. *Relations Industrielles/Industrial Relations*, 75(4), 796–817. https://doi.org/10.7202/1074565ar

Grace Garnett, A. (2023, May 18). How smart contracts work with blockchain: A step-by-step guide. *Britannica Money*. https://www.britannica.com/money/how-smart-contracts-work

Gupta, V. (2023). The impact of blockchain technology on HR processes. *Economic Times*. https://hrme.economictimes.indiatimes.com/news/hrtech/the-impact-of-blockchain-technology-on-hr-processes/103978267

Gupta, V. (2023, September 27). The impact of blockchain technology on HR processes. ETHRWorld.com. https://hrme.economictimes.indiatimes.com/news/hrtech/the-impact-of-blockchain-technology-on-hr-processes/103978267

Haque, S.. (2023). The impact of remote work on HR practices: Navigating challenges, embracing opportunities. *European Journal of Human Resource Management Studies*. 7. https://doi.org/10.46827/ejhrms.v7i1.1549.

Hosking, A. (2023, March 20). 5 ways blockchain technology can impact human resource management - HR future. *HR Future*. https://www.hrfuture.net/talent-management/technology/5-ways-blockchain-technology-can-impact-human-resource-management/

Howell, B. E., & Potgieter, P. H. (2021). Uncertainty and dispute resolution for blockchain and smart contract institutions. *Journal of Institutional Economics*, 1–15. https://doi.org/10.1017/s1744137421000138

Howell, B., & Potgieter, P. H. (2021). Uncertainty and dispute resolution for blockchain and smart contract institutions. *Journal of Institutional Economics*, 17(4), 545–559. https://doi.org/10.1017/s1744137421000138

Hrrkoin. (2023, July 31). Unlocking HR's potential: How blockchain and AI are changing the game. *LinkedIn*. https://www.linkedin.com/pulse/unlocking-hrs-potential-how-blockchain-ai-changing-game-hrrkoin

Hughes, C., Swaminathan, V., & Brooks, G. (2019). Driving brand engagement through online social influencers: An empirical investigation of sponsored blogging campaigns. *Journal of Marketing*, 83(5), 78–96. https://doi.org/10.1177/0022242919854374

Jenkins, A. (2023, April 6). Blockchain in manufacturing: How tech is changing the industry. *NetSuite*. Retrieved from https://www.netsuite.com/portal/resource/articles/inventory-management/blockchain-in-manufacturing.shtml

Kashyap, S., & Gupta, S. (2023, July 4). Legal implications of remote work. King, Stubb & Kasiva. Mondaq Ltd. https://www.mondaq.com/india/employee-rights-labour-relations/1336724/legal-implications-of-remote-work

Khan, F., & Mer, A. (2023). Embracing artificial intelligence technology: Legal implications with special reference to European Union initiatives of data protection. In Simon Grima, Eleftherios Thalassinos, Graţiela Georgiana Noja, Theodore V. Stamataopoulos, Tatjana Vasiljeva, and Tatjana Volkova (eds) *Digital Transformation, Strategic Resilience, Cyber Security and Risk Management* (pp. 119–141). Emerald Publishing Limited.

Kirkwood, J., & Chaisse, J. (2022, January 6). Smart courts, smart contracts, and the future of online dispute resolution. *Stanford Journal of Blockchain Law & Policy*. Available at SSRN: https://ssrn.com/abstract=4344466

Kişi, N. (2022). Exploratory research on the use of blockchain technology in recruitment. *Sustainability*, 14(16), 10098. MDPI AG. Retrieved from https://dx.doi.org/10.3390/su141610098

Koncheva, V. A., Odintsov, S. V., & Khmelnitski, L. (2019, December). Blockchain in HR. In *Proceedings of the International Scientific and Practical Conference on Digital Economy (ISCDE 2019)* (pp. 504–507). Atlantis Press. https://doi.org/10.2991/iscde-19.2019.154

Kral, T. R. A., Davis, K., Korponay, C., Hirshberg, M. J., Hoel, R., Tello, L. Y., Goldman, R. I., Rosenkranz, M. A., Lutz, A., & Davidson, R. J. (2022). Absence of structural brain changes from mindfulness-based stress reduction: Two combined randomized controlled trials. *Science Advances,* 8(20), eabk3316. https://doi.org/10.1126/sciadv.abk3316

Král, P., Janoskova, K., & Dawson, A. (2022). Virtual skill acquisition, remote working tools, and employee engagement and retention on blockchain-based metaverse platforms. *Psychosociological Issues in Human Resource Management.* Addleton Academic Publishers. https://www.ceeol.com/search/article-detail?id=1052540

Král, P., Janoskova, K., & Dawson, A. (2022). Virtual skill acquisition, remote working tools, and employee engagement and retention on blockchain-based metaverse platforms. *Psychosociological Issues in Human Resource Management*, 10(1), 92. https://doi.org/10.22381/pihrm10120227

Lauslahti, K., Mattila, J., & Seppälä, T. (2017). Smart contracts how will blockchain technology affect contractual practices? *Social Science Research Network.* https://doi.org/10.2139/ssrn.3154043

Levi, S. D., & Lipton, A. B. (2018, May 26). An introduction to smart contracts and their potential and inherent limitations. *Harvard Law School Forum on Corporate Governance.* Retrieved from https://corpgov.law.harvard.edu/

Mallick, M., Sengupta, A., Ingawale, S., & Aljapurkar, A. (2022). Using blockchain technology for recruitment effectiveness in industry 4.0. *Prayukti – Journal of Management Applications*, 02(01), 52–57. https://doi.org/10.52814/pjma.2022.2107

Martín, D. (2021, July 16). Solving gender inequality by using blockchain technology. *OpenHR.* https://www.openhr.cloud/en/blog/solving-gender-inequality-by-using-blockchain-technology

Mazour, V. (2023, July 15). eXo Rewards: A blockchain solution to boost employee engagement. *eXo Platform.* https://www.exoplatform.com/blog/exo-rewards-a-blockchain-solution-to-boost-employee-engagement/

McGimpsey, P. (2023, October 17). Smart contracts explained. *Forbes Advisor Australia.* https://www.forbes.com/advisor/au/investing/cryptocurrency/smart-contracts-explained/

Mer, A. (2022). A study on antecedents and consequences of work engagement with special reference to NGOs in Uttarakhand. https://shodhganga.inflibnet.ac.in/handle/10603/359946

Mer, A. (2023). Artificial intelligence in human resource management: Recent trends and research agenda. In Grima, S., Thalassinos, E. I., Noja, G. G., Stamataopoulos, T. V., Vasiljeva, T., Volkova, T., (eds) *Digital Transformation, Strategic Resilience, Cyber Security and Risk Management* (Vol. 111, pp. 31–56). Emerald Publishing Limited.

Mer, A., & Srivastava, A. (2023). Employee engagement in the new normal: Artificial intelligence as a buzzword or a game changer? In Tyagi, P., Chilamkurti, N., Grima, S., Sood, K., & Balusamy, B. (eds) *The Adoption and Effect of Artificial Intelligence on Human Resources Management, Part A* (pp. 15–46). Emerald Publishing Limited.

Mer, A., & Virdi, A. S. (2023). Navigating the paradigm shift in HRM practices through the lens of artificial intelligence: A post-pandemic perspective. In Tyagi, P., Chilamkurti, N., Grima, S., Sood, K., & Balusamy, B. (eds) *The Adoption and Effect of Artificial Intelligence on Human Resources Management,* Part *A* (pp. 123–154), Emerald Publishing Limited.

Mer, A., Virdi, A. S., & Sengupta, S. (2023). Unleashing the antecedents and consequences of work engagement in NGOs through the lens of JD-R Model: Empirical evidence from India. *VOLUNTAS: International Journal of Voluntary and Nonprofit Organizations*, 34(4), 721–733.

Mishunin, D. (2023, July 6). What makes Smart Contracts "smart"? *Forbes*. https://www.forbes.com/councils/forbestechcouncil/2023/07/05/what-makes-smart-contracts-smart/

Neiheiser, R., Inácio, G., Rech, L., & Da Silva Fraga, J. (2019). HRM smart contracts on the blockchain. In *2019 IEEE Symposium on Computers and Communications (ISCC)*. https://doi.org/10.1109/iscc47284.2019.8969692

Neiheiser, R., Inácio, G., Rech, L., & Da Silva Fraga, J. (2020). HRM smart contracts on the blockchain: Emulated vs native. *Cluster Computing*, 23(3), 2105–2122. https://doi.org/10.1007/s10586-020-03063-9

Nurhasanah, Y., Prameswari, D., & Fachrunnisa, O. (2020). Blockchain-based solution for effective employee management. In Pattnaik, P.K., Sain, M., Al-Absi, A.A., Kumar, P. (eds) *Proceedings of International Conference on Smart Computing and Cyber Security. SMARTCYBER 2020*. Lecture Notes in Networks and Systems (pp. 147–154). Springer, Singapore. https://doi.org/10.1007/978-981-15-7990-5_14

Obu, U., Ambekar, Y., Lingam, R., Borikar, Y., Yadav, R., & Dongre, S. (2023). Blockchain system against gender bias and other discriminatory practices in workplaces. In *2023 IEEE 3rd International Conference on Technology, Engineering, Management for Societal Impact Using Marketing, Entrepreneurship and Talent (TEMSMET)*. https://doi.org/10.1109/temsmet56707.2023.10150193

Onik, M. H., Miraz, M. H., & Chul-Soo, K. (2018). A recruitment and human resource management technique using blockchain technology for industry 4.0. In *Smart Cities Symposium 2018*. https://doi.org/10.1049/cp.2018.1371

Owocki, K. (2022, August 26). Gitcoin launches to push open source forward for the Web3 generation. https://www.gitcoin.co/blog/gitcoin-launches-to-push-open-source-forward-for-the-web3-generation

Pachahara, S., & Maheshwari, C. (2022, April). Dispute resolution on blockchain: An opportunity to increase efficiency of business dispute resolution? *Conflict Studies Quarterly*, 39. chrome-extension://efaidnbmnnnibpcajpcglclefindmkaj/http://www.csq.ro/wp-content/uploads/5-S.-PACHAHARA-C.-MAHESHWARI.pdf

Pinna, A., & Ibba, S. (2018). A blockchain-based decentralized system for proper handling of temporary employment contracts. *Intelligent Computing*, 1231–1243. https://doi.org/10.1007/978-3-030-01177-2_88

Ray, A. (2023). *Dispute Resolution for Smart Contracts: Challenges and Opportunities*. Winsavvy.

Shojaei, A., Flood, I., Moud, H.I., Hatami, M., & Zhang, X. (2020). An implementation of smart contracts by integrating BIM and blockchain. In Arai, K., Bhatia, R., Kapoor, S. (eds) *Proceedings of the Future Technologies Conference (FTC) 2019. FTC 2019. Advances in Intelligent Systems and Computing*, vol 1070. Springer, Cham. https://doi.org/10.1007/978-3-030-32523-7_36

Taherdoost, H. (2023). Smart contracts in blockchain technology: A critical review. *Information*, 14(2), 117. MDPI AG. Retrieved from https://doi.org/10.3390/info14020117

Tai, E. T. T. (2019). Challenges of smart contracts. In Cambridge University Press eBooks (pp. 80–101). https://doi.org/10.1017/9781108592239.005

The Hummer. (2023, September 4). Blockchain in HR and recruitment. *Hiring and Recruitment*. Retrieved from https://www.peoplehum.com/blog/blockchain-in-hr-recruitment

Torvekar, G. (2021, February). Can blockchain eliminate unconscious bias in recruitment? *Unleash*. https://www.unleash.ai/emerging-tech/can-blockchain-eliminate-unconscious-bias-in-recruitment/

Tranfield, D., Denyer, D., & Smart, P. (2003). Towards a methodology for developing evidence-informed management knowledge by means of systematic review. *British Journal of Management*, 14(3), 207–222. https://doi.org/10.1111/1467-8551.00375

Voss, W. G. (2021, June 3). Data protection issues for smart contracts. In Corrales, M., Fenwick, M., Wrbka, S. (eds), *Smart Contracts: Technological, Business and Legal Perspectives* (pp. 79–100). Hart Publishing/Bloomsbury. Retrieved from https://www.bloomsbury-collections.com/book/smart-contracts-technological-business-and-legal-perspectives/

Wiles, J. (2019, August 27). 5 Ways blockchain will affect HR. *Human Resources Insights*. Retrieved from https://www.gartner.com/smarterwithgartner/5-ways-blockchain-will-affect-hr

Wright, B. (2019, January 25). Levi Strauss to pilot blockchain for factory worker welfare. *Just-Style*. Retrieved from https://www.just-style.com/news/levi-strauss-to-pilot-blockchain-for-factory-worker-welfare/?cf-view

Yi, C. S. S., Yung, E., Fong, C., & Tripathi, S. (2020). Benefits and use of blockchain technology to human resources management: A critical review. *International Journal of Human Resource Studies*, 10(2), 131. https://doi.org/10.5296/ijhrs.v10i2.16932

Zhao, R., Wang, J., & Xue, F. (2023). A blockchain-based token incentive mechanism for ESG in the construction industry. In *2023 European Conference on Computing in Construction*, Heraklion, https://ec-3.org/publications/conferences/EC32023/papers/EC32023_235.pdf

Zheng, Z., Xie, S., Dai, H., Chen, W., Chen, X., Weng, J., & Imran, M. (2020). An overview on smart contracts: Challenges, advances and platforms. *Future Generation Computer Systems*, 105, 475–491. https://doi.org/10.1016/j.future.2019.12.019

Zielinski, D. (2021, May 24). How blockchain benefits recruiters, job candidates. *SHRM*. https://www.shrm.org/resourcesandtools/hr-topics/technology/pages/how-blockchain-benefits-recruiters-job-candidates.aspx

6 Robotics' Place in HR
Developments, Trends, and Effects

Shabana Azami and Deepa Gupta

6.1 INTRODUCTION

In the developing scene of India's worldwide economy, robotics has turned into a basic component, fundamentally impacting different areas. The integration of trend setting innovations, especially robotics, is changing the manner in which organizations work, tending to numerous human touchpoints with imaginative arrangements [1]. The exhibition qualities of robots, for example, their capacity to deal with dreary assignments, oversee broad data sets, save time, and surpass human efficiency in critical thinking, are reshaping businesses. For entrepreneurs, putting resources into robotics is viewed as an essential, once consumption that can yield long haul benefits by smoothing out tasks and upgrading generally speaking productivity [2].

6.1.1 Objectives

- To analyse the role of robotics in Human Resources (HR).
- To explore the advantages and limitations of Robotic Process Automation (RPA).
- To examine the implementation of RPA in HR practices."

6.2 LITERATURE REVIEW

A review coordinated by Infosys BPM, a main overall player in IT, re-appropriating, and errands, includes the uncommon impact of automation on HR processes [3]. The client, an overall organization with an enormous workforce spread across various overall work environments, stood up to troubles in managing HR works capably. The rising volume of HR works out, crucial for employee satisfaction, mentioned more suitable correspondence with the leaders, adherence to essential business necessities, and consistency with quality rules.

Infosys BPM recognized automation as a solution for lessening the heaviness of manual processes, which were dreary and leaned to botches [4]. By introducing RPA, a couple of HR processes saw basic redesigns:

- Establishment Check for New Employees: The process, which included wide sweeps across various informational indexes for affirming contender information, was streamlined using RPA [5]. The automation decreased the

DOI: 10.1201/9781032619651-6

time expected as well as discarded the prerequisite for manual intervention, ensuring perfect and exact report age.

- Creating Course of action Letters for New Joiners: In advance, this process required cautious manual effort, expecting close to 15 minutes for each employee [6]. RPA lessened processing time by 90%, completing the entire system while adhering to each and every managerial need.
- Full and Last Settlement for Pulling out Employees: Money processing, which included really taking a look at exceptional portions across workplaces, was improved by RPA [7]. The automation extended process efficiency by 95%, restricting botches and ensuring consistence.

The execution of RPA by Infosys BPM achieved critical benefits, recollecting a 70% decline in troublesome work, a 55% reduction in lead times, and an immense improvement in accuracy [8]. This case addresses the capacity of RPA to redesign productivity and manufacture solid areas for a case for extra automation.

6.3 ROBOTICS

Robots, known for their capacity to perform endeavours commonly managed by humans, are changing business undertakings by giving shrewd game plans [9]. They are particularly effective in separating gigantic informational indexes and offering helpful objectives to useful troubles. In various pieces of business, robots are surpassing human capacities, driving associations to place resources into robotics advancement across various regions, including retail, gathering, activities, and creation network of the chiefs [10].

No matter what the capacity of robotics, its adoption in assisting organizations with HR has been slow. In any case, as associations dynamically see the upsides of robotics, the development is being embraced across a greater extent of purposes [11].

6.4 ROBOTICS IN HR

The conversation around the gig of robotics in HR centres around whether these progressions can supersede or extend standard human positions [12]. Various HR abilities, particularly those that are standard and rule-based, are suitable for automation. By modernizing these endeavours, affiliations can allow employees to focus on extra fundamental locales, similar to methodology headway, talent the board, and employee maintenance [13].

According to a Deloitte report, 42% of organizations participating in an overall report on human capital improvement have gained basic progress in planning robotics into their workforce, with expected cost save assets of up to 20%. This integration has enabled the improvement of programming bots that direct normal tasks capably [14].

6.4.1 Current Trends and Impact of Robotics in HR and Industry

- Straightforward Integration: RPA is a by and large protected, painless development that can be helpfully planned into existing structures, establishing the groundwork for extra movements in artificial intelligence (AI) [15].

- Extended Efficiency: By diminishing the obligation on employees, RPA grants relationships to help overall productivity, enabling employees to focus on more creative and high-regard tasks [16].
- Cost-Feasibility: RPA is a pragmatic game plan, offering long stretch advantages with to some degree low starting endeavours [17].
- Precision: In tasks like data assessment, RPA conveys results with higher precision and exactness compared to human undertakings [18].
- Helpful Work: RPA redesigns the efficiency and reasonableness of processes in various undertakings, conveying extraordinary outcomes with fewer slip-ups [19].
- Executing Lean Processes: Robotics maintains the execution of lean processes by propelling efficiency and killing trivial chips away at, inciting cost save reserves and speedier benefits from hypothesis (profit from starting capital speculation) [20] (Figure 6.1).

In any case, hardships, for instance, high maintenance and foundation costs, particularly for little and medium endeavours, and potential work adversities on account of automation ought to be painstakingly considered [21]. The social repercussions of occupation dislodging and the impact on unambiguous occupations, as clinical assessment, furthermore warrant thought.

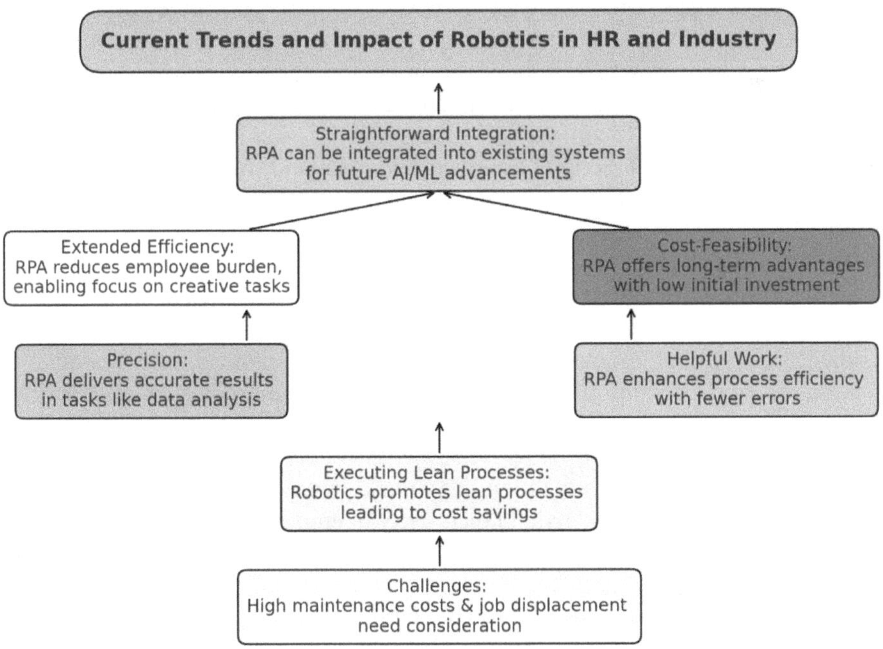

FIGURE 6.1 Current trends and impact of robotics in HR and industry.

6.5 DIGITIZATION IN HUMAN RESOURCES

AI and robotics hold the possibility to modernize numerous HR processes, from recruitment to talent on the board. Gartner research proposes that by 2020, AI could make 2.1 million new positions, balancing the 1.8 million positions that automation could kill [23]. This shift features the developing interest for experts gifted in AI and robotics.

The digitization of HR is generally changing the manner in which associations deal with their workforce. By utilizing trend setting innovations like man-made consciousness (AI), AI (ML), and RPA, HR offices can smooth out processes, upgrade direction, and work on by and large efficiency [22].

Enlistment and Ability Obtaining: One of the primary effects of digitization in HR is tracked down in enrolment. Now, AI-controlled devices can look at resumes, look at the skills of candidates, and, surprisingly, use chatbots to direct early-on gatherings. These advances empower HR social affairs to rapidly perceive top ability, diminishing the time and cost related to standard enrolment strategies. Furthermore, computer-based intelligence calculations can dispose of ignorant tendency in using, pushing a more remarkable and complete work area [25].

Upgraded Effectiveness and Precision: The coordination of robotics and RPA in HR rehearses has brought about huge enhancements in productivity and exactness. Dull undertakings, for example, continued screening, personal investigations, and finance handling, have been smoothed out, permitting HR experts to zero in on additional essential drives [24]. Mechanization guarantees consistency and diminishes the probability of human mistakes, which is especially essential in compliance-related tasks [26].

Cost Reserve Funds and Efficiency: Robotization in HR processes offers significant expense reserve funds by decreasing the requirement for physical work and limiting functional expenses [27]. Robotics additionally upgrades efficiency by getting done with responsibilities quicker than people, adding to the general productivity of the association [32].

Further developed Direction: Robotics and computer-based intelligence give HR offices information driven bits of knowledge, considering better dynamic in regions like ability the board, representative commitment, and labour force arranging. Progressed examination empowers HR experts to foresee patterns, recognize expertise holes, and configuration designated improvement programs, working on authoritative execution [31].

Influence on Ability/Talent Procurement: The utilization of computer-based intelligence and robotics in ability securing has changed enrolment processes. Robotized frameworks can check a huge number of resumes and evaluate up-and-comers' reasonableness in a small portion of the time, guaranteeing that the best ability is distinguished rapidly [28]. In addition, man-made intelligence can lessen oblivious predisposition, advancing variety and inclusivity in employing [25].

Difficulties of Robotization: In spite of the advantages, there are difficulties related to the execution of robotics in HR. High starting arrangement costs and continuous support costs can be a weight for little and medium-sized undertakings (SMEs) [32]. Also, there are worries about work removal, as robotization can supplant some conventional HR jobs, prompting likely joblessness [24].

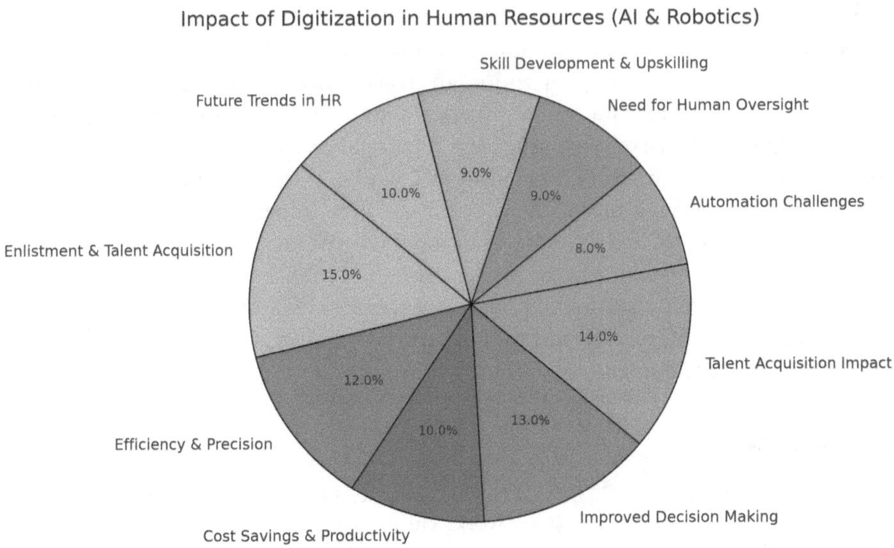

FIGURE 6.2 Impact of digitalization in HR.

Need for Human Oversight: While robotics can deal with numerous standard errands, there is as yet a requirement for human oversight, particularly in dynamic cycles that require compassion and nuanced judgment. HR works like compromise, representative turn of events, and hierarchical culture-building depend on human communication, which computerization can't completely recreate [30].

Ability Improvement and Upskilling: As mechanization turns out to be more predominant, HR offices should zero in on reskilling and upskilling their labour force to stay serious. Representatives should foster new abilities, for example, overseeing mechanized frameworks and dissecting information, to actually work close by robots [29].

Future Patterns: The procedure with advancement of simulated intelligence, AI, and robotics will additionally change HR rehearses. The fate of HR will probably see more prominent cooperation among people and machines, where cutting-edge innovations improve, as opposed to supplant, human jobs in the working environment. HR divisions should get ready for this shift by putting resources into innovation and encouraging a culture of flexibility and constant learning [33] (Figure 6.2).

6.6 CONCLUSIONS

Robotic computerization is changing the scene of human assets by offering upgraded productivity, accuracy, and cost-adequacy. As organizations embrace robotics and simulated intelligence-driven advancements, HR cycles, for example, ability procurement, worker onboarding, finance, and consistency have become fundamentally more smoothed out. These advancements diminish the weight of redundant, tedious assignments, permitting HR experts to focus on essential capabilities like representative turn of events, commitment, and maintenance. In any case, notwithstanding the various benefits, including further developed navigation and quicker execution, the broad reception of robotization raises difficulties. High arrangement and support costs, especially for more modest undertakings, and the expected relocation of occupations because of computerization are basic worries that associations should address. The requirement for human oversight stays basic, particularly in jobs that request sympathy, decisive reasoning, and relational association. Also, as mechanization turns out to be more implanted in HR works, upskilling the labour force to oversee and team up with these advancements will be imperative. Looking forward, the eventual fate of HR lies in a mixture model where human mastery and machine effectiveness work connected at the hip, encouraging a defter and useful business climate. This beneficial interaction of people and robots won't just reshape conventional HR rehearses but additionally add to more extensive authoritative achievement and public financial development.

REFERENCES

1. Abraham, M., Niessen, C., Schnabel, C., Lorek, K., Grimm, V., Moslein, K., & Wrede, M. (2019). Electronic monitoring at work: The role of attitudes, functions, and perceived control for the acceptance of tracking technologies. *Human Resource Management Journal*, 29(4), 657–675. https://doi.org/10.1111/1748-8583.12250
2. Agarwal, S., & Gupta, D. (2024). *Digital Analytics Applications for Sustainable Training and Education* (1st ed.). Apple Academic Press.
3. Agarwal, S., Gupta, D., & Gupta, M. (2023). Techno pedagogical concept with digital skills. In Manna, M. S., Balusamy, B., Sood, K., Chilamkurti, N. & George, I. R. (eds) *Edutech Enabled Teaching* (pp. 129–152). Chapman and Hall/CRC.
4. Anuj, K, Gupta, D., Gupta, M., & Srivastava, G. (2021). India an emerging leader after pandemic: A strategy for the development of new India. *Global Journal of Enterprise Information System*, 13(1), 60–70. https://www.gjeis.com/index.php/GJEIS/article/view/629
5. Araujo, T. (2018). Living up to the chatbot hype: The influence of anthropomorphic design cues and communicative agency framing on conversational agent and company perceptions. *Computers in Human Behavior*, 85, 183–189. https://doi.org/10.1016/j. chb.2018.03.051
6. Bondarouk, T., & Brewster, C. (2016). Conceptualising the future of HRM and technology research. *The International Journal of Human Resource Management*, 27(21), 2652–2671. https://doi.org/10.1080/09585192.2016.1232296
7. Chao, G. T., & Kozlowski, S. W. (1986). Employee perceptions on the implementation of robotic manufacturing technology. *Journal of Applied Psychology*, 71(1), 70–76.
8. De Kock, F. S., Lievens, F., & Born, M. P. (2020). The profile of the 'Good Judge' in HRM: A systematic review and agenda for future research. *Human Resource Management Review*, 30(2), 100667. https://doi.org/10.1016/j.hrmr.2018.09.003
9. Feldman, D. C., & Klaas, B. S. (2002). Internet job hunting: A field study of applicant experiences with on-line recruiting. *Human Resource Management*, 41(2), 175–192. https://doi.org/10.1002/hrm.10030
10. Gaur, A., & Kumar, M. (2018). A systematic approach to conducting review studies: An assessment of content analysis in 25 years of IB research. *Journal of World Business*, 53(2), 280–289. https://doi.org/10.1016/j.jwb.2017.11.003
11. Gupta, D., & Agarwal, S. (2018). Skill development initiative-literature review. *Inspira-Journal of Modern Management and Entrepreneurship (JMME)*, 8(2), 319–322.
12. Gupta, D., & Agarwal, S. (2018). Training prospects in power sector in India. *International Journal of Research in Engineering, IT and Social Sciences*, 8(Special Issue), 305–314.

13. Gupta, D., Gupta, M., & Rani, S. (2022). A study on training of workmen in a manufacturing organization—With reference to aluminium foundry. In: Dvivedi, A., Sachdeva, A., Sindhwani, R., Sahu, R. (eds) *Recent Trends in Industrial and Production Engineering*. Lecture Notes in Mechanical Engineering. Springer, Singapore. https://doi.org/10.1007/978-981-16-3330-0_19
14. Hooper, R. S., Galvin, T. P., Kilmer, R. A., & Liebowitz, J. (1998). Use of an expert system in a personnel selection process. *Expert Systems with Applications*, 14(4), 425–432. Huang, M. H., & Rust, R. T. (2018). Artificial intelligence in service. *Journal of Service Research*, 21(2), 155–172. https://doi.org/10.1177/1094670517752459
15. Golden, A. G., & Geisler, C. (2007). Work–life boundary management and the personal digital assistant. *Human Relations*, 60(3), 519–551. https://doi.org/10.1177/0018726707076698.
16. Kumar, V., Gupta, M., & Gaur, S. (2023). Intrusion detection for the Internet of Things. In Kaushik, K., Dahiya, S., Bhardwaj, A., Maleh, Y. (eds), *Internet of Things and Cyber Physical Systems Security and Forensics* (1st ed., pp. 183). CRC Press.
17. Lawler, J. J., & Elliot, R. (1996). Artificial intelligence in HRM: An experimental study of an expert system. *Journal of Management*, 22(1), 85–111. https://doi.org/10.1177/014920639602200104
18. Malik, A., Budhwar, P., Srikanth, N. R., & Varma, A. (2019). May the Bots Be with You! Opportunities and Challenges of Artificial Intelligence for Rethinking Human Resource Management Practices. Paper Accepted for presentation BAM 2019. https://www.bam.ac.uk/sites/bam.ac.uk/files/contribution294_0.pdf
19. Markus, M. L. (2015). New games, new rules, new scoreboards: The potential consequences of big data. *Journal of Information Technology*, 30(1), 58–59. https://doi.org/10.1057/jit.2014.28
20. Marler, J. H., & Boudreau, J. W. (2017). An evidence-based review of HR analytics. *The International Journal of Human Resource Management*, 28(1), 3–26. https://doi.org/10.1080/09585192.2016.1244699
21. Park, R. (2018). The roles of OCB and automation in the relationship between job autonomy and organizational performance: A moderated mediation model. *The International Journal of Human Resource Management*, 29(6), 1139–1156. https://doi.org/10.1080/09585192.2016.1180315
22. Rani, S., Gupta, M., & Gupta, D. (2020). Artificial intelligence and personalized banking. In *Transforming Management Using Artificial Intelligence Techniques* (1st ed., pp. 24). CRC Press. https://doi.org/10.4324/9781003032410
23. Ravid, D. M., Tomczak, D. L., White, J. C., & Behrend, T. S. (2020). EPM 20/20: A review, framework, and research agenda for electronic performance monitoring. *Journal of Management*, 46(1), 100–126. https://doi.org/10.1177/0149206319869435
24. Singh, S., Gupta, D., & Gupta, M. (2022). Optimized task allocation technique using mathematical fuzzy logic in heterogeneous distributed computational system. In *2022 International Conference on Computational Intelligence and Sustainable Engineering Solutions (CISES)* (pp. 37–45), Greater Noida, India, 2022, https://doi.org/10.1109/CISES54857.2022.9844410
25. Sajjadiani, S., Sojourner, A. J., Kammeyer-Mueller, J. D., & Mykerezi, E. (2019). Using machine learning to translate applicant work history into predictors of performance and turnover. *Journal of Applied Psychology*, 104(10), 1207–1225. https://doi.org/10.1037/apl0000405
26. Singh, J., Brady, M., Arnold, T., & Brown, T. (2017). The emergent field of organizational frontlines. *Journal of Service Research*, 20(1), 3–11. https://doi.org/10.1177/1094670516681513

27. Singh, S., & Gupta, D. (2023). Module allocation model in distributed computing system by implementing fuzzy C-means clustering technique. In: Agrawal, R., Mitra, P., Pal, A., Sharma Gaur, M. (eds) *International Conference on IoT, Intelligent Computing and Security*. Lecture Notes in Electrical Engineering, vol 982, pp. 157–172, Springer, Singapore. https://doi.org/10.1007/978-981-19-8136-4_14
28. Agarwal, S., Gupta, D., & Gupta, M. (2023). Impact of training method on trainees learning and implementation on job – A study with special reference to power sector. *AIP Conference Proceedings*, (27 February 2023) 2427(1), 020020. https://doi.org/10.1063/5.0100893
29. Thomaz, F., Salge, C., Karahanna, E., & Hulland, J. (2020). Learning from the Dark Web: Leveraging conversational agents in the era of hyper-privacy to enhance marketing. *Journal of the Academy of Marketing Science*, 48(1), 43–63. https://doi.org/10.1007/s11747-019-00704-3
30. Tranfield, D., Denyer, D., & Smart, P. (2003). Towards a methodology for developing evidence-informed management knowledge by means of systematic review. *British Journal of Management*, 14(3), 207–222. https://doi.org/10.1111/1467-8551.00375
31. Van Doorn, J., Mende, M., Noble, S. M., Hulland, J., Ostrom, A. L., Grewal, D., & Petersen, J. A. (2017). Domo arigato Mr. Roboto: Emergence of automated social presence in organizational frontlines and customers' service experiences. *Journal of Service Research*, 20(1), 43–58. https://doi.org/10.1177/1094670516679272
32. Wall, T. D., Jackson, P. R., & Davids, K. (1992). Operator work design and robotics system performance: A serendipitous field study. *Journal of Applied Psychology*, 77(3), 353–362. https://doi.org/10.1037/0021-9010.77.3.353
33. Wang, X., Wang, L., Zhang, L., Xu, X., Zhang, W., & Xu, Y. (2017). Developing an employee turnover risk evaluation model using case-based reasoning. *Information Systems Frontiers*, 19(3), 569–576. https://doi.org/10.1007/s10796-015-9615-9

7 A Study of Ethical, Social and Legal Implications of Emerging Technologies in HRM

Himani Grewal, Aditi Vishnoi, Avinash Saxena, and Mukul Gupta

7.1 INTRODUCTION

The advent of new information on people and machines has revolutionized organizational management. Enterprises are constantly seeking to pinpoint opportunities for enhancement and expanding their market share (Khan, 2007). Modern, cutting-edge technologies are rapidly reshaping the worldwide human resource management (HRM) scene (Vrontis et al., 2021).

The "changing world of work," which refers to how technology is affecting the workplace, has drawn a lot of attention lately, particularly from consultants and the media. Naturally, technological change is not new in and of itself; ever since the steam engine propelled the first industrial revolution, it has been a defining aspect of labor and society (Parry & Battista, 2023).

Information technologies are changing HRM-related processes; one prominent example is the introduction of e-recruitment, e-training, or e-competence management. These developments have a favorable effect on the caliber of HRM services supplied by both domestic and international businesses (Vrontis et al., 2021). There is renewed concern about how automation may affect the quantity and quality of jobs due to the new technologies' rapid development and systemic integration. Seeing that we are living in a period of unmatched technological development is now ordinary (Halteh et al., 2018). Future labor will be impacted by technology in two ways: positively and negatively (Holland & Bardoel, 2016). Since the beginning of time, technological developments have altered how the sector operates (Adeney, 1994).

In the last sixty years, HR academics have accumulated a tremendous amount of splendid knowledge relating to the interacting effects of technology and HRM. They have used the most innovative methodological techniques to conduct research, watched the latest technical state-of-the-art changes of their time closely, and provided practically useful insights (Shamim et al., 2016; Kim et al., 2021). In the realm of human resource management, there has been an integration of high-end advanced technologies like AI among others, which no longer

DOI: 10.1201/9781032619651-7

serve as tools but a lot more than that. According to Ivanov and Webster (2019), emerging technologies are arriving in employee training and development. With the help of augmented reality and virtual reality, training experience has become immersive and engaging. Malik et al. (2020). This reduces costs associated with traditional methods while improving learning results in the process. Moreover, technology's role in performance reviews and feedback is also increasingly changing how companies deal with employee performance. Real-time feedback, continuous performance monitoring, and data-driven insights offer HR professionals quicker and more personalized responses to employees, which help in growth and development. But all over again, some challenges need to be considered with the adoption of such technologies (Abraham et al., 2019). Assuring is here in taking up the issues of data security, privacy issues, and the potential bias that emanates from the algorithms themselves.

7.2 LEGAL IMPLICATIONS OF EMERGING TECHNOLOGIES IN HRM

The growth of emerging technologies establishes one such revolution with extensive effects in various sectors including HRM as well. The capacity of these technologies is that programmed devices are able to perform routine tasks that used to be completed by the manual workforce (Scherer, 2016). With regards to HRM practices, adoption of emerging technologies means that various HRM activities like recruitment & selection, training & development, performance appraisal, compensation planning, etc. could become programmed to a significant extent (Sadok et al., 2022). Technology is reforming how organizations are managing their workforce, creating schedules, measuring productivity, growing efficiency, providing feedback, and improving their overall participation (Sadok et al., 2022).

The introduction of emerging technologies such as artificial intelligence to HRM, however, also poses some significant challenges, mostly at the level of managing employee–employer and labor–supervisor relations from a legal perspective within a group (Nankervis et al., 2019). Nondiscriminatory rules cover staffing procedures, the rules and norms associated with the employment contract, the provision of reimbursement and rewards, and the making of decisions relating to relocation, termination, and dismissal (Melnychenko, 2020). Moreover, technology is responsible to come in at vital moments of the employment relation, such as during the stage of workplace safety measurement, granting social benefits to employees, performance appraisal, and beyond all this the assessment of employee harassment in an organization, which is one of the most judiciary involvement decisions (Stefano, 2019).

There is a frequent demand that HR managers proactively update the employees about their rights in this regard, so that employees might be in a state to pursue legal redress for their issues (Pandya, 2019). There is a chance that biased conclusions will be reached when personnel decisions are made using algorithms that process raw data since there may be an indirect correlation between traits protected by antidiscrimination laws and characteristics that appear to be nondiscriminatory.

It is certain that under these conditions, decisions that are fundamentally biased will be made. As a result, HR departments will have the difficult challenge of implementing effective bylaws that include safeguards to prevent these kinds of outcomes (Sadok et al., 2022).

7.3 ETHICAL IMPLICATIONS OF EMERGING TECHNOLOGY IN HRM

The correlation between ethics and human resource management is becoming a topic of significant scholarly investigation. Because the handling of people is at the heart of human resource management, it is an intrinsically moral activity. As such, conceptualizing HRM naturally brings up ethical issues. The ethical management of employees was not a topic of discussion in the realm of business ethics until quite recently (Winstanley & Woodall, 2000). The firm's temporal and physical boundaries are shifting due to the introduction of new technologies, and a new organizational structure is arising from the redefining of working hours and workplace. These adjustments are paying off in numerous ways, particularly when it comes to low-cost transactional solutions like outsourcing and vertical integration (Hitt et al., 1999; Afuah, 2003). Without a doubt, technology has greatly benefited humanity. There are countless ways in which automation, communication that is quick and efficient, accuracy and quality, etc., have all contributed to an increase in living quality. For these reasons, businesses will keep searching for more cutting-edge technology to add value to their offerings of goods and services. The alignment of an organization's procedures with an ethical culture can be emphasized through the implementation of ethical human resource management. Organizations must set an example for their employees by treating them fairly and with respect if they want them to treat customers—both internal and external—fairly, respect the integrity of freely entered contracts, and respect third parties' rights. Companies should be very concerned about the ethical implications of technology in the workplace if they wish to be humanistic or moral enterprises (Gupta et al., 2024). This is particularly the responsibility of the company's human resource management or that individual. The following regions have greatly benefited from new and updated technology:

a. Data Privacy: HR departments may now gather and examine enormous volumes of employee data because of the development of AI and big data. This brings up moral concerns around permission and privacy.
b. AI Bias: AI is being utilized more and more in HR for functions like hiring performance prediction and resume screening. However, if the information utilized to hone these algorithms is skewed, the AI might reinforce these prejudices.
c. Job Automation: Many HR-related duties are becoming automated, which may result in job losses. It is critical to think about ways to assist staff members who may be affected by this.
d. Technologies for Remote Work: As remote work becomes more common, technologies like surveillance software are being employed to keep an eye on staff members. This brings up moral questions regarding privacy and trust (Agarwal & Gupta, 2024; Agarwal et al., 2023).

7.4 SOCIAL IMPLICATIONS OF EMERGING TECHNOLOGY IN HRM

For millennia, people have been observing and documenting the impact of technology on civilization. We can observe the effects of technical innovation on civilization arbitrarily because of the discoveries of fire and the wheel, two inventions that had a major influence on society and the survival of the human species (Kostakos et al., 2005).

It would be exhilarating to ponder over how the upcoming technology in HRM is going to influence society. Technology keeps changing and is changing how firms handle HR processes. New technologies are making their entrance in changing the sector of HR: from hiring to training from appraisal to data analysis. Impact on work responsibilities and requirements for new skills is one of the major social impacts.

The automation and artificial intelligence emerging in organizations can automate certain functions that were once done by HR professionals. It may mean that the job and its responsibilities are going to change, and some retraining or upskilling is necessary to cope with the fast-evolving technology environment. Ethics and privacy of data are other important considerations. Most importantly, HR departments are collecting and processing a lot of data about the employees; it is vital to ensure that the information cannot be exploited without their consent and will not fall into the wrong hands. Many business matters increasingly depend on employee data protection and transparency in its processing. In addition, the pursuit of inclusion and diversity by HR can be further enhanced through emerging technology (Rajvanshi, P.R. et al., 2022).

AI-driven solutions can help eradicate some of the biased approaches toward hiring and build a culture of inclusion and diversity at work. At any given time, even at the said unbiased meetings, it is always necessary to keep a watch on various biases associated with algorithms and to keep assessing and updating such technologies. Social implications of adopted emergent technologies within human resources management are generally taking multiple facets. While these technologies boast of several advantages, such as well-informed decision-making and efficiency, it is equally important to present or remedy any potential drawbacks in the utility of such facilities by implementing them in a nondiscriminatory and ethical way (Rajvanshi et al., 2022).

The field of recruitment has undergone DISC technology. Now, with the application of AI-heavy algorithms and data analytics in HR departments, significantly faster searching, filtering, and selection of candidates can be achieved. This may further lead to objectivity in recruitment processes and efficiency, putting an emphasis on promoting diversity and inclusion within a company. Considering this, the social implications of new technologies in the area of HR administration remain amazing (Singh et al., 2022). Fascinatingly, one now sees how technology is transforming HR processes to open doors toward more efficient, inclusive, data-driven strategies.

7.5 MITIGATING ETHICAL, SOCIAL, AND LEGAL RISKS

On one hand, the changing world of human resource management opens new perspectives to increase efficiency, simplify procedures, and enhance decision-making ability, thanks to the rapid diffusion of emergent technologies. On the other hand, it increases ethical, social, and legal challenges that are related to the integration of

AI, Machine Learning (ML), and Machine Learning (RPA). Consequently, the need for proactive strategies from HR leaders is constantly changing to mitigate all potential risks. This chapter discusses how to develop technology HRM solutions that are ethical and transparent, and conform to the law, while enhancing social responsibility through a flexible workforce.

7.5.1 Ethics in Developing AI/ML Models

One of the core challenges in integrating AI and ML into the process of HRM is ensuring that these models operate ethically and are free from bias. The most important thing about HR algorithms is that they often create a direct impact on one's career, like hiring, promotion, and compensation. If these models are not well-designed, AI, when learning from biased or prejudiced information from historical data, may cause unfair and discriminatory outcomes. In particular, this calls for prioritizing the ethical development of AI, whereby organizations create a variety of data sets that represent all kinds of demographics; regularly audit algorithms for bias; and design models with fairness and transparency in mind. Fairness, inclusiveness, and human dignity require cross-functional collaboration across HR professionals, data scientists, and ethicists throughout the AI life cycle.

7.5.2 Applying Transparently and Equitably Data Use Policies

Considering that HRM is increasingly a field of data-driven decisions, it goes without saying that organizations are under the obligation to clearly establish policies regarding the use of data in a manner that is nondiscriminatory and clearly understandable. Employee data are particularly sensitive; information misuse may amount to violation of privacy rights and destruction of trust between employees and employers. Transparency, for this reason, calls for assurance that an employee understands how his or her private data are collected, kept, and used. Organizations should clearly explain to employees the policies of fair data usage, consent forms taken before collecting personal information, and limitations on data usages (Gupta et al., 2022). Two principles can be maintained for ethical data usages: data minimization and purpose limitation. In the case of data minimization, only that data are collected which are necessary to be collected. In the case of purpose limitation, data are used only for the purposes for which they are intended to be used. Auditing data practices routinely can ensure compliance with these standards and foster trust through enhanced employee privacy.

7.5.3 Legal Compliance in AI Implementation in HRM

Even so, the legal framework in which AI and automation operate within HRM is constantly evolving. Certain existing laws, such as those against data protection-enumerated under General Data Protection Regulation (GDPR), or antidiscrimination laws, have to be addressed during the implementation of AI-powered human resources solutions. More specifically, legal risks associated with AI engaged in hiring and performance evaluation occur in the context of compliance with extant labor and employment laws. It involves having organizations collaborate with experts in the legal fields to ensure AI solutions are developed and deployed within the boundaries of data privacy laws and equal employment opportunity standards. For example, when organizations utilize AI tools in conducting recruitments, it rests upon them to ensure such AI tools applied do not result in disproportionate exclusions of candidates from protected groups. In addition, accountability structures relating to AI-driven decisions made by HR teams must be established in a way that human judgment is not completely removed from decision-making, particularly on high-stake issues involving employee terminations and promotions.

7.5.4 Encouraging Workforce Education and Technological Adaptation

The fast pace of the technological shift in human resource management contributes to a skill gap, where the employees lack the basic knowledge or perhaps the capacity to use newer tools. In that way, it has enhanced inequalities at workplaces and has made others lag behind. Workforce education with technological adaptation is highly necessary to ensure equal benefits for all workers. The corporate world should give them the relevant training to work in tandem with artificial intelligence, RPA, or any other technology. It includes digital literacy, fluency with AI, and interpretation of data analytics. Upskilling/reskilling efforts are valued since this will not only help employees become successful in a technology-driven workplace but also create an inclusive environment for them to grow as individuals (Gupta & Agarwal, 2018).

7.5.5 Ensuring Human Oversight in Automated HR Processes

Automation gives speed and efficiency, but there is also a more worrying question about how this chips away at the presence of human judgment around decision-making. Fully automated systems—think AI-powered recruitment tools or performance-evaluating algorithms—let in mistakes or bias if not caught. Thus, to be fair, accountable, and ethical, human oversight of automated processes becomes very important in HR. It would be prudent for organizations to implement human-in-the-loop systems where automated decisions would be reviewed regularly by HR professionals. This deepens the scrutiny of machine-generated outcomes and leaves room for the human judgment factor that might want to alter certain unwanted effects of such decisions. Where AI makes high-impact decisions, like those on hiring or disciplinary actions, it is of utmost import that such decisions should be reviewed and their validity checked by humans regarding alignment with organizational values and ethical standards.

7.5.6 Technology-Driven Corporate Social Responsibilities in Human Resource Management

The trend of adopting emerging technologies in human resource management should be carried out in concert, not only with a focus on operational efficiency but also in line with broader corporate social responsibility goals. Organizations have the obligation to be concerned about the social relevance of AI and automation to their workforce and the communities in which they operate—things like preventing

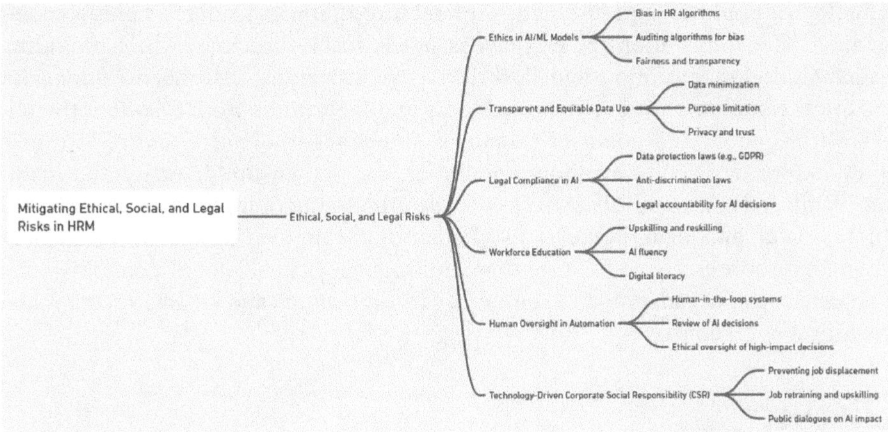

FIGURE 7.1 Mitigating ethical, social, and legal risks in HRM.

job displacement, just treatment of employees across the board, and healing the ills in society. In this case, the incorporation of Corporate Social Responsibility (CSR) into technology-driven HRM will be implemented by companies that absorb shock through automation to employees with job retraining, upskilling programs, or career transition opportunities. Another way organizations can reach ethical use of technology in HR is by joining public dialogues concerning AI implications and reflecting on how their respective practices contribute back towards societal good. Companies can also help create a corporate citizenry culture by adopting technology solutions that no doubt benefit business outcomes yet foster diversified persuasion, equity, and social good (Figure 7.1).

7.6 CONCLUSION

Basically, controlling ethical, social, and legal risks of arising technologies in HRM has manifold directions. In particular, it includes the development of ethical models of AI technologies, legitimacy and transparency of data use, observing legal regulations, ensuring workforce education, keeping human capital at the center, and integrating CSR into organizations' practice to let organizations gain full power from the technology hand in hand with the principles of fairness, responsibility, and inclusion. These will prove to be salient strategies as the face of HRM continues to change and ensure that the technology benefits the organization and its employees on a sustainable and socially responsible basis.

The various developments of technology in HRM pose several complex legal, social, and ethical issues. It is exceptionally important that these be dramatically thought of by the enterprise as technology continues to develop in order to meet all necessary and required needs. Legally, HR departments will have to make sure that laws on privacy and data protection are observed when employee data are gathered and analyzed. They also have to be aware of the possible legal implications of integrating advanced technologies into the practice of HR. Socially, emerging technologies could change the nature of required human resource competencies and jobs. The implication for employees needs to be discussed while providing opportunities for retraining and upskilling. Organizations also need to consider the ethical implications of AI-enabled tools and algorithms for HR so that the latter are transparent and nondiscriminatory. Processes to identify and reduce bias should be put in place to avoid any potential bias and ensure diversity and inclusion. While weighing up all factors, due care and attention must be given to the ethical, social, and legal implications of emerging technologies in the management of human resources. By addressing these consequences in advance, technology can be applied to aid organizations to enhance HR procedures and by law, socially, and ethically stay on course.

REFERENCES

Abraham, M., Niessen, C., Schnabel, C., Lorek, K., Grimm, V., Möslein, K., & Wrede, M. (2019). Electronic monitoring at work: The role of attitudes, functions, and perceived control for the acceptance of tracking technologies. *Human Resource Management Journal*, 29(4), 657–675.

Adeney, B. T. (1994). The dark side of technology. *Transformation*, 11(2), 21–25.

Afuah, A. N. (2003). Redefining firm boundaries in the face of the internet: Are firms really shrinking? *Academy of Management Review*, 28(1), 34–53.

Agarwal, S., & Gupta, D. (2024). *Digital Analytics Applications for Sustainable Training and Education* (1st ed.). Apple Academic Press.

Agarwal, S., Gupta, D., & Gupta, M. (2023). Techno pedagogical concept with digital skills. In Manpreet Singh Manna, Balamurugan Balusamy, Kiran Sood, Naveen Chilamkurti, Ignisha Rajathi George (eds) *Edutech Enabled Teaching* (pp. 129–152). Chapman and Hall/CRC.

Gupta, D., & Agarwal, S. (2018). Skill development initiative-literature review. *Inspira-Journal of Modern Management and Entrepreneurship (JMME)*, 8(2), 319–322.

Gupta, D., Gupta, M., & Gupta, P. M. (2024). *HR Analytics: The Future of HR* (p. 404). PHI Learning Pvt. Ltd., New Delhi, India.

Gupta, D., Gupta, M., & Rani, S. (2022). A study on training of workmen in a manufacturing organization—With reference to aluminium foundry. In Dvivedi, A., Sachdeva, A., Sindhwani, R., Sahu, R. (eds) *Recent Trends in Industrial and Production Engineering. Lecture Notes in Mechanical Engineering*. Springer, Singapore. https://doi.org/10.1007/978-981-16-3330-0_19

Halteh, J., Arrowsmith, J., Parker, J., Zorn, T. E., & Bentley, T. (2018). The impact of technology on employment: A research agenda for New Zealand and beyond. *Labour & Industry: A Journal of the Social and Economic Relations of Work*, 28(3), 203–216.

Hitt, M. A., Ireland, R. D., Camp, M. & Sexton, D. L. (1999). Strategic entrepreneurship: integrating entrepreneurial and strategic management perspectives, (Chapter One), available at www.blackwellpublishing.com/pdf/HittSE001.pdf.

Holland, P., & Bardoel, A. (2016). The impact of technology on work in the twenty-first century: Exploring the smart and dark side. *The International Journal of Human Resource Management*, 27(21), 2579–2581.

Ivanov, S., & Webster, C. (2019). *Robots, Artificial Intelligence and Service Automation in Travel, Tourism and Hospitality*. Emerald Publishing, Bingley.

Khan, S. A. (2007). The future of HR function and the challenges before the HR managers. *Indian Journal of Industrial Relations*, 42(3), 430–444.

Kim, S., Wang, Y., & Boon, C. (2021). Sixty years of research on technology and human resource management: Looking back and looking forward. *Human Resource Management*, 60(1), 229–247.

Kostakos, V., O'Neill, E., Little*, L., & Sillence, E. (2005). The social implications of emerging technologies. *Interacting with Computers*, 17(5), 475–483. doi:10.1016/j.intcom.2005.03.001

Malik, A., Budhwar, P., & Srikanth, N. R. (2020). Gig economy, 4IR and artificial intelligence: Rethinking strategic HRM. In Kumar, P., Agrawal, A., Budhwar, P. (eds) *Human & Technological Resource Management (HTRM): New Insights into Revolution 4.0.* Emerald Publishing, Bingley.

Melnychenko, O. (2020). Is artificial intelligence ready to assess an enterprise's financial security? *Journal of Risk and Financial* Management, 13(9), 191.

Nankervis, A., Connell, J., Cameron, R., Montague, A., & Verma, P. (2019). 'Are we there yet?' Australian HR professionals and the Fourth Industrial Revolution. *Asia Pacific Journal of Human Resources*, 59(1), 3–19.

Pandya, D. B. (2019). *A Competency Framework for Virtual HR Professionals in an Artificial Intelligence Age.* Diamond Scientific Publication, Barcelona.

Parry, E., & Battista, V. (2023). The impact of emerging technologies on work: A review of the evidence and implications for the human resource function. *Emerald Open Research*, 1(4).

Rajvanshi, P. R., Singh, T., Gupta, D., & Gupta, M. (2022). Blockchain technology for pharmaceutical drug supply chain management (book chapter). In Singh, P., Mishra, D., & K. Seth (eds) *Transformation in Healthcare with Emerging Technologies* (1st ed., pp. 217–230). CRC Press.

Sadok, H., Sakka, F., & El Maknouzi, M. E. H. (2022). Artificial intelligence and bank credit analysis: A review. *Cogent Economics & Finance*, 10(1), 2023262.

Scherer, M. U. (2016). Regulating artificial intelligence systems: Risks, challenges, competencies, and strategies. *Harvard Journal of Law & Technology*, 29(2), 353–400.

Shamim, S., Gang, S., & Yu, H. (2016, December). Influencers of information system usage among employees for knowledge creation. A future research agenda. In *2016 10th International Conference on Software, Knowledge, Information Management & Applications (SKIMA)* (pp. 134–141), Chengdu, China. IEEE.

Singh, S., Gupta, D., & Gupta, M. (2022). Optimized task allocation technique using mathematical fuzzy logic in heterogeneous distributed computational system. In *2022 International Conference on Computational Intelligence and Sustainable Engineering Solutions (CISES)* (pp. 37–45). Greater Noida, India, 2022. https://doi.org/10.1109/CISES54857.2022.9844410.

Stefano, V. D. (2019). "Negotiating the algorithm": Automation, artificial intelligence and labour protection. *Comparative Labor Law & Policy Journal*, 41(1), 1–34.

Vrontis, D., Christofi, M., Pereira, V., Tarba, S., Makrides, A., & Trichina, E. (2021). Artificial intelligence, robotics, advanced technologies and human resource management: A systematic review. *International Journal of Human Resource Management, Early View*. https://doi.org/10.1080/09585192.2020.1871398.

Winstanley, D., & Woodall, J. (2000). The ethical dimension of human resource management. *Human Resource Management Journal*, 10(2), 5.

8 Revolutionizing Workforce Management

The Future of HRM in the Digital Era

Mukul Gupta, Deepa Gupta, Nitin Agrawal, and Parth Mukul Gupta

8.1 INTRODUCTION: THE CHANGING FACE OF HRM

Human Resource Management (HRM) has for some time been a foundation of hierarchical achievement, overseeing representative relations, enrolment, pay, and improvement. Customarily, HRM rehearses have zeroed in on manual cycles, individual interactions, and hierarchical management designs to guarantee operational productivity and worker fulfilment. However, HRM's job and practices are undergoing significant change as innovation continues to reshape every aspect of business operations [18]. This section looks at how HRM is evolving as a result of digital disruption and the pressing need for businesses to adapt to a world that is increasingly driven by innovation.

8.1.1 Overview of Traditional HRM Practices

HRM has typically been established through one-on-one interactions and manual cycles, laying the groundwork for many years for hierarchical operations. For example, enlistment was a long and labour-intensive process in which HR professionals were tasked with examining genuine resumes, directing face-to-face gatherings, and making decisions based on commonly profound guidelines. HR departments relied on private associations, real-time job postings on sheets, and local advertisements to attract capacity without the benefits of computerized tools [9]. In the recruitment interaction, the absence of data-driven moves frequently slowed and increased inclination rather than productivity. Similar methods were used to delegate responsibility, with HR professionals relying on individual communications and annual information studies to determine employee satisfaction and effectiveness [9]. In today's fast-paced workplaces, where constant improvement and criticism are essential to maintaining representative commitment and authoritative arrangement, this active approach lacked the adaptability and speed required.

The standard systems for execution management further highlight the limitations of early HRM practices. Generally, execution reviews were led on a yearly or semiannual premise, intensely depending on regulatory information and mental

 DOI: 10.1201/9781032619651-8

evaluations. This approach customarily neglected to get consistent execution plans, offering what is happening for dependable examination or changes after some time. As a consequence of this, representatives were frequently kept in the dark about their presentation until the subsequent cycle of surveys, which may have stifled their expert turn of events. Also, learning and development (L&D) programs were usually set up in a way that was the same for everyone, with agents going to the same studios or educational gatherings [9]. These social events, while useful for general knowledge building, often did not address individual advancement needs or the rapidly evolving skill requirements that many industries now face.. This distinction between traditional preparation methods and current workforce requirements presented challenges for representatives seeking advancement and organizations seeking to remain competitive in a rapidly shifting business environment.

Administrative capacities, similar to funding the executives, benefits association, and consistent oversight, were also well thought and leaned to inadequacies under standard HRM models. HR departments relied on actual documents or fundamental calculation sheet instruments to monitor fundamental representative data, and these assignments were frequently handled physically. This has not simply worked on the likelihood of slip-ups in money and benefits calculations yet furthermore consumed a basic piece of HR's time and assets, diverting thought from extra fundamental drives. The limits of these manual cycles became increasingly apparent as organizations grew in size and complexity [18]. The serious need for HR departments to advance was highlighted by the inability to scale effectively and the risks of rebelliousness due to human error. Even though the conventional, work-focused approach to HRM is useful in less specific or modest circumstances, it simply cannot keep up with the demands of a cutting-edge, innovation-driven business environment [9]. Mechanization, artificial intelligence (AI), and data analysis are increasingly being incorporated into HR cycles to further develop proficiency, precision, and key independent direction as a result of this recognition [6].

8.1.2 The Impact of Technology on Workforce Management

The approach of trend setting innovations like man-made consciousness (artificial intelligence, AI), machine learning (ML), huge information investigation, and distributed computing has reformed the scene of HRM [6]. These innovations have presented computerization, information-driven experiences, and continuous interaction in workforce management, on a very basic level modifying how HR experts approach their work.

- Enlistment: computer-based intelligence-controlled candidate global positioning frameworks (ATS) have robotized continued screening, radically lessening the time spent on starting up-and-comer surveys [16]. Digital stages empower organizations to arrive at a worldwide ability pool, leveraging calculations to coordinate up-and-comers with employment opportunities.
- Information-Driven Direction: Enormous information examination permits HR groups to anticipate worker turnover, survey group efficiency, and screen commitment progressively, empowering more essential workforce arranging [9].

The coordination of these advancements into HR processes has expanded proficiency, decreased authoritative weight, and permitted HR experts to zero in additional on essential drives, likeability improvement, and hierarchical culture [6]. Furthermore, the capacity to leverage information has prompted a more educated and straightforward direction, making a more customized and responsive HRM capability [9].

8.1.3 The Need for Digital Transformation in HRM

As organizations keep on developing in the digital era, there is a developing requirement for HR divisions to go through digital change [16]. The speed of mechanical headway, the ascent of remote work, and the changing assumptions for representatives require HRM to move past conventional practices and take on new instruments and approaches [24].

- Adjusting to Remote and Cross Breed Work Models: The Coronavirus pandemic accelerated the shift to remote work, pushing associations to reconsider workforce management [26]. Cloud-based HR frameworks and digital specialized instruments have become fundamental for overseeing appropriate groups, guaranteeing efficiency, and keeping up with worker commitment [26].
- Upgrading Representative Experience: Workers today anticipate more customized and adaptable workplaces. Digital HR apparatuses can offer customized professional improvement plans, on-request learning, and continuous criticism, upgrading the overall worker experience [16].
- Tending to the Abilities Hole: As occupation jobs become more particular, there is a rising requirement for constant learning and upskilling [2]. Digital stages make it simpler to give designated preparation programs that meet the particular necessities of workers and the association [2].
- Information-Driven Experiences: The shift towards information-driven navigation is basic for HR to stay applicable. With the immense measure of representative information accessible, associations need to leverage examination to settle on informed choices, whether in enrolment, maintenance, or worker improvement [9].
- Guaranteeing Consistence and Security: With the ascent of digital HR devices comes the requirement for elevated consideration regarding information protection and security. Consistence with worldwide information insurance guidelines, like General Data Protection Regulation - European Union (GDPR) and Digital Personal Data Protection Act (DPDP), is fundamental to protecting delicate representative data [24].

The change of HRM in the digital era is presently not a choice however a need for associations to stay cutthroat [6]. By embracing innovation and reconsidering customary HR rehearses, organizations can make more coordinated, productive, and representative-driven HR works that line up with the requests of the advanced workforce [16].

8.1.4 Literature Review

The development of HRM in the digital era has been a significant area of examination, with various examinations featuring the developing significance of innovation in changing workforce management rehearses [18].

As indicated by Repel and Tyson (2011), the reception of e-HRM frameworks has altogether upgraded authoritative productivity via mechanizing routine HR cycles like finance and representative information management. These frameworks give ongoing information, work with self-administration functionalities, and backing more essential decision-production inside HR divisions [18].

The joining of man-made intelligence into HR capabilities has acquired significant consideration lately [16]. As McKinsey and Company (2019) report, simulated intelligence advances are changing ability procurement by empowering prescient examination, which assists companies with better surveying applicant appropriateness. This shift is moving HR from a receptive to a more proactive and vital job. Essentially, Bersin (2020) [6] stressed that AI and ML consider personalization in representative improvement programs, guaranteeing that preparation is lined up with individual vocation ways and hierarchical objectives [6].

Information-driven direction is one more significant progression in HRM. Davenport et al. (2010) recommended that information investigation is revolutionizing HR rehearses by giving bits of knowledge into workforce patterns, worker commitment, and execution measurements. This empowers organizations to upgrade their human capital and make a lither workforce.

In addition, digital stages/platforms that help remote and mixed work have extended the conceivable outcomes of workforce management. As indicated by a concentrate by Spreitzer et al. (2017) [24], the reception of adaptable work courses of action upheld by digital instruments helps representative fulfilment as well as upgrades efficiency. This pattern has been accelerated by the Coronavirus pandemic, which featured the significance of digital HR arrangements in keeping up with business congruity (Waizenegger et al., 2020) [26].

8.2 KEY DRIVERS OF DIGITAL HRM TRANSFORMATION

The field of human resources (HRM) is going through a huge change in the speedy computerized universe of today. Headway is through and through influencing how affiliations deal with their workforce, from choice and onboarding to expert obligation and execution of the board. We should investigate five key drivers framing the inevitable destiny of HRM:

8.2.1 Artificial Intelligence (AI) and Machine Learning (ML)

AI and ML are becoming increasingly important to HR operations. These advances help HR specialists with analysing gigantic proportions of data and seek additional keen decisions. Screening resumes, coordinating candidates with ongoing income sources, and even anticipating agent execution are all carried out using computerized reasoning. Over the long haul, man-made intelligence/AI estimations can give more precise bits of

TABLE 8.1
Benefits of AI and ML in HRM along with Examples

Benefits of AI and ML in HRM	Examples
Faster recruitment process	AI tools can screen thousands of resumes in minutes
Predicting employee performance	AI can analyse past data to forecast future productivity
Personalized learning and development	ML can suggest relevant training programs based on employee needs
Enhancing employee engagement	Chatbots can provide 24/7 assistance and answer HR-related queries

knowledge into delegate conduct and examples like worker turnover [6,7]. Table 8.1 given below depicts various benefits of AI and ML in HRM along with suitable examples.

8.2.2 Big Data Analytics

Big Data has reformed HRM by engaging HR divisions to gather, process, and dissect immense measures of information from various sources, empowering more educated and vital direction. HR professionals now have access to a comprehensive, 360-degree view of their workforce thanks to the capability to gather real-time data from a variety of platforms, such as employee satisfaction surveys, performance metrics, and even interactions on social media [8,12]. This abundance of information permits HR groups to move past conventional premonition draws near, moving toward information-driven bits of knowledge that can fundamentally improve hierarchical results. When Big Data analytics are incorporated into HRM, deeper insights into employee behaviour, preferences, and performance are made possible [7]. These insights can be used to predict trends, personalize employee experiences, and improve overall workforce management. Table 8.2 depicts the Key Use Cases of Big Data in HRM and their benefits.

8.2.3 Cloud Computing

Cloud computing has upset the manner in which HR oversees data. With cloud-based frameworks, associations can get to representative data from any place, empowering adaptable workplaces. Cloud stages likewise guarantee data are secure and effectively available, which is particularly significant for worldwide or remote groups [16]. Various benefits of Cloud Computing in HRM are illustrated in the Table 8.3.

8.2.4 Automation and Robotic Process Automation (RPA)

Mechanization and RPA are assisting HR divisions with turning out to be more productive by taking over dreary, tedious errands like finance handling, leave management, and worker onboarding [7,13]. With computerization, HR experts can zero in on essential undertakings that require a human touch, like representative commitment and improvement [17]. Table 8.4 highlights the various advantages of Automation in HRM and their Impact on HR.

TABLE 8.2
Key Use Cases of Big Data in HRM and Their Benefits

Key Use Cases of Big Data in HRM	Benefits
Predicting employee turnover	HR can identify patterns in employee data to prevent attrition
Performance tracking and improvement	Continuous monitoring of employee performance metrics
Enhancing employee satisfaction and retention	Data-driven insights help improve workplace culture and policies

TABLE 8.3
Benefits of Cloud Computing in HRM

Benefits of Cloud Computing in HRM	Description
Accessibility from anywhere	HR teams can access data from any location, fostering remote work
Centralized employee data management	All employee information is stored securely in one place
Streamlined HR processes	Cloud systems make it easier to manage payroll, benefits, and more

TABLE 8.4
Advantages of Automation in HRM

Advantages of Automation in HRM	Impact on HR
Reducing administrative workload	Automated payroll and leave processing save time and effort
Faster employee onboarding	Automation speeds up background checks and document submissions
Improved accuracy and compliance	Automated systems minimize human errors in data entry

8.2.5 Internet of Things (IoT) and Its Influence on HR

The Internet of Things (IoT) interfaces gadgets and frameworks, permitting associations to screen and gather continuous data on worker conduct and work area utilization [26]. IoT can assist HR divisions with improving office spaces, track representative well-being and health, and guarantee work environment security [19]. Table 8.5 explains various IoT Applications in HRM and their benefits.

The future of HRM is progressively digital, and the incorporation of simulated intelligence, Big Data, cloud computing, mechanization, and IoT is changing the way in which HR groups operate [6,7,16]. These innovations make HR more proficient as well as give further bits of knowledge into workforce elements, assisting organizations with making a more useful and drawn-in workforce [24].

TABLE 8.5
IoT Applications in HRM

IoT Applications in HRM	Benefits
Monitoring workspace usage	Optimizes office layouts and improves resource management
Tracking employee wellness	IoT wearables can monitor employee health, reducing sick leaves
Ensuring safety in the workplace	IoT sensors can detect unsafe conditions and prevent accidents

8.3 THE ROLE OF AI IN HRM

AI has reformed numerous businesses, and HRM is no special case. AI's effect on HR is reshaping the way that associations draw in, hold, and deal with their workers [6,16].

8.3.1 AI in Recruitment and Talent Acquisition

Enlistment is possibly one of the most time-consuming HR tasks. The interaction can be overwhelming when it comes to selecting promising candidates from among the numerous resumes. This has changed as a result of man-made intelligence devices automating many of the tedious tasks associated with enlistment. Organizations can check a lot of resumes in a few seconds using man-made intelligence, choose the best competitors based on skills, experience, and abilities, and even use chatbots driven by man-made intelligence to start meetings [7]. This recuperation spotters time and ensures a more objective method for managing contender assurance, reducing the potential outcomes of human error or inclination [6]. Table 8.6 depicts the various benefits of AI in Recruitment.

8.3.2 AI-Powered Employee Assessments and Performance Tracking: AI in Performance Tracking

See Table 8.7

TABLE 8.6
Benefits of AI in Recruitment

Traditional Recruitment	AI-Powered Recruitment
Manual resume screening	AI scans resumes quickly and efficiently
Human-driven candidate shortlisting	AI algorithms shortlist based on data
Lengthy interview scheduling	AI chatbots schedule interviews instantly
Potential for unconscious bias	Data-driven decisions reduce bias

TABLE 8.7
Traditional Vs AI-Powered Assessment

Traditional Assessment	AI-Powered Assessment
Annual performance reviews	Continuous, real-time feedback
Manager's subjective observations	Data-driven, objective evaluations
Limited scope of tracking	Comprehensive tracking using AI tools

8.3.3 Overhauling Delegate Responsibility with Reproduced Insight-Based Mechanical Assemblies

Delegate responsibility is an essential process for any connection's flourishing. By giving individualized encounters, man-made insight gadgets assist organizations with keeping representatives associated. Man-made information can break down worker data to propose arranging, flourishing undertakings, and occupation improvement open entrances custom-fitted to individual necessities [6,16]. Man-made consciousness chatbots, for example, can help delegates with requests in regards to organization techniques or advantages, and re-enacted knowledge-fuelled stages, then again, can furnish representatives with individualized learning content in view of their vocation objectives. This individualization helps representative joy by causing them to feel esteemed and upheld at work (Table 8.8).

8.3.4 Ethical Considerations and Biases in AI-Driven HRM

HRM reaps a number of benefits from man-made knowledge understanding, but it also faces challenges. The possibility of predisposition in simulated intelligence calculations is a major concern. Predispositions, such as orientation or racial segregation, that are reflected in the actual data may be propagated or attempted to intensify by computer-based intelligence systems [7,18]. These structures depend on information that can be confirmed. For example, if a PC-based information device is prepared for past-choice data that are oriented toward a particular piece, it may continue to focus on promising newcomers from that party, resulting in incorrect results.

Security is another moral thought. A great deal of worker information is habitually isolated by man-made knowledge structures, which raises worries about how that information is utilized and taken care of. To stay aware of specialists, associations should ensure straightforwardness and reasonableness while incorporating re-enacted information into HR (Table 8.9).

TABLE 8.8
AI's Impact on Engagement

Traditional Engagement Practices	AI-Driven Engagement
Generic training programs	Personalized learning and development
Limited interaction with HR	24/7 AI chatbots for employee support
One-size-fits-all career paths	AI-tailored career advancement plans

TABLE 8.9
Ethical Challenges of AI in HR

Potential Issue	Explanation
Bias in hiring algorithms	AI can learn and repeat historical biases in recruitment
Lack of transparency in decision making	Employees may not understand how AI makes decisions
Privacy concerns with employee data	Collecting and analysing large amounts of personal data

Simulated intelligence is changing HR by making processes speedier, more useful, and information driven. From enlistment to execution following and specialist responsibility, man-made insight is transforming into a basic contraption for HR workplaces. However, organizations should be aware of moral considerations, ensuring decency, simplicity, and the reliable use of AI to create a future in which innovation and human potential work together [22,23].

8.4 DATA-DRIVEN DECISION MAKING IN WORKFORCE MANAGEMENT

Workforce management has undergone a significant transformation in the digital age of the present. Associations are finished relying solely upon impulse or past experiences to arrive at decisions about their workers/employees. Taking everything into account, they're going to information to coordinate their choices. Data-driven independent direction is a method that is transforming the way businesses interact with their workforce [9,10].

8.4.1 Why Data-Driven Decision Making Matters

Generally, HR choices were made in view of manual surveys, meetings, or chiefs' perspectives. While these strategies gave some understanding, they frequently needed precision and objectivity [10]. By utilizing data, organizations can now:

- Pursue More Educated Choices: Data offer an unmistakable image of worker conduct, execution, and inclinations.
- Foresee Patterns: Data assist organizations with distinguishing designs, for example, turnover rates or ability holes, and address them before they become issues.
- Upgrade Representative Experience: By investigating input and commitment data, HR can make enhancements that lead to a higher fulfilment and maintenance.

8.4.2 Types of Data Used in Workforce Management

There are many sorts of data that organizations gather to actually deal with their workforce [8] as shown in Table 8.10:

TABLE 8.10
Types of Data Used in Workforce Management

Data Type	Description
Performance data	Tracks employee productivity, project completion, and quality of work
Engagement data	Measures employee satisfaction and involvement through surveys or feedback
Turnover data	Analyses employee exits and reasons for leaving the company
Recruitment data	Tracks recruitment metrics such as time-to-hire, source of hire, and success rates
Skills and training data	Shows what skills employees have and what training programs are effective

8.4.2.1 Example: Predicting Employee Turnover

One of the most significant purposes of data-driven navigation is foreseeing which representatives could leave the organization. By gathering and examining data on work execution, commitment, and outer variables, HR groups can recognize designs that show somebody is probably going to leave. This permits organizations to act right on time by offering help, learning experiences, or tending to any worries workers could have.

8.4.3 Benefits of Data-Driven Workforce Management

- Better Employing Choices: Utilizing data to evaluate applicants guarantees that HR recruits the perfect individuals to make it happen, in light of abilities and potential [6].
- Further Developed Worker Maintenance: Examining data on representative fulfilment assist associations with working on their working environment and diminish turnover [6].
- Improved Execution Management: Continuous data provide supervisors with a superior comprehension of representative execution, assisting them with giving opportune criticism and backing [10].

8.5 CLOUD-BASED HR SYSTEMS

Cloud-based HR frameworks are changing the manner in which associations deal with their workforce. In contrast to customary HR frameworks that necessitate actual servers and were just open from specific areas, cloud-based frameworks can be gotten to from any place, giving continuous HR management on a worldwide scale [16].

8.5.1 What is a Cloud-Based HR System?

A cloud-based HR framework is programming facilitated on the web, permitting organizations to oversee HR capabilities like finance, advantages, enlistment, and representative data through a solitary stage. These frameworks are adaptable, meaning they can develop with the organization's requirements, and they wipe out the requirement for actual foundation [16,22].

8.5.2 Key Features of Cloud-Based HR Systems

1. Centralized Data Management: All worker data, from individual data to execution audits, are put away in one spot [8].
2. Real-Time Access: HR groups and workers can access significant data from any place and at any time [16].
3. Automation of Routine Assignments: Cloud frameworks can robotize undertakings like finance handling, participation following, and leave management [16].
4. Scalability: As an organization develops, cloud-based frameworks can undoubtedly increase without the requirement for huge foundation changes [17].

8.5.3 Benefits of Cloud-Based HR Systems

Cloud-Based HR Systems have numerous benefits, and the main benefits of Cloud-Based HR Systems are shown in the Table 8.11.

8.5.3.1 Example: Streamlining Payroll and Benefits with Cloud HR

One of the most widely recognized utilizations of cloud-based HR frameworks is smoothing out finance and advantages organization. For instance, a worker can sign into the framework, demand downtime, and see their accessible leave balance right away. The finance office can likewise get to these data progressively, guaranteeing exact compensation computations. This decreases desk work and wipes out the opportunity of mistakes.

8.5.4 The Future of Cloud HR

As organizations keep on embracing remote work and worldwide groups, cloud-based HR frameworks will turn out to be much more fundamental. They give adaptability, security, and productivity, making them a basic device for present day workforce management.

8.6 AUTOMATING ROUTINE HR PROCESSES

Organizations are finding it increasingly challenging to physically oversee routine HR tasks in the current fast-paced world. Motorization offers major areas of strength for helping HR divisions with focusing on fundamental tasks like capacity

TABLE 8.11
Benefits of Cloud-Based HR Systems

Benefit	Description
Cost-effective	Cloud systems reduce the need for expensive hardware and maintenance
Increased accessibility	Employees and HR professionals can access the system from anywhere
Improved data security	Modern cloud systems offer high-level security measures to protect sensitive data
Real-time updates	Any changes in employee data, payroll, or leave balances are updated instantly
Easier compliance	These systems help companies stay compliant with local and global labour laws

improvement and worker's/employee's responsibility, rather than concentrating profoundly on excess activities. We ought to research how motorizing routine HR cycles can make a major difference [23].

8.6.1 Why Automate HR Processes?

HR tasks like money management, offboarding, specialist onboarding, and investment following are critical for any business. In any case, when performed physically, these cycles can be tedious and prone to human error. These tasks are smoothed out by robots, increasing proficiency and precision while freeing up HR teams' time to focus on more important tasks.

8.6.2 Common HR Processes That Can Be Automated

Mechanization has the potential to have a rapid impact in the following key areas as shown in Table 8.12.

8.7 THE IMPACT OF REMOTE WORK ON WORKFORCE MANAGEMENT

The climb of remote work has certainly affected how affiliations manage their labour force. HR departments have had to adapt to new methods and tools because representatives are currently spread out across a variety of areas [6,24].

8.7.1 The Rise of Remote Workplaces

During the Coronavirus pandemic, remote work became a necessity [26]. However, even though things are back to normal, many businesses have decided to permanently adopt remote or hybrid work arrangements. HR's oversight of representatives has changed from enrolling to execution management as a result of this shift [6,16].

TABLE 8.12
HR Processes That Can Be Automated

HR Process	Traditional Approach	Automated Approach	Benefits
Payroll processing	Manual calculations and data entry	Automated payroll software	Faster processing, fewer errors
Attendance tracking	Paper-based or spreadsheet systems	Digital attendance systems (e.g., biometrics, online apps)	Accurate, real-time tracking
Leave management	Employee emails or paper requests	Automated leave management systems	Easy approval process, clear tracking
Employee onboarding	Paperwork, manual orientations	Automated onboarding portals and chatbots	Faster onboarding, better experience
Performance reviews	Yearly manual reviews, often inconsistent	Continuous automated feedback and review systems	Real-time feedback, transparency

TABLE 8.13
Various Challenges of Remote Workforce Management

Challenge	Description	Solution
Communication	Difficulties in keeping remote employees connected and informed	Use collaboration tools like Slack, Microsoft Teams, and Zoom
Employee engagement	Remote employees may feel isolated or disconnected from the company culture	Regular check-ins, virtual team-building activities, engagement tools
Productivity tracking	Difficult to monitor productivity of employees not in a physical office	Use productivity tracking software and set clear performance metrics
Work–life balance	Remote workers may struggle to separate work and home life	Encourage flexible hours and promote mental health initiatives

8.7.2 Challenges of Remote Workforce Management

Dealing with a far-off workforce presents special difficulties for HR groups, for example (Table 8.13),

8.7.3 The Role of Technology in Managing Remote Work

Innovation plays had an essential impact in assisting organizations with adjusting to remote work. Here are a few devices and arrangements that have become fundamental for dealing with a far-off workforce:

- Cloud-based HR Frameworks: Cloud stages like BambooHR or Normal business day permit HR groups to oversee worker data, finance, and advantages from any place [16].
- Specialized Instruments: Video conferencing (Zoom, Google Meet) and informing stages (Slack, Groups) keep workers associated and locked in [8].
- Cooperation Apparatuses: Venture management instruments like Asana, Trello, and Monday.com guarantee groups stay adjusted and useful, regardless of where they are [8].
- Execution Management Programming: Apparatuses like 15Five and Grid give nonstop criticism and track worker execution, in any event, while working from a distance [8] (Figure 8.1).

8.8 EMPLOYEE WELL-BEING AND DIGITAL HR TOOLS

In the present high-speed and digitally determined workplace, worker prosperity has turned into a focal concentration for organizations hoping to construct a sound, useful, and fulfilled workforce. Worker prosperity goes past actual well-being — it's tied in with establishing a climate where representatives feel intellectually, inwardly, and socially upheld. With the assistance of digital HR apparatuses, associations are currently better prepared to screen, make due, and upgrade the prosperity of their representatives in manners that were impractical previously [6,7].

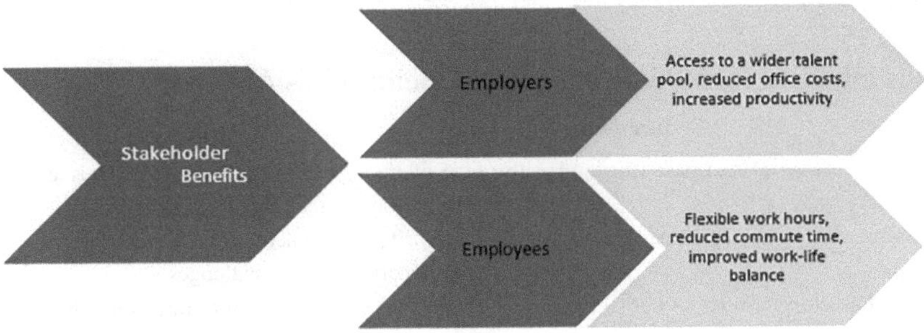

FIGURE 8.1 Benefits of remote work for employers and employees.

8.8.1 Why Employee Well-being Matters

Representative prosperity is straightforwardly connected to efficiency, maintenance, and overall work fulfilment. At the point when workers feel significantly better, both intellectually and genuinely, they are bound to perform at their best. Overlooking this can prompt burnout, low assurance, truancy, and high turnover rates, which can cost organizations as far as lost efficiency and expanded enrolment costs.

8.8.2 The Role of Digital Tools in Employee Well-being

Digital HR apparatuses have arisen as important resources in supporting worker prosperity. These devices assist representatives with overseeing pressure, track their well-being, and remain associated in significant ways—whether they are working in the workplace, from a distance, or in a mixed arrangement [10]. The following are a few key regions where digital instruments assume a part (Table 8.14):

8.8.3 Popular Digital Well-being Tools

8.8.3.1 Case Study: Digital Tools Enhancing Employee Well-being

We should accept a model from an enormous tech organization that presented a thorough representative prosperity program utilizing digital HR devices [11]. This is the way they made it happen (Table 8.15):

TABLE 8.14
Well-being Aspect Where Digital Instruments Assume a Part

Well-being Aspect	Digital HR Tool
Mental health	Mental health apps (e.g., Calm, Headspace) [1]
Physical health	Fitness tracking apps, wellness programs [7]
Emotional support	Employee Assistance Programs (EAPs) [5]
Work–life balance	Flexible scheduling and leave management [18]
Financial well-being	Financial education platforms [20]
Social connection	Virtual team-building platforms [26]

TABLE 8.15
Various Initiative for Which Digital Well-Being Tools Are Used

Initiative	Tool Used	Result
Mindfulness and stress reduction program	Headspace (mental health)	60% of employees reported reduced stress levels and higher focus after using the app daily
Physical fitness challenge	Fitbit (fitness tracker)	Increased physical activity with over 70% participation in step challenges
Financial well-being workshops	Smart Dollar (financial education)	Employees improved savings rates and felt more in control of their personal finances

These drives assisted the organization with expanding worker commitment and fulfilment, decreasing non-attendance, and lifting efficiency.

8.8.4 Benefits of Using Digital Well-being Tools

1. Convenience: With versatile applications and online stages, representatives can get to prosperity resources whenever and anyplace. This is especially valuable for remote and cross breed workforces [24].
2. Confidentiality: Devices like EAPs guarantee that representatives can look for help in a private and secure way, lessening the disgrace related to emotional well-being support [10].
3. Improved Commitment: Representatives who feel upheld are bound to be participated in their work, bringing about better execution and occupation fulfilment [21].

8.8.5 Challenges in Implementing Digital Well-being Tools

While digital HR apparatuses offer huge advantages, there are likewise difficulties that associations might confront (Table 8.16):

TABLE 8.16
Challenges & Solutions in Implementing Digital Well-Being Tools

Challenge	Solution
Adoption resistance	Provide training and clear communication on the benefits
Data privacy concerns	Ensure compliance with data privacy laws and transparency
Technology overload	Limit the number of tools and integrate them seamlessly into daily workflows

8.9 UPSKILLING AND RESKILLING THROUGH DIGITAL PLATFORMS: EMPOWERING THE WORKFORCE OF TOMORROW

In the present quickly impacting world, innovation is reshaping the way that organizations operate and how individuals work. With the ascent of robotization, AI, and digital change, many positions are advancing, and new jobs are arising [6]. Accordingly, the requirement for upskilling and reskilling has become more basic than at any other time. Digital stages are presently driving the charge in assisting workers/employees with securing new abilities and remain cutthroat in this new era [3,4,15].

8.9.1 What is Upskilling and Reskilling?

- Upskilling: This alludes to working on current abilities to improve execution in the current work, for example, learning progressed data examination strategies in the event that you're as of now a data examiner.
- Reskilling: This is mastering completely new abilities to change to an alternate work or job, for instance, changing from a customary promoting job to a digital showcasing one.

8.9.2 Why Are Upskilling and Reskilling Significant?

1. Adapting to Mechanical Changes: With AI and mechanization assuming control over routine assignments, workers/employees need to master further developed abilities to stay important [6].
2. Job Security: Acquiring new abilities assists workers/employees with staying aware of occupation market requests, decreasing the gamble of employment cutback [24].
3. Career Development: Learning new things opens ways to advancements and authority potential open doors [17].
4. Employee Fulfilment: When workers feel that they are developing and learning, they are more fulfilled and persuaded [9].

8.9.3 Digital Platforms Leading the Way

Digital stages have made learning simpler, quicker, and more open [2]. These stages offer a great many courses, certificates, and involved encounters to help workers/employees upskill and reskill [7] (Table 8.17).

These stages are open to anybody, whether they are hoping to work on their ongoing abilities or acquire something completely new.

8.9.4 How Digital Platforms Are Changing Learning

1. Adaptability and Accommodation

   Not at all like customary learning techniques, digital stages permit individuals to gain at their own speed and from any place [24]. Whether it's watching an instructional exercise on a mid-day break or finishing a

TABLE 8.17
Digital Platforms/Stages and Their Key Features

Platform Name	Key Features	Example Courses
Coursera	University-level courses, industry certifications	Data Science, AI, Business Strategy
Udemy	Affordable, wide range of subjects	Web Development, Marketing, Design
LinkedIn Learning	Focuses on professional skills and career growth	Project Management, Leadership
edX	Offers programs from top universities	Machine Learning, Cybersecurity
Khan Academy	Free courses, mainly academic subjects	Mathematics, Economics

confirmation throughout the end of the week, digital stages offer unparalleled adaptability [8].

2. Customized Learning Ways

   Numerous stages use computer-based intelligence to suggest custom-fitted learning ways. In the event that you're a showcasing proficient needing to move into data examination, stages like LinkedIn Learning can propose courses that match your objectives [16].

3. Cooperation and Systems Administration

   Most stages offer gatherings, conversation gatherings, and companion audits where students can associate with others. This joint effort improves advancement as well as helps in building an expert organization [8,9].

4. Active Learning with Certifiable Ventures

   It's one thing to learn about an idea, and one more to apply it in fact. Digital stages like Coursera and Udacity offer capstone tasks and genuine contextual analyses, permitting students to apply their abilities in reasonable situations [8].

8.9.4.1 Key Benefits for Companies

Table 8.18 illustrates how the associations/companies are likewise exploiting digital stages to upskill and reskill their workforce.

TABLE 8.18
Benefits of Digital Platforms for the Companies

Benefit	Explanation
Cost-Effective Training	Digital platforms reduce the costs associated with in-person training programs
Scalability	Large teams can learn simultaneously, making it easier to train a global workforce
Keeping Up with Industry Trends	Helps employees stay updated with the latest skills and industry standards
Employee Retention	Employees are more likely to stay with companies that invest in their development

8.9.5 The Future of Upskilling and Reskilling

The future is clear—constant learning will be an indispensable piece of each and every expert's excursion. As innovation develops, digital stages will assume a considerably bigger part in assisting people and organizations with remaining ahead [1].

To remain serious, people need to assume responsibility for their own learning processes, and organizations should put resources into their workforce by leveraging these stages [11].

Upskilling and reskilling through digital stages are presently not discretionary—they are fundamental for progress in the digital era. With the adaptability, personalization, and certifiable learning presented by these stages, the workforce can ceaselessly develop, guaranteeing that the two people and associations flourish from here on out [2,24].

Whether you're hoping to remain serious in your ongoing job or change to a completely new vocation, there will never be been a superior opportunity to embrace learning through digital stages [7,14].

8.10 COMPLIANCE AND GOVERNANCE IN DIGITAL HRM

As associations adopt digital transformation in workforce management, ensuring compliance and governance becomes a key priority. In the computerized period, HR specialists ought to investigate a stunning scene of rules, information security guidelines, and moral principles, all while using development to manage their work force capably. Maintaining moral standards, protecting employee data, and ensuring that all HR practices are carried out are at the heart of Digital HRM's consistency and administration [3].

8.10.1 Why Compliance and Governance Matter

1. Security and Insurance for Data: With the rise of Cloud-Based HR Systems and digital devices, businesses now manage a lot of sensitive employee data.
2. In dynamic cycles, ensuring simplicity facilitates working relationships with representatives of the company.
3. Global and Neighbourhood Guidelines: With the workforce turning out to be more worldwide, organizations should comply with various guidelines in different areas [18]. HR experts need to remain refreshed with work regulations, charge arrangements, and other locale explicit guidelines to keep away from legitimate issues [6] (Table 8.19).

8.10.1.1 Digital Tools for Governance and Compliance

Digital HR frameworks assist with robotizing numerous consistence undertakings, making it more straightforward for organizations to remain within lawful limits. For instance, AI can screen HR strategies for consistence infringement, while cloud-based frameworks can naturally track and record worker working hours to guarantee consistence with work regulations [3].

TABLE 8.19
Key Areas of Compliance in Digital HRM

Compliance Area	Focus	Examples
Data privacy and security	Protecting employee data from breaches and ensuring lawful processing	GDPR, DPDP, data encryption, secure cloud storage [8]
Equal employment opportunities	Ensuring fair and unbiased hiring practices	AI fairness in hiring, avoiding discrimination in algorithms [7]
Labour laws and employee rights	Adhering to labour laws, employee contracts, and overtime regulations	Local labour laws, wage and hour compliance [18]
Health and safety	Ensuring workplace safety, both physically and digitally	Digital tools for tracking employee well-being and safety [7]
Whistleblowing and reporting	Providing secure channels for reporting unethical behaviour	Anonymous reporting platforms, protection from retaliation [6]

8.10.1.2 Challenges in Digital HR Compliance

While advanced HR instruments bring efficiency, they in like manner present hardships. Motorized systems could coincidentally make inclinations, and information breaks can uncover fragile specialist information [7]. Human resource professionals should put a strong emphasis on security and ethical practices to counteract growth [25].

Consistency and management in HRM go beyond following the rules in the digital age [24]. It's connected to protecting delegates' opportunities, building trust, and making a fair workplace. Companies can ensure that their workforce has access to a consistent and secure HR environment by regularly updating policies and mindfully using digital devices.

8.11 CHALLENGES IN IMPLEMENTING DIGITAL HRM

Computerized HRM instruments and systems can essentially further develop capability, yet they likewise accompany their own arrangement of difficulties. One of the most difficult obstacles is safeguarding oneself against change. It very well might be trying for delegates, especially the people who are familiar with customary procedures, to conform to pristine computerized structures. This much of the time prompts delay or even resistance, which rolls out the improvement amazing sluggish.

An additional test involves mechanical constraints. Not all affiliations have the resources to place resources into first in class improvement or combine new devices with their continuous designs. As a result, HR operations on a daily basis may suffer [9,16].

8.12 FUTURE TRENDS IN DIGITAL HRM

Development is forming the fate of HRM, and it is modifying the way in which we regulate people in the work environment. As we move forward, digital tools will continue to transform HR, making processes more productive and representative-focused.

One of the most important patterns is AI, or simulated intelligence. PC-based knowledge won't just work with quicker enrolment by interfacing contenders to open positions; however, it will likewise customize specialist encounters by giving individualized learning and advancement programs. Imagine working in an environment where your preparation is tailored specifically to your strengths and interests.

Another important development is the rise of data-driven navigation. HR meetings will use a lot of data to anticipate patterns like agent turnover or problems with proficiency. By better understanding the needs of representatives, businesses can reduce burnout and increase employee satisfaction at work [25].

Robotization will continue to streamline audits of execution, leave requests, and finances. This empowers HR experts to focus on extra significant regions like cultivating a positive workplace and helping delegates in their turn of events.

Remote work and cloud-based HR stages are both long-term solutions. These devices make it more straightforward to direct gatherings regardless of where they are, empowering facilitated exertion and ensuring that even representatives who live far away feel like they are important to the organization.

Finally, representative prosperity will take over as the primary focus. With the help of advanced gadgets, associations will place more in close to home prosperity, well-being ventures, and harmony among fun and serious exercise drives.

The eventual fate of HRM is awe inspiring, with advancement working on both capability and the human experience. The consideration will remain on people, yet with cannier, faster, and more modified help."

8.13 CONCLUSION: EMBRACING THE FUTURE OF HRM

As we step into the future, obviously HRM is going through a huge change. Innovation is reshaping the manner in which we work, convey, and oversee groups. In any case, in the midst of the relative multitude of headways, one thing stays steady: individuals are at the core of each and every association. The job of HR is turning out to be a higher priority than at any other time, as it overcomes any barrier between state-of-the-art innovation and human association. The future of HRM isn't just about computerization, man-made intelligence, or data. It's tied in with utilizing these devices to make a seriously captivating, comprehensive, and steady work environment where representatives feel esteemed and engaged. Digital stages can assist with smoothing out errands and make processes quicker, yet they can likewise assist HR experts with zeroing in on the main thing—figuring out individuals' necessities, supporting their development, and encouraging a culture of coordinated effort.

For associations, the street ahead is energizing however brimming with difficulties. Adjusting to new innovations expects receptiveness to change, interest in upskilling, and a guarantee of representative prosperity. While innovation offers enormous potential outcomes, achievement will really rely on how associations offset the digital with the human touch. In this excursion, HRM will assume a critical part in forming the workforce of tomorrow—one that is versatile, various, and prepared to flourish in the digital era. By embracing this future, associations can make a more effective work environment, yet one that genuinely focuses on its kin, helping them develop and succeed together.

REFERENCES

1. Agarwal, S., & Gupta, D. (2023). An analytical study of HDI among India and its adjoining nations with reference to the relationship of literacy rate. *International Journal of Indian Culture and Business Management*, 28(1), 85–100.
2. Agarwal, S., & Gupta, D. (2024). Digital analytics applications for sustainable training and education. In K. Sood, P. Kalia, S. Grima, & A. Chaudhary (Eds.), *Digital Analytics Applications for Sustainable Training and Education* (p. 25). Apple Academic Press, New Delhi, India.
3. Agarwal, S., Gupta, D., & Gupta, M. (2023). Techno pedagogical concept with digital skills. In M. S. Manna, B. Balusamy, K. Sood, N. Chilamkurti, & I. R. George (eds) *Edutech Enabled Teaching* (pp. 129–152). Chapman and Hall/CRC, Boca Raton, FL.
4. Agarwal, S., Gupta, D., & Verma, P. (2019). Impact of employment on GDP contribution of various sectors in India. *Global Journal of Enterprise Information System*, 11(1), 47–53.
5. Kumar, A., Gupta, D., Gupta, M., & Srivastava, G. (2021). India an emerging leader after pandemic: A strategy for the development of new India. *Global Journal of Enterprise Information System*, 13(1), 60–70. Retrieved from https://www.gjeis.com/index.php/GJEIS/article/view/629
6. Bersin, J. (2020). *The Future of Work: The Transformation of Talent Management*. Deloitte Insights, New York, NY.
7. Binns, R., Veale, M., Van Kleek, M., & Shadbolt, N. (2018). 'It's reducing a human being to a percentage': Perceptions of justice in algorithmic decisions. *Proceedings of the 2018 CHI Conference on Human Factors in Computing Systems*, Montreal, Canada, pp. 1–14.
8. CIPD. (2019). *People Analytics: Driving Business Performance with People Data*. Chartered Institute of Personnel and Development, London, UK.
9. Davenport, T. H., Harris, J., & Shapiro, J. (2010). Competing on talent analytics. *Harvard Business Review*, 88, 52.
10. Srivastava, G., & Gupta, D. (2022). Determining the relationship between job satisfaction and job burnout of the faculties of business school in Delhi. *International Journal of Indian Culture and Business Management*, 26(2), 276–286.
11. Gupta, D., & Agarwal, S. (2018). Skill development initiative-literature review. *Inspira-Journal of Modern Management and Entrepreneurship (JMME)*, 8(2), 319–322.
12. Gupta, D., Gupta, M., & Gupta, P. M. (2024). *HR Analytics: The Future of HR* (p. 404), PHI Learning Pvt. Ltd.; New Delhi, India.
13. Gupta, D., Gupta, M., & Rani, S. (2022). A study on training of workmen in a manufacturing organization—With reference to aluminium foundry. In A. Dvivedi, A. Sachdeva, R. Sindhwani, & R. Sahu (Eds.), *Recent Trends in Industrial and Production Engineering. Lecture Notes in Mechanical Engineering*. Springer, Singapore. https://doi.org/10.1007/978-981-16-3330-0_19
14. Gupta, D., Gupta, M., Tiwari, S., & Singh, N. (2021). Motivation due to fear of failure is a key contributor in maximizing workers' productivity in today's competitive arena. *International Journal of Indian Culture and Business Management*, 23(2), 193–217. https://doi.org/10.1504/IJICBM.2021.115895

15. Kumar, V., Gupta, M., & Gaur, S. (2023). Intrusion detection for the Internet of Things. In K. Kaushik, S. Dahiya, A. Bhardwaj, & Y. Maleh (Eds.), *Internet of Things and Cyber Physical Systems Security and Forensics* (1st ed., pp. 183). CRC Press, Boca Raton, FL.
16. McKinsey & Company. (2019). AI in Talent Management: From Acquisition to Retention. https://www.mckinsey.com/featured-insights/mckinsey-explainers/what-is-talent-management
17. Mittal, S., Srivastava, P., & Gupta, D. (2022). Emotional intelligence: Assessing its impact on financial productivity in an organization. In V. V. Rao, A. Kumaraswamy, A. Kalra, & A. Saxena (Eds.), *Computational and Experimental Methods in Mechanical Engineering*. Smart Innovation, Systems and Technologies, vol 239. Springer, Singapore. https://doi.org/10.1007/978-981-16-2857-3_22
18. Parry, E., & Tyson, S. (2011). Desired goals and actual outcomes of e-HRM. *Human Resource Management Journal*, 21(3), 335–354.
19. Rajvanshi, P. R., Singh, T., Gupta, D., & Gupta, M. (2022). Blockchain technology for pharmaceutical drug supply chain management. In P. Singh, D. Mishra, & K. Seth (Eds.), *Transformation in Healthcare with Emerging Technologies* (pp. 217–230). CRC Press, Boca Raton, FL.
20. Rajvanshi, P. R., Singh, T., Gupta, D., & Gupta, M. (2022). Cybersecurity and data privacy in the insurance market. In K. Sood, B. Balusamy, S. Grima, & P. Marano (Eds.), *Big Data Analytics in the Insurance Market* (pp. 1–20). Emerald Publishing Limited, Bingley. https://doi.org/10.1108/978-1-80262-637-720221001
21. Rani, S., Gupta, M., & Gupta, D. (2020). Artificial intelligence and personalized banking. In R. Agrawal, & V. Garg (Eds.), *Transforming Management Using Artificial Intelligence Techniques* (1st ed., pp. 24). CRC Press, Boca Raton, FL. https://doi.org/10.4324/9781003032410
22. Singh, S., Gupta, D., & Gupta, M. (2022). Optimized task allocation technique using mathematical fuzzy logic in heterogeneous distributed computational system. *2022 International Conference on Computational Intelligence and Sustainable Engineering Solutions (CISES)*, Greater Noida, India, 2022, pp. 37–45. https://doi.org/10.1109/CISES54857.2022.9844410
23. Singh, S., & Gupta, D. (2023). Module allocation model in distributed computing system by implementing fuzzy C-means clustering technique. In R. Agrawal, P. Mitra, A. Pal, & M. Sharma Gaur (Eds.), *International Conference on IoT, Intelligent Computing and Security*. Lecture Notes in Electrical Engineering, vol 982. Springer, Singapore. https://doi.org/10.1007/978-981-19-8136-4_14
24. Spreitzer, G., Cameron, L., & Garrett, L. (2017). Alternative work arrangements: Two images of the new world of work. *Annual Review of Organizational Psychology and Organizational Behavior*, 4, 473–499.
25. Agarwal, S., Gupta, D., & Gupta, M. (2023). Impact of training method on trainees' learning and implementation on job – A study with special reference to power sector. *AIP Conference Proceedings*, 2427(1), 020020. https://doi.org/10.1063/5.0100893
26. Waizenegger, L., McKenna, B., Cai, W., & Bendz, T. (2020). An affordance perspective of team collaboration and enforced working from home during COVID-19. *European Journal of Information Systems*, 29(4), 429–442.

9 Promotion Decision Process in Private Company Using Neutrosophic Fermatean Similarity Measures

R. Narmada Devi, Yamini Parthiban, Nagadevi Bala Nagaram, and Kala Raja Mohan

9.1 INTRODUCTION

In our everyday experiences, uncertainty often arises, whether it's the outcome of flipping a coin or making decisions in ambiguous situations. To aid decision-making in such scenarios, various theories have been proposed over time. Zadeh introduced fuzzy sets (FSs) in 1965 [23], followed by the concept of Interval-Valued Fuzzy Set (IVFS). Atanassov contributed to the idea of Intuitionistic Fuzzy Set (IFS) in 1986 [1], and Atanassov and Gorgov introduced IVIFSs in 1989 [2,11]. In 1998, Smarandache introduced Neutrosophic Sets (NS), which encompass elements of truthfulness, indeterminacy, and falseness [16]. Wang et al. introduced Single-Valued Neutrosophic Sets (SVNSs) to address practical challenges in applying NSs [18].

Across domains like education, medicine, societal issues, and conflict resolution, NSs and their extensions have found utility and thorough examination. Similarity computation between FSs has been a significant focus, initiated by Wang [18] and further explored by researchers like Chen [6,7]. However, these methods have limitations in handling uncertainty. Various similarity metrics for SVNS and NS have been extensively discussed in the literature [3,4,8,19–21]. Broumi and Smarandache extended Hausdorff distance to NSs, with applications in practical fields like computer-assisted surgery [4].

Several similarity measures for SVNSs have been proposed, including those by Kharal [10], Ye [19], and others, with applications in decision-making problems. Different similarity measures have been devised for various types of sets, such as IFSs, INS, and IVNSs.

Jafar and colleagues have effectively applied fuzzy, Intuitionistic, and neutrosophic logics in diverse decision-making scenarios [9,12,13], while Saqlain et al. have researched decision-making problems using neutrosophic theory. Researchers have made notable strides in addressing Multiple Criteria Decision-Making problems under uncertain conditions [14,15,17,22], often leveraging Fermatean NS [5].

DOI: 10.1201/9781032619651-9

This book chapter provides the fundamental prerequisites for comprehending Fermatean NS, with a focus on utilizing tangent and cotangent similarity metrics. It also explores critical characteristics and attributes. To demonstrate its practical utility, a numerical case study is elucidated, involving the selection of an Assistant Manager from a pool of three Project Heads.

9.2 PRELIMINARY

9.2.1 Definition

Let $^\circ F$ be a non-empty set and $\mathcal{Q}$ is said to be an NS. Then

$$\mathcal{Q}=\left\{\left\langle p,\aleph_{\mathcal{Q}}(p),\partial_{\mathcal{Q}}(p),\Upsilon_{\mathcal{Q}}(p)\right\rangle : p\in {}^\circ F\right\}$$

where $\aleph_{\mathcal{Q}},\partial_{\mathcal{Q}},\Upsilon_{\mathcal{Q}} : {}^\circ F\rightarrow[0,1]$ and $0\leq\aleph_{\mathcal{Q}}(p)+\partial_{\mathcal{Q}}(p)+\Upsilon_{\mathcal{Q}}(p)\leq 3$ Here $\aleph_{\mathcal{Q}}(p),\partial_{\mathcal{Q}}(p)$, and $\Upsilon_{\mathcal{Q}}(p)$ are the degree of true membership, degree of indeterminacy, and degree of falsity.

9.2.2 Definition

Let $^\circ F$ be a non-empty set and $\mathcal{Q}$ is said to be a neutrosophic Fermatean set (NFS). Then

$$\mathcal{Q}=\left\{\left\langle p,\aleph_{\mathcal{Q}}(p),\partial_{\mathcal{Q}}(p),\Upsilon_{\mathcal{Q}}(p)\right\rangle : p\in {}^\circ F\right\} \text{ where } \aleph_{\mathcal{Q}},\partial_{\mathcal{Q}},\Upsilon_{\mathcal{Q}} : {}^\circ F\rightarrow[0,1] \text{ and}$$

$$0\leq\aleph_{\mathcal{Q}}(p)^3+\breve{\partial}_{\mathcal{Q}}(p)^3+\Upsilon_{\mathcal{Q}}(p)^3\leq 2, 0\leq\aleph_{\mathcal{Q}}(p)^3+\Upsilon_{\mathcal{Q}}(p)^3\leq 1 \text{ and } 0\leq\partial_{\mathcal{Q}}(p)^3\leq 1.$$

9.2.3 Definition

Let $\mathcal{Q}$ be a Fermatean neutrosophic set over an non-empty set $^\circ F$ then (and + is called Universe Fermatean Neutrosophic set and Empty Fermatean Neutrosophic Set such that

$$\boxplus=\left\{\left\langle p,1,1,0\right\rangle : p\in {}^\circ F\right\} \text{ and } \blacksquare=\left\{\left\langle p,0,0,1\right\rangle : p\in {}^\circ F\right\}$$

9.2.4 Definition

Let $\mathcal{Q}$ and $\mathcal{S}$ be a two NFS over a non-empty set $^\circ F$ is of the form

$$\mathcal{Q}=\left\{\left\langle p,\aleph_{\mathcal{Q}}(p),\partial_{\mathcal{Q}}(p),\Upsilon_{\mathcal{Q}}(p)\right\rangle : p\in {}^\circ F\right\}\cdot \text{ and}$$
$$\mathcal{S}=\left\{\left\langle p,\aleph_{\mathcal{S}}(p),\partial_{\mathcal{S}}(p),\Upsilon_{\mathcal{S}}(p)\right\rangle : p\in {}^\circ F\right\}.$$

Then

i. $\mathcal{Q} \cup \mathcal{S}$
$$= \left\{ \left\langle \text{p}, \max\left(\aleph_{\mathcal{Q}}(\text{p}), \aleph_{\mathcal{S}}(\text{p})\right), \max\left(\partial_{\mathcal{Q}}(\text{p}), \breve{\partial}_{\mathcal{S}}(\text{p})\right), \min\left(\Upsilon_{\mathcal{Q}}(\text{p}), \Upsilon_{\mathcal{S}}(\text{p})\right) \right\rangle : \text{p} \in {}^{\circ}\text{F} \right\}.$$

ii. $\mathcal{Q} \cap \mathcal{S} =$
$$\left[\left\langle \text{p}, \min\left(\aleph_{\mathcal{Q}}(\text{p}), \aleph_{\mathcal{S}}(\text{p})\right), \min\left(\overset{\frown}{\mathcal{Q}}(\text{p}), \partial_{\mathcal{S}}(\text{p}) \right), \max\left(\Upsilon_{\mathcal{Q}}(\text{p}), \Upsilon_{\mathcal{S}}(\text{p})\right) \right\rangle : \text{p} \in {}^{\circ}\text{F} \right\}.$$

iii. $\mathcal{Q}^c = \left\{ \left\langle \text{p}, \Upsilon_{\mathcal{Q}}(\text{p}), 1 - \partial_{\mathcal{Q}}(\text{p}), \aleph_{\mathcal{Q}}(\text{p}) \right\rangle : \text{p} \in {}^{\circ}\text{F} \right\}.$

iv. $\mathcal{S} \cup \blacksquare = \mathcal{S}$

v. $\mathcal{S} \cup \boxplus = \boxplus$

vi. $\mathcal{S} \cap \blacksquare = \blacksquare$

vii. $\mathcal{S} \cap \boxplus = \mathcal{S}$

viii. $\mathcal{Q} \cup \mathcal{Q} = \mathcal{Q} \cap \mathcal{Q} = \mathcal{Q}$

ix. $\mathcal{Q} \cup \mathcal{S} = \mathcal{S} \cup \mathcal{Q}$

x. $\mathcal{S} \cap \mathcal{Q} = \mathcal{Q} \cap \mathcal{S}$

xi. $\left(\mathcal{Q}^c\right)^c = \mathcal{Q}$

x. $\boxplus^c = \blacksquare$

xi. $\blacksquare^c = \boxplus$

9.3 NFS FOR TANGENT AND COTANGENT SIMILARITY MEASURE

Consider two neutrosophic Fermatean sets $\mathcal{Q}$ and $\mathcal{S}$ over ${}^{\circ}$F. To establish a similarity metric that assesses the likeness between these sets based exclusively on their alignment, without taking into account the separation between them. Then,

(i) **Tangent Similarity Measure:**

$$\rho(\mathcal{Q}, \mathcal{S}) = \frac{1}{n}\left(\sum_{\text{i}=1}^{n} 1 - \tan\left[\frac{\pi\left[\left|\aleph_{\mathcal{Q}}(\text{p}) - \aleph_{\mathcal{S}}(\text{p})\right| + \left|\partial_{\mathcal{Q}}(\text{p}) - \partial_{\mathcal{S}}(\text{p})\right| + \left|\Upsilon_{\mathcal{Q}}(\text{p}) - \Upsilon_{\mathcal{S}}(\text{p})\right| \right]}{12} \right] \right)$$

(ii) **Cotangent Similarity Measure:**

$$\rho^{*}(\mathcal{Q}, \mathcal{S}) = \frac{1}{n}\left(\sum_{\text{i}=1}^{n} \cot\left[\frac{\pi}{4} + \frac{\pi\left[\left|\aleph_{\mathcal{Q}}(\text{p}) - \aleph_{\mathcal{S}}(\text{p})\right| + \left|\partial_{\mathcal{Q}}(\text{p}) - \partial_{\mathcal{S}}(\text{p})\right| + \left|\Upsilon_{\mathcal{Q}}(\text{p}) - \Upsilon_{\mathcal{S}}(\text{p})\right| \right]}{12} \right] \right)$$

9.3.1 Proposition

The defined tangent similarity ($\rho(\mathcal{Q},\mathcal{S})$) for the two NFS $\mathcal{Q}$ and $\mathcal{S}$ over a non-empty set $^{\circ}F$. Then it satisfies the properties

i. $0 \le \rho(\mathcal{Q},\mathcal{S}) \le 1$
ii. $\rho(\mathcal{Q},\mathcal{S}) = 1$ iff $\mathcal{Q} = \mathcal{S}$
iii. $\rho(\mathcal{Q},\mathcal{S}) = \rho(\mathcal{S},\mathcal{Q})$

Proof:

i. Since the membership, indeterminacy, and non-membership functions of the NFS fall within the interval [0,1], and the tangent function also operates within that same interval, the resulting similarity measure based on the tangent function will likewise yield values within [0,1].

   Hence $0 \le \rho(\mathcal{Q},\mathcal{S}) \le 1$

ii. For any two NFS $\mathcal{Q}$ and $\mathcal{S}$ IF $\mathcal{Q} = \mathcal{S}$ this implies

$$\aleph_{\mathcal{Q}}(p) = \aleph_{\mathcal{S}}(p), \partial_{\mathcal{Q}}(p) = \partial_{\mathcal{S}}(p), \Upsilon_{\mathcal{Q}}(p) = \Upsilon_{\mathcal{S}}(p)$$

Then $|\aleph_{\mathcal{Q}}(p) - \aleph_{\mathcal{S}}(p)| = 0, |\partial_{\mathcal{Q}}(p) - \partial_{\mathcal{S}}(p)| = 0, |\Upsilon_{\mathcal{Q}}(p) - \Upsilon_{\mathcal{S}}(p)| = 0$

Thus $\rho(\mathcal{Q},\mathcal{S}) = 1$

Conversely, $\rho(\mathcal{Q},\mathcal{S}) = 1$

Then $|\aleph_{\mathcal{Q}}(p) - \aleph_{\mathcal{S}}(p)| = 0, |\partial_{\mathcal{Q}}(p) - \partial_{\mathcal{S}}(p)| = 0, |\Upsilon_{\mathcal{Q}}(p) - \Upsilon_{\mathcal{S}}(p)| = 0$

$$\Rightarrow |\aleph_{\mathcal{Q}}(p) - \aleph_{\mathcal{S}}(p)| = 0, |\partial_{\mathcal{Q}}(p) - \partial_{\mathcal{S}}(p)| = 0, |\Upsilon_{\mathcal{Q}}(p) - \Upsilon_{\mathcal{S}}(p)| = 0$$

$$\Rightarrow \mathcal{Q} = \mathcal{S}$$

iii. From the definition we know that,

$$\rho(\mathcal{Q},\mathcal{S}) = \frac{1}{n}\left(\sum_{i=1}^{n} 1 - \tan\left[\frac{\pi\left[|\aleph_{\mathcal{Q}}(p) - \aleph_{\mathcal{S}}(p)| + |\partial_{\mathcal{Q}}(p) - \partial_{\mathcal{S}}(p)| + |\Upsilon_{\mathcal{Q}}(p) - \Upsilon_{\mathcal{S}}(p)|\right]}{12}\right]\right)$$

$$= \frac{1}{n}\left(\sum_{i=1}^{n} 1 - \tan\left[\frac{\pi\left[|\aleph_{\mathcal{S}}(p) - \aleph_{\mathcal{Q}}(p)| + |\partial_{\mathcal{S}}(p) - \partial_{\mathcal{Q}}(p)| + |\Upsilon_{\mathcal{S}}(p) - \Upsilon_{\mathcal{Q}}(p)|\right]}{12}\right]\right)$$

$$= \rho(\mathcal{S},\mathcal{Q})$$

$$\Rightarrow \rho(\mathcal{Q},\mathcal{S}) = \rho(\mathcal{S},\mathcal{Q})$$

9.3.2 Proposition

The defined cotangent similarity ($\rho^*(\mathcal{Q},\mathcal{S})$) for the two NFS $\mathcal{Q}$ and $\mathcal{S}$ over an non-empty set $^\circ F$. Then it satisfies the properties

i. $0 \le \rho^*(\mathcal{Q},\mathcal{S}) \le 1$

ii. $\rho^*(\mathcal{Q},\mathcal{S}) = 1$ iff $\mathcal{Q} = \mathcal{S}$

iii. $\rho^*(\mathcal{Q},\mathcal{S}) = \rho^*(\mathcal{S},\mathcal{Q})$

Proof. The claim can be easily deduced from Proposition 3.1.

9.4 ALGORITHM

Step 1: Collection of data

Consider $\mathfrak{m}$ attributes $\mathcal{A}_1, \mathcal{A}_2, \mathcal{A}_3, \ldots, \mathcal{A}_\mathfrak{m}$, $\mathfrak{n}$ replacement $\mathcal{C}_1, \mathcal{C}_2, \mathcal{C}_3, \ldots, \mathcal{C}_\mathfrak{n}$, and $\mathfrak{p}$ replacement $\mathcal{D}_1, \mathcal{D}_2, \mathcal{D}_3, \ldots, \mathcal{D}_\mathfrak{p}$ $(\mathfrak{n} \le \mathfrak{p})$ for multi-attributes decision-making problem.

$\mathcal{D}_\mathfrak{p} \setminus \mathcal{A}_i$	$\mathcal{A}_1$	$\mathcal{A}_2$	.	.	.	$\mathcal{A}_m$
$\mathcal{D}_1$	$\eth_{11}$	$\eth_{12}$	.	.	.	$\eth_{1m}$
$\mathcal{D}_2$	$\eth_{21}$	$\eth_{22}$	.	.	.	$\eth_{2m}$
$\mathcal{D}_3$	$\eth_{31}$	$\eth_{32}$	.	.	.	$\eth_{3m}$
.	.	.	.	.	.	.
.	.	.	.	.	.	.
$\mathcal{D}_p$	$\eth_{p1}$	$\eth_{p2}$	.	.	.	$\eth_{pm}$

$\mathcal{A}_i \setminus \mathcal{C}_j$	$\mathcal{C}_1$	$\mathcal{C}_2$	.	.	.	$\mathcal{C}_n$
$\mathcal{A}_1$	$\mathfrak{a}_{11}$	$\mathfrak{a}_{12}$	.	.	.	$\mathfrak{a}_{1n}$
$\mathcal{A}_2$	$\mathfrak{a}_{21}$	$\mathfrak{a}_{22}$	.	.	.	$\mathfrak{a}_{2n}$
$\mathcal{A}_3$	$\mathfrak{a}_{31}$	$\mathfrak{a}_{32}$	.	.	.	$\mathfrak{a}_{3n}$
.	.	.	.	.	.	.
.	.	.	.	.	.	.
$\mathcal{A}_m$	$\mathfrak{a}_{m1}$	$\mathfrak{a}_{m2}$	.	.	.	$\mathfrak{a}_{mn}$

Step 2: Calculation

Calculating the tangent and cotangent similarity measure with collected data.

Step 3: Final Decision

Pick the highest tangent measure from each row.

9.5 NUMERICAL APPLICATION

The heart of any organization lies in its human resources, providing vital support for its development and advancement. In the absence of an exceptional team, a company's ability to progress is significantly constrained. Hence, the primary imperative for any organization is the cultivation of a highly skilled workforce.

From the organizational perspective, the act of promoting employees represents a highly coveted milestone, contingent upon meeting a meticulously defined set of criteria laid out by the human resources department. When viewed through the lens of the organization, the ultimate aim of promoting employees is to identify and elevate well-qualified individuals from diverse positions, endowing them with more prestigious roles marked by heightened titles, expertise, and compensation packages. This strategic maneuver is designed to maximize their potential contributions to the organization. Consequently, the "results" and "validity" of employee promotions emerge as pivotal factors that determine the course of an organization's growth and its successful ascent.

A comparable circumstance arises within a privately held company as they aim to formalize the list of promotions for a trio of project leaders. Their goal is to designate one employee to assume the position of Assistant Manager. To navigate this situation, they are employing the tangent and cotangent similarity measures.

$$\text{Employee} = \{L, M, N\},$$
$$\text{Criteria} = \{\text{ Work Quality, Honesty, Skills, Punctuality, Team Work}\}$$
$$\text{Position} = \{\text{Selected, Non-Selected}\}$$

9.6 SELECTION FOR ASSISTANT MANAGER

Tables 9.1–9.5 formed with collected data:

TABLE 9.1
Relation between Employees and Criteria

$\breve{\Upsilon}$	Work Quality	Honesty	Skills	Punctuality	Team Work
L	$(0.8, 0.3, 0.1)$	$(0.5, 0.4, 0.1)$	$(0.6, 0.4, 0.1)$	$(0.6, 0.2, 0.2)$	$(0.7, 0.3, 0.2)$
$\bar{M}$	$(0.7, 0.3, 0.2)$	$(0.7, 0.4, 0.0)$	$(0.7, 0.3, 0.2)$	$(0.8, 0.2, 0.1)$	$(0.7, 0.4, 0.1)$
N	$(0.8, 0.2, 0.2)$	$(0.9, 0.1, 0.1)$	$(0.9, 0.1, 0.2)$	$(0.5, 0.4, 0.2)$	$(0.6, 0.4, 0.1)$

TABLE 9.2
Relation between Criteria and Position

$\breve{W}$	Non-selected	Selected
Work quality	$(0.7, 0.1, 0.3)$	$(0.5, 0.3, 0.3)$
Honesty	$(0.6, 0.3, 0.2)$	$(0.6, 0.3, 0.2)$
Skills	$(0.7, 0.2, 0.1)$	$(0.7, 0.3, 0.1)$
Punctuality	$(0.7, 0.4, 0.1)$	$(0.8, 0.0, 0.2)$
Team work	$(0.8, 0.0, 0.2)$	$(0.8, 0.3, 0.1)$

TABLE 9.3
Tangent Similarity Measure

ρ^*	Selected	Non-selected
L	0.9001	**0.9265**
M	0.9053	**0.9377**
N	**0.8787**	0.8628

TABLE 9.4
Cotangent Similarity Measure

ρ	Selected	Non-Selected
L	0.8189	**0.8382**
M	0.8289	**0.8645**
N	**0.7862**	0.7685

TABLE 9.5
Summary

Project Head	Result
L	Not selected
M	Not selected
N	Selected

9.7 CONCLUSION

In this chapter, the focus is on the practical implementation of tangent and cotangent similarity measures within neutrosophic Fermatean sets. It provides clear definitions and discusses the essential properties associated with these measures. Moreover, it presents a real-world case study concerning the selection process for an Assistant Manager position, where the analysis identifies employee 'N' as the most suitable candidate among three project leaders. Additionally, the chapter explores how these similarity measures are applied in various fields that handle uncertain information.

REFERENCES

1. Atanassov, K., (1986). Intuitionistic fuzzy sets, *Fuzzy Sets and Systems*, 20:87–96.
2. Atanassov, K., and Gargov, G., (1989). Interval valued intuitionistic fuzzy sets, *Fuzzy Sets and System*, 31:343–349.
3. Biswas, P., Pramanik, S., and Giri, C.B., (2015). Cosine similarity measure based multiattribute decision making with trapezoidal fuzzy neutrosophic numbers, *Neutrosophic Sets and System*, 8:47–58.
4. Broumi, S., and, Smarandache, F., (2013). Several similarity measures of neutrosophic sets, *Neutrosophic Sets and Systems*, 1:54–62.
5. Broumi, S., Sundareswaran, R., Shanmugapriya, M., Nordo, G., Talea, M., Bakali, A., and Smarandache, F., (2022). Interval-valued fermatean neutrosophic graphs. Collected Papers. Volume XIII: On Various Scientific Topics, 496.
6. Chen, M.S., Yeh, M.S., and Hsiao, H.P., (1995). A comparison of similarity measure of fuzzy value, *Fuzzy Sets and System*, 72:79–89.
7. Chen, M.S., (1998). A new approach to handling fuzzy decision making problems, *IEEE Transactions on Systems Man and Cybemetics*, 8:1012–1016.
8. Devi, R.N., and Parthiban, Y., (2023). Decision making process over neutrosophic pythagorean soft sets using measure of correlation. *Southeast Europe Journal of Soft Computing*, 12(2), 09–09.
9. Jafar, N.M, Faizullah, Shabbir, S, Alvi, F.M.S., and Shaheen, L., (2020). Intuitionistic fuzzy soft matrices, compliments and their relations with comprehensive study of medical diagnosis, *International Journal of Latest Engineering Research and Applications*, 5(1):23–30.
10. Kharal, A., (2013). A neutrosophic multi-criteria decision-making method, *New Mathematics and Natural Computation*, 10(2):143–162. Creighton University USA.
11. Mondal, K., and Pramanik, S., (2015). Intuitimistic fuzzy similarity measure based on tangent function and its application to multi attribute decision, *Global Journal of Advanced Research*, 2(2):404–471. 8
12. Murugesan, R., Parthiban, Y., Devi, R., Mohan, K.R., and Kumarave, S.K., (2023). A comparative study of fuzzy cognitive maps neutrosophic cognitive maps on Covid variants. *Neutrosophic Sets Systems*, 55(1):20.
13. Pramanik, S., and Roy, K.T., (2014). Neutrosophcic game theoretic approach to Indo-Pak conflict over JammuKashmir, *Neutrosophic Sets and Systems*, 2:82–101.
14. Riaz, M., Saeed, M., Saqlain, M., and Jafar, N., (2019). Impact of water hardness in instinctive laundry system based on fuzzy logic controller, *Punjab University Journal of Mathematics*, 51(4):73–84.
15. Saeed, M., Zulqarnain, M., and Dayan, F., (2018). TOPSIS analysis for the prediction of diabetes based on general characteristics of humans. *International Journal of Pharmaceutical Sciences and Research*, 9:2932–2939.
16. Salama, A.A., and Smarandache, F., (2015). *Neutrosophic Crisp Set Theory.* Infinite Study.

17. Tian, M.Y., (2012). A new fuzzy similarity based on cotangent function for medical diagnosis, *Advanced Model Option*, 5(2):151–156.
18. Wang, J.W., (1997). New similarity measure on fuzzy sets and element, *Fuzzy Sets and System*, 85:305–309.
19. Ye, J., (2013). Multicriteria decision making method using the correlation coefficient using single valued neutrosophic environment, *International Journal of General System*, 42(4):386–394.
20. Ye, J., and Zhang, Q., (2012). Single valued neutrosophic similarity measures for multiple attribute decision making, *Neutrosophic Sets and System*, 2:48–54.
21. Ye, J., (2014). Similarity measures between interval neutrosophic sets and their multi criteria decision making method, *Journal of Intelligent and Fuzzy Systems*, 26:165–172.
22. Ye, J., (2014). Vectors similarity measure of simplified neutrosophic sets and their application in multi criteria decision making, *International Journal of Fuzzy Systems*, 16(2):204–215.
23. Zadeh, A.L., (1965). Fuzzy sets, *Information and Control*, 8:338–353.

10 Transforming Performance Management System (PMS)

Influence of Digitalization

Preeti Malhotra, Deepa Gupta, and Rajesh Kumar Dhanaraj

10.1 INTRODUCTION

A performance management system (PMS) is needed by an organization for comprehensive and continuous improvement. The most essential role of PMS is to provide a thoughtful and dedicated process of continuous evaluation and feedback. Organizations use PMSs as a tool to evaluate their performance as a whole and as well as their employees' performance in relation to standards or goals established.

PMS has been regarded as a vital tool for organizations. The information provided by it is highly useful in strategic planning and in making decisions related to personnel aspects such as promotions, increments, training needs, and compensation.

Performance management is a process required for improvement to occur. Without assessment and feedback, we have no basis for guiding our efforts to improve. Performance management should be done with management by objective, which helps the organization to align its and its employees' performance with the organization's vision, mission and organizations objectives.

George Odiorne defines Management by Objectives (MBO) as a systematic process whereby people at top, middle, and lower management work together to define their organizational goals, identify each employee's prime responsibilities in terms of output expected, and use this as evaluation matrix which can be used as guide for managing the whole organizational and assessing the contribution of each employee.

The PMS is done through MBO in the following steps:

Step 1: Understanding the vision (long-term aspiration) of an organization
Step 2: Derive mission to make the vision predictable and achievable
Step 3: Set organization objective(s) (the annual targets of the organization)
Step 4: Set the department(s) objectives (segregating the organization objectives on the basis of specialization to each department)
Step 5: Segregate the departmental objectives for each employee of the department based on their competencies (set individual targets or Key Responsibility areas)

DOI: 10.1201/9781032619651-10

MBO is a famous technique for managing performance as it involves setting specific, measurable, achievable, relevant, and time-bound objectives for employees. It also helps in a holistic and complete evaluation of the organization. The other modern methods being used by organizations for evaluating performance are the Behavioural anchored rating scale, Assessment centre, Human accounting method, psychological appraisal method, 360-degree, and 720-degree methods.

The long-term achievement of organizations in meeting their strategic objectives rests on their ability to manage employee performance and make sure that performance measures are appropriate to the organization's needs (Mello, 2013). Performance management is a continual process of identifying, evaluating, and improving an individual's or team's performance and aligning their performance with the organization's objectives, vision, and mission.

10.2 EVOLUTION OF PMS IN DISTINCT TIME FRAME

The PMS is evolving in many industries to meet the demand present scenario. PMS has now become an imperative component for evaluating organization and employee's performance (Table 10.1).

10.2.1 PMS in 21st Century

In the competitive and uncertain environment, organizations are using customized PMSs to match the needs of the time. Organizations have been trying to implement the system in such a way that they can manage the performance of their employees efficiently. Depending on the organization's size and nature, different organizations have varied approaches to PMS (Rath, 2018). Over the past few years, enhancing the

TABLE 10.1
Overview of Evolution of Performance Management Systems in a Distinct Time Frame

Era	Methods	Measures
3rd AD	Qualitative evaluation on traits	Attitude
Pre 1800s	First examples of trait/competencies	Attitude
1800s	Narrative report analysis	Attitude and character
1920s	Task-based output	Observation on target completion
1950s	Trait-based, critical incident analysis	Attitude and behaviour
1960s	Management by objective	Key responsibility area (KRA) and accomplishment of common goal(s)
1970s	Assessment centre	Attitude
1980s	Hybrid	Scale for attitude and qualitative for behaviour
1990s	Performance management	Attitude, Behaviour, KRA
	Competency development	Skill enhancement
	360-Degree feedback	Holistic improvement
	Balanced scorecard	Attitude, Behaviour, KRA

efficiency of PMS and the appraisal procedure has been one of the prime functions for human resource (HR) practitioners. Many organizations are utilizing PMS as a tool for organizational transformation in addition to its conventional uses such as goal setting, performance review, identifying performance gap areas, and rewarding employees (Dessler and Varrkey, 2011).

10.2.2 PMS in the Era of Digitalization

PMS has metamorphosed to expand conventional boundaries. It currently covers several elements such as goal setting, annual compensation, and performance planning. The system must continually accommodate organization objectives as well as a millennial mindset, which despises conformity, and transparency, and is ravenous for constructive feedback aimed at personal growth. Organizations are taking all measures to cater to new trends and technology is providing the platform that enables them to use modern-day performance management with integration of multiple needs (Gupta et al., 2022). Technology enables PMSs to not only measure performance but also track it.

Technological tools available for PMSs are Success Factors by SAP, Taleo by Oracle, Workday, and Sum Total by Skillsoft.

10.2.3 Impact of Technology on Business Processes

Technology has fundamentally transformed business processes across industries, driving efficiency, enhancing decision-making, and fostering innovation. Digital tools and technologies have redefined how organizations operate, communicate, and manage resources. Below is an overview of the key impacts:

1. **Automation of Repetitive Tasks**
   - Technology automates routine processes like data entry, payroll, and reporting.
   - Software solutions like RPA (Robotic Process Automation) enhance accuracy, reduce errors, and speed up processes.
2. **Enhanced Communication and Collaboration**
   - Tools like Slack, Microsoft Teams, and Zoom facilitate real-time communication across departments and geographies.
   - Cloud-based collaboration platforms like Google Workspace and SharePoint enable teams to work together seamlessly from anywhere.
3. **Data-Driven Decision-Making**
   - The integration of big data and analytics allows businesses to make informed decisions based on real-time data.
   - Predictive analytics help forecast trends, enabling proactive business strategies.
4. **Streamlined Supply Chain Management**
   - Technology optimizes supply chain processes through automation, IoT (Internet of Things), and artificial intelligence (AI)-driven analytics.
   - Real-time tracking of shipments and inventory leads to more efficient logistics and reduced costs.

TABLE 10.2
Impact of Key Technologies on Business Processes

Technology	Business Process Impact	Key Benefits
Automation (RPA)	Automates repetitive tasks (e.g., data entry, billing)	Time savings, reduced errors, cost efficiency
Cloud Computing	Enables remote work, data access, and storage	Scalability, flexibility, cost reduction
AI and Machine Learning	Enhances decision-making through predictive insights	Accurate forecasting, process optimization
Big Data Analytics	Supports data-driven strategies and real-time monitoring	Improved decision-making, trend identification
IoT	Monitors supply chain and equipment performance in real-time	Enhanced operational efficiency, reduced downtime
CRM Systems	Personalizes customer interactions and streamlines marketing	Increased customer satisfaction, sales growth

5. **Improved Customer Experience**
   - Customer Relationship Management (CRM) systems provide personalized interactions, improving customer satisfaction.
   - AI-powered chatbots offer instant responses to customer queries, enhancing service quality.
6. **Increased Agility and Innovation**
   - Cloud computing provides scalability and flexibility, allowing businesses to quickly adapt to changing market demands.
   - Agile methodologies and DevOps practices enable faster product development and delivery cycles (Table 10.2).

10.2.4 Key Drivers of Digital Transformation in Performance Management Systems (PMS)

Digital transformation in PMS has become imperative as organizations strive to enhance employee productivity, engagement, and alignment with business objectives (Sugandha et al., 2023). Below are the key drivers of digital transformation in PMS:

1. **Need for Real-Time Feedback and Continuous Improvement**
   - Traditional PMS often relies on annual reviews, which are inadequate for today's fast-paced environment.
   - Digital PMS systems offer real-time feedback loops, enabling continuous employee development and performance adjustments (Gupta and Agarwal, 2018a).
2. **Data-Driven Performance Evaluation**
   - The integration of AI and analytics into PMS allows for objective, data-driven performance assessments.
   - Organizations can track KPIs (Key Performance Indicators) in real-time and make more informed decisions on promotions and development.

3. **Employee Engagement and Retention**
   - Modern digital tools like mobile apps allow employees to actively participate in their performance management.
   - Employees can set personal goals, track progress, and receive regular updates, increasing ownership and engagement.
4. **Customization and Personalization**
   - Digital PMS systems offer personalized performance metrics and development plans, tailored to individual employee needs.
   - AI-driven personalization fosters a sense of individual growth, boosting motivation and retention.
5. **Scalability and Flexibility**
   - Digital PMS solutions are scalable, making it easy to manage large teams across multiple locations.
   - Cloud-based systems offer flexibility, allowing employees and managers to access performance data from anywhere.
6. **Compliance and Transparency**
   - Digital PMS platforms ensure compliance with industry standards and internal policies by automating documentation and tracking processes.
   - Transparency in performance assessments builds trust between employees and management (Figure 10.1 and Table 10.3).

The impact of technology on business processes is profound, driving efficiency, enhancing decision-making, and fostering collaboration. In PMS, digital transformation is primarily driven by the need for real-time feedback, data-driven evaluations, and enhanced employee engagement (Gupta et al., 2024). By leveraging AI, cloud computing, and big data, organizations can develop a more scalable, flexible, and transparent PMS that aligns with modern workforce expectations.

10.3 PMS IN THE ERA OF AI

AI's ability to provide sophisticated analytics, automation, and quick understanding will play a crucial role in enhancing PMSs.

Business leaders and HR practitioners see a lot of potential in the performance management trends with AI and what it can bring to the future of their companies. AI-driven performance management software can measure results and can transform business processes. It will help employees to get free from redundant tasks so they can do more productive tasks.

People are becoming more technologically savvy. Teams are choosing automated PMSs that can reduce repetitive tasks, keep good track of employees' performance, and provide required assessments for improvement (Rajvanshi et al., 2022).

10.3.1 The Role of AI in PMSs

1. Data Analysis and Observation: AI has the capability to analyse large amounts of data pertaining to employee performance, including KPIs, individual targets, accomplishments, feedback, and historical data. By identifying patterns,

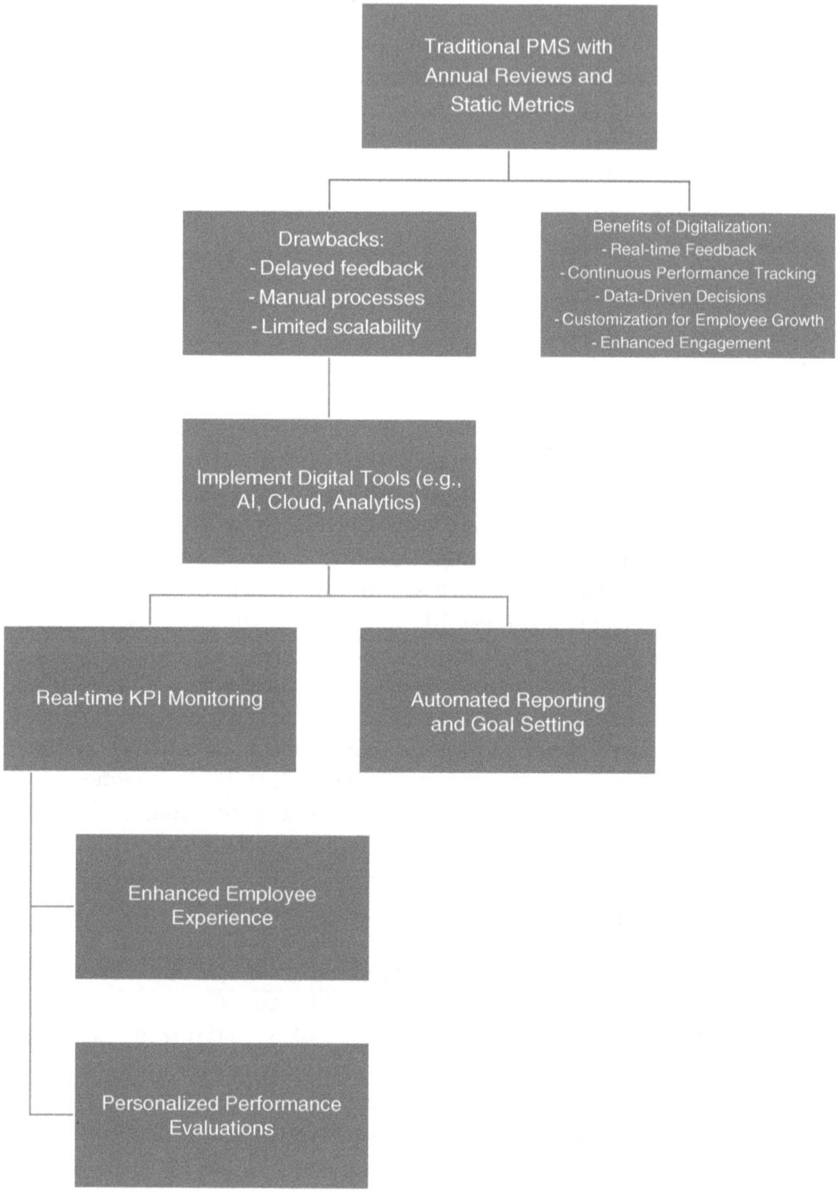

FIGURE 10.1 Flowchart depicting Digital Transformation in Performance Management Systems.

trends, correlation, and regression within the data, AI can generate valuable output that HR practitioners, managers, and staff can use to make informed decisions and effectively address performance gaps. This upgraded technology makes the decision process efficient and empowers the organization to optimize performance management strategies (Singh et al., 2022).

TABLE 10.3
Key Drivers of Digital Transformation in PMS

Driver	Impact on PMS	Benefits
Real-time feedback	Enables continuous employee development	Faster performance improvements, better alignment
Data-driven evaluation	Objective assessment based on data and analytics	Fairer evaluations, reduced bias
Employee engagement	Encourages active participation and goal setting	Higher retention rates, increased motivation
Customization	Tailored performance metrics and development plans	Boosts employee satisfaction and personal growth
Scalability	Handles large teams across geographies easily	Flexibility, better resource management
Compliance and transparency	Automated documentation and transparent evaluation process	Improved trust, easier compliance with regulations

2. Real-Time Feedback and Mentoring: PMS powered by AI can offer employees real-time feedback and coaching. AI can offer instant feedback on performance by analysing various data sources such as task progress and completion on time, customer satisfaction, employee behaviour, etc. This allows for the identification of areas for improvement and recognition of employee achievements providing real-time inputs; AI helps employees to track their performance and progression, allows them to make required adjustments and improvements, and ultimately fosters continuous performance enhancement (Gupta and Agarwal, 2018b).
3. Personalized Development Plans: AI helps to create customized development plans by analysing the performance data and career objectives. By utilizing AI algorithms, organizations can provide personalized training programs, learning resources, and counselling sessions that align with an individual's strengths, weaknesses, and areas of improvement. This tailored approach to professional development boosts employee engagement and obtains a culture of continuous growth within employees (Agarwal and Gupta, 2024).
4. Bias Detection and Alleviation: Unconscious bias that affects assessments and decision-making is one of the issues in performance management. AI plays an important role in promoting equality and objectivity in decision-making. It helps to identify and reduce bias by impartially analysing performance data without any predetermined biases. By analysing feedback, ratings, and suggestions, AI can identify patterns of biases and provide valuable insights to ensure fair evaluation and decision-making processes.
5. Predictive Analytics: By utilizing the power of predictive analysis, PMS have the ability to anticipate future performance trends and outcomes. AI can identify the key factors that lead to high performance levels and predict

the likelihood of achieving specific goals by analysing historical data. This helps HR practitioners and managers to proactively address performance gaps and make informed, logical, and data-driven decisions that optimize performance (Gupta et al., n.d.).

6. Automate and Organize: AI helps to streamline routine administrative work related to performance management like data collection, performance tracking, and report generation. By automating these tasks, AI allows valuable time for HR practitioners and managers to focus on the strategic aspects of performance management such as coaching, talent development, and employee engagement. Thus, AI allows to improve the efficiency of organizations and enables their leaders to strategic initiatives.

   Hence, AI enhances PMSs with enhanced analytics, automation, and tailored insights, enabling fair assessments, data-driven decision-making, and continual development. It enables firms to efficiently accomplish their strategic goals and optimize performance and employee engagement (Agarwal et al., 2023).

10.3.2 Challenges for Implementing AI for PMSs

1. Data Quality: AI relies on data for performance analysis. Therefore, it is essential to provide reliable and accurate data and also to ensure uniformity and uprightness of data to prevent any biases that can affect the results (Rani et al., 2020).
2. Comprehensibility and Transparency: AI systems can often be difficult to comprehend and demonstrate. Therefore, it is essential to have a clear understanding of how these systems reach specific conclusions and suggestions in order to establish faith and reception among employees.
3. Employee Reception: It is important to understand that some employees may not feel comfortable about the use of AI in their performance appraisal process. To address this concern, organizations must focus on transparent communication, address any concerns they arise, and work to build trust among employees. By encouraging the environment of openness and understanding, organizations can ensure that the employees feel confident and accept the role of AI in the evaluations (Gupta et al., 2021).
4. Appropriate Balance: It is essential to create a right balance between AI-driven insights and human judgement. Relying too much on AI tools without considering human context and expertise can lead to poor decision-making and employee withdrawal.
5. Ethical Considerations: It is important to address ethical considerations such as privacy, data security, and algorithm equity when integrating AI into PMSs. These factors must be carefully monitored and regulated to ensure the ethical use of AI tools in the workplace.

10.4 CONCLUSION

The conception, administration, and implementation of PMSs have evolved significantly over time. The future of managing employees' performance is bright due to the AI-driven PMS. AI in PMSs will transform the way organizations evaluate and track performance and provide real-time, continuous feedback to employees. It will also help employees with emotional and mental well-being. Moreover, an AI-driven PMS saves cost, resources, and time. It will become a more efficient source of evaluation. Hence, organizations should overcome the challenges and cultivate the culture of real-time feedback and continuous improvement to enrich performance, commitment, and favourable outcomes.

REFERENCES

Agarwal, S., & Gupta, D. (2024). Digital analytics applications for sustainable training and education. In: Sood, K., Kalia, P., Grima, S., & Chaudhary, A. (eds) *Digital Analytics Applications for Sustainable Training and Education* (p. 25). Apple Academic Press, New Delhi, India.

Dessler, G., & Varkkey, B. (2011). *Human Resource Management*, Twelfth Edition, Pearson Publication, Delhi, India.

Gupta, D., & Agarwal, S. (2018a). Skill development initiative-literature review. *Inspira-Journal of Modern Management and Entrepreneurship (JMME)*, 8(2), 319–322.

Gupta, D., & Agarwal, S. (2018b). Training prospects in power sector in India. *International Journal of Research in Engineering, IT and Social Sciences*, 8, 305–314.

Gupta, D., Gupta, M., & Gupta, P. M. (2024). *HR Analytics: The Future of HR* (p. 404), Delhi, India.

Gupta, D., Gupta, M., & Rani, S. (2022). A study on training of workmen in a manufacturing organization—With reference to aluminium foundry. In: Dvivedi, A., Sachdeva, A., Sindhwani, R., Sahu, R. (eds) *Recent Trends in Industrial and Production Engineering*. Lecture Notes in Mechanical Engineering. Springer, Singapore. https://doi.org/10.1007/978-981-16-3330-0_19

Gupta, D., Gupta, M., Tiwari, S., & Singh, N. (2021). Motivation due to fear of failure is a key contributor in maximizing workers' productivity in today's competitive arena. *International Journal of Indian Culture and Business Management*, 23(2), 193–217. https://doi.org/10.1504/IJICBM.2021.115895

Gupta, M., Gupta, D., Rai, P. (2024). Digital payment systems and financial inclusion: Examine how digital payment systems, such as mobile wallets and digital currencies, can improve financial inclusion by providing access to banking services for the unbanked and underbanked population. In: Fortino, G., Kumar, A., Swaroop, A., Shukla, P. (eds) *Proceedings of Third International Conference on Computing and Communication Networks. ICCCN 2023*. Lecture Notes in Networks and Systems, vol 917. Springer, Singapore. https://doi.org/10.1007/978-981-97-0892-5_57

Mello, J. A. (2013). *Strategic Management of Human Resources*, Third Edition, Cengage Learning, Boston, MA.

Rajvanshi, P. R., Singh, T., Gupta, D., & Gupta, M. (2022). Blockchain technology for pharmaceutical drug supply chain management. In Singh, P., Mishra, D., & Seth, K. (eds) *Transformation in Healthcare with Emerging Technologies* (1st ed., pp. 217–230). CRC Press.

Rani, S., Gupta, M., & Gupta, D. (2020). Artificial intelligence and personalized banking. In: Agrawal, R., & Garg, V. (eds) *Transforming Management Using Artificial Intelligence Techniques* (1st ed., pp. 24). CRC Press, Boca Raton, FL. https://doi.org/10.4324/9781003032410

Singh, S., Gupta, D., & Gupta, M. (2022). Optimized task allocation technique using mathematical fuzzy logic in heterogeneous distributed computational system. *2022 International Conference on Computational Intelligence and Sustainable Engineering Solutions (CISES)*, Greater Noida, India, 2022, pp. 37–45. https://doi.org/10.1109/CISES54857.2022.9844410

Sugandha, A., Gupta, D., & Gupta, M. (2023). Impact of training method on trainees learning and implementation on job – A study with special reference to power sector. *AIP Conference Proceedings*, 2427(1), 020020. https://doi.org/10.1063/5.0100893

11 HR Process Automation
Current State and Future Directions

Rakesh Kumar Dixit, Pushpendra Pal Singh, and Balamurugan Balusamy

11.1 INTRODUCTION

Human Resource Management has experienced a sensationally rapid evolution in the past few years mainly because of the evolution of automation technologies such as Artificial Intelligence (AI), Machine Learning (ML), and Robotic Process Automation (RPA). These newly introduced changes have in a broad sense realigned the general features of the HR tasks, giving new ways of improving process and efficiency. Due to the pressure that associations have faced in enhancing tasks and eradicating cost implications in processes, HR divisions have opted for automation as a main strategy. This has enabled the extraction of HR/post specialists from several time-confining administrative tasks—namely finance processing, recruitment, and evaluation of implementation—enabling the experts to instead focus on more 'value' enhancing tasks.

In general, Human Resource Management (HRM) has been implemented in manual processes where a higher level of people involvement was required, particularly for enrollment and for employee execution management in regions. This has now shifted with the use of automation where frameworks are now capable of doing errands that require a lot of investment and effort. For instance, it is now possible for firms to filter thousands of resumes within a moment through the use of AI-controlled frameworks, thereby affirmatively cutting down the time spent on the screening of candidates. The mechanized apparatuses for execution assessments feedback continuously and make use of analyses to predict imminent execution trends. Therefore, associations are in a better position to arrive at factual choices in a bid to enhance worker commitment and, generally, authoritative effectiveness.

As shown by the above benefits, the implementation of automation in the HRM is not without difficulties. One very large concern is the ethical considerations that are associated with the application of AI in management. Despite the effectiveness of AI frameworks, AI risks feeding off the biased input data that might result in discriminated hiring rehearses or prejudiced execution evaluation. Besides, the increasing usage of data in the automation process remains a concern as it makes it easy for firms to infringe data privacy and security laws such as the Overall Data Assurance Regulation (GDPR) in Europe. These moral and lawful difficulties ought to be

DOI: 10.1201/9781032619651-11

contemplated by associations intentionally to ensure that won't flagrant the standards of being reasonable and simplistic for the benefit of automating the process.

The current state of affairs of HR automation which is existent, however, serves merely the first step in the continuum. Advanced innovations such as cognitive AI, blockchain, and other advanced data analytics may have the potential to change HRM even further. For example, Cognitive AI opens the opportunity to integrate the ability to comprehend people on the deepest level into the HR processes; thus, frameworks can understand and satisfy the employees' needs more individually and empathetically. You will learn that blockchain has promised to revolutionize the clarity and security of HR transactions, particularly with regard to finance, and check on employees. These advancements are probably going to play a basic role in the future of HRM despite the fact that they are as of now in their early stages (Podgorodnichenko et al., 2022).

The center ideal of this paper is to offer an appraisal of the current state of development in the aspect of HR automation and likely directions that this field might consider in the coming future. Examining various models, and constructing hypothetical scenarios, it will be possible to determine how the developments that are still in their infancy could revolutionize HR even more. Also, we shall discuss the challenges that may hinder the implementation of these innovations based on moral issues, data privacy concerns, and enhancing new frameworks that fit in existing authoritative architectures. As such, this paper contributes to the current discussions on how innovation is redefining the area of HRM by presenting a clear picture of the current and the future state of automation in the field.

11.2 CURRENT STATE OF HR PROCESS AUTOMATION

There has recently been a great leap in the condition of automating HR processes; changing administrative tasks, procurement of talents, and even strategic HR functions. Use of new technologies in Human Resource processes like AI, Machine learning (ML), and RPA has revolutionized the HR processes, and it helps associations to accomplish higher efficiencies, reduce costs, and go with additional intelligent decisions (Abbas et al., 2022; Heizmann and Fox, 2019).

Some of the key activities such as finance processing, employee records management, and leave records are some of the activities that have been most impacted on through automation. For instance, while RPA automates repetitive tasks, it gives time to the HR specialists and frees them to sharpen their focus on other more complex functions (Fukuda, 2020). Tools such as SAP SuccessFactors, tools for mastering work processes that involve work onboarding and execution, help in the completion of functional skills (Dhanpat et al., 2020). However, the integration of these frameworks is never an easy task and requires a lot of attention. The maintainability of data is still an ever-present concern, as even the computerized systems are still often managed and overseen by people; thus the accuracy of exemptions or when the system addresses complex compliance issues related to work regulations remains a concern (Benade, 2020).

Talent management automation, driven by AI and ML, has changed enrollment and employee engagement processes. AI-fueled frameworks, for example,

LinkedIn Talent Arrangements have streamlined the resume screening process by matching candidates to sets of expectations all the more proficiently (Adekoya, 2022). Regular Language Processing (NLP) advancements survey candidates' capabilities and their social fit in light of data from resumes and web-based entertainment profiles (Amey and Eddy, 2023). Nonetheless, the test of algorithmic bias is ever-present. In the event that AI frameworks are trained on biased verifiable data, they can propagate inequalities, leading to discriminatory hiring rehearses (Triana et al., 2021). Normal reviews and fairness checks are important to guarantee that AI frameworks remain evenhanded and unbiased (Biswas et al., 2021).

Strategic HR automation addresses the cutting edge of HR innovation, where AI, predictive analytics, and cognitive automation intersect to give HR divisions data-driven dynamic capacities. Predictive analytics assist HR with forecasting patterns, for example, employee turnover and efficiency changes, identifying designs that permit associations to design proactively (He et al., 2019). Cognitive AI frameworks broaden these capacities by incorporating the ability to appreciate anyone on a deeper level into direction, allowing HR experts to screen employee feeling and engagement progressively (Bennett and McWhorter, 2021). These advances, however promising, accompany difficulties connected with data privacy and compliance with regulations like GDPR (Harney and Collings, 2021).

While administrative and talent management automation offers clear advantages as far as productivity and cost decrease, associations should address difficulties like data integrity, algorithmic bias, and administrative compliance to completely use the upsides of HR process automation (Graham and Colin, 2023). As these innovations continue to create, the potential for HR divisions to add to strategic dynamic will develop, positioning HR as a basic driver of hierarchical achievement.

11.3 MODEL FOR STRATEGIC AUTOMATION

The intricacy and dynamic nature of strategic HR automation demand a thorough model to guarantee the seamless integration of different HR capabilities. This model is organized into three key layers, each serving a distinct reason within the general framework. At its establishment, the Data Accumulation and Automation Layer gathers and processes broad measures of data, both internal (e.g., employee execution records, finance data, and engagement overviews) and outer (e.g., work market analytics) (Fukuda, 2020). RPA mechanizes essential capabilities like data section and record-keeping in this primary layer, ensuring that data are precise and promptly available for more significant level examination (Tschang and Almirall, 2021). Normal reviews assist with maintaining data integrity, which is pivotal for dynamic processes. Similarly, predictive analytics also play a comparatively less basic function in this layer, developing insights that help HR specialists to make a profound predictive decision on the management and planning of the workforce (Aiginger and Rodrik, 2020). These predictive models yield papers and recommendations that are audited by HR groups in order to provide comfortable interventions.

The last level in this model is the Cognitive AI and Choice Help Layer which further interprets the results of ML and predictive analytics. From a cognitive AI framework perspective, outcomes are estimated and the identification of precise measures provided is also highlighted. Such could be ideas for progression, retention mechanisms, or training programs for employees based on continuous data (El-Farr and Hosseingholizadeh, 2019). Hence, these frameworks invariably learn from criticism and modify the dynamic process in order to ensure that the HR interventions are meaningful and feasible.

11.3.1 Strategic HR Automation in Action

A good example of strategic HR automation would be evident in a context where an organization experiences high turnover rates among mid-level supervisors. In such a case, the mechanized framework starts with gathering valid data on engagement, execution, non-attendance, outer work market trends, or factors affecting the employees and the organization. ML calculations investigate these data to foresee which employees are probably going to leave the organization, in light of elements like declining position fulfillment or terrible showing audits (Carroll and Conboy, 2020). The cognitive AI layer then suggests tailored interventions, for example, authority training amazing open doors or adaptable work courses of action, aimed at improving position fulfillment and retention. As these procedures are carried out, the framework continuously screens their effect, adjusting proposals as new data open up. This proactive, data-driven approach improves the organization's capacity to retain significant employees while ensuring HR assumes a strategic part in shaping the association's drawn out progress (Miller, 2023).

11.3.2 Challenges in Strategic HR Automation

Regardless of the critical advantages presented by strategic HR automation, a few difficulties should be addressed to understand its potential completely. Data privacy and security is a central issue, especially given the delicate idea of the data involved, for example, well-being records, execution assessments, and employee feeling. Compliance with regulations like the Overall Data Insurance Regulation (GDPR) is fundamental to stay away from lawful punishments and guarantee that employee data are handled mindfully (Harney and Collings, 2021). Associations should carry out stringent data assurance strategies to defend against breaks.

One more test lies in the moral contemplations and bias inherent in AI frameworks. AI models trained on biased authentic data can propagate discriminatory practices, particularly in regions like hiring and advancements. For instance, an AI framework that has been trained on data reflecting past orientation or racial biases might continue to incline toward certain gatherings except if the data are consistently examined and differentiated (Triana et al., 2021). Addressing this issue requires ongoing endeavors to moderate bias through thorough model reviews and the inclusion of different data sets.

Furthermore, protection from change is a typical boundary to the reception of strategic HR automation. Numerous HR experts and employees are careful about AI frameworks, fearing that these advances might supplant human judgment and lessen individual interaction in HR processes (Graham and Colin, 2023). It is vital to accentuate that AI and cognitive automation are intended to increase human independent direction, providing HR experts with data-driven insights that improve their capacity to make very much informed, strategic choices, instead of replacing their skills.

11.4 FUTURE DIRECTIONS OF HR PROCESS AUTOMATION

The eventual fate of HR process automation is ready to go through significant changes, driven by the more deeply integration of cutting edge innovations like AI, blockchain, and cognitive computing. These improvements will change HR from a predominantly administrative job to one of strategic significance. By leveraging these innovations, HR divisions will actually want to settle on constant data-driven choices, further develop employee engagement, and make secure, straightforward records of HR exchanges (Parry and Battista, 2023).

11.4.1 AI-Driven Decision-Making

11.4.1.1 Hypothesis

AI frameworks will develop past automating routine undertakings and begin to offer strategic insights that empower associations to make informed, ongoing choices. These AI frameworks won't simply streamline HR works yet will effectively add to basic business choices like workforce planning, authority progression, and employee advancement methodologies.

11.4.1.2 Model

11.4.1.2.1 Tier 1: Administrative Automation

Administrative undertakings, like finance and onboarding, will be completely mechanized using RPA. This will guarantee that monotonous, tedious undertakings are handled with minimal human intervention, leading to cost and time efficiencies.

11.4.1.2.2 Tier 2: AI and ML Models for Prediction

AI models will examine authentic and constant data to foresee patterns like employee turnover, truancy, and execution plunges. For instance, AI could distinguish employees who are probably going to leave in light of declining engagement levels and suggest designated retention procedures (Bennett and McWhorter, 2021).

11.4.1.2.3 Tier 3: Cognitive AI for Strategic Insights

Cognitive AI devices will take predictive analytics a stride further by providing strategic insights. These apparatuses won't just anticipate occasions but additionally suggest activities for initiative progression planning, abilities advancement, and even emotional well-being interventions. For instance, AI could assist HR chiefs with identifying expected pioneers within the association and propose tailored advancement programs for those individuals (Repel and Battista, 2023) (Figure 11.1).

11.4.1.3 Real-Life Scenario

A multinational organization could carry out this AI-driven model to foresee which divisions might confront high employee turnover in view of ongoing execution and engagement data. The cognitive AI instrument would recommend customized retention programs, including compensation changes, proficient improvement open doors, or adaptable work plans (Kuknor and Bhattacharya, 2022). Along these lines,

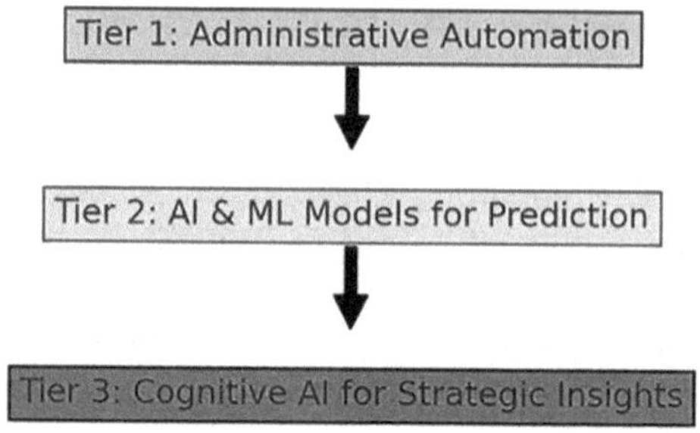

FIGURE 11.1 AI-driven decision-making model.

AI helps HR address current difficulties as well as expect future necessities, positioning HR as a vital strategic accomplice in hierarchical achievement.

11.4.2 Blockchain for HR Transactions

11.4.2.1 Hypothesis

Blockchain innovation will reform HR by creating straightforward, changeless records of HR exchanges. These records, especially for finance and employee check, will give an unrivaled degree of safety and trust, ensuring data integrity and compliance with worldwide regulations.

11.4.2.2 Model

11.4.2.2.1 Decentralized HR Framework

All employee records, including finance, execution assessments, and confirmations, will be put away on a solid blockchain record. Blockchain's decentralized nature guarantees that records can't be changed or messed with, consequently preventing misrepresentation and ensuring straightforwardness.

11.4.2.2.2 Brilliant Agreements for Finance and Employee Advantages

Finance and employee advantages can be overseen through brilliant agreements that consequently execute installments and advantages once predefined conditions are met. For instance, rewards and incentives could be consequently dispersed in view of employee execution assessments without the requirement for manual intervention (Fukuda, 2020) (Figure 11.2).

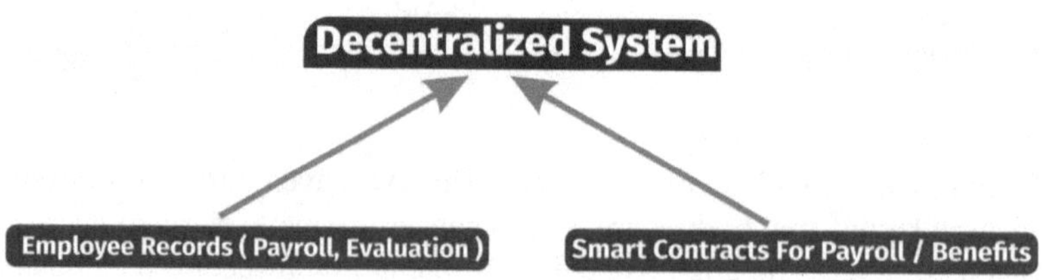

FIGURE 11.2 Blockchain for the HR transactions model.

11.4.2.3 Real-Life Scenario

A worldwide enterprise could execute blockchain to deal with its finance across different nations. Savvy agreements would consequently execute installments in view of the terms of business contracts, ensuring compliance with nearby work regulations. Also, blockchain would permit the organization to confirm employee qualifications and affirmations safely, making it simpler to hire employees from various districts without the gamble of extortion.

11.4.3 Employee Engagement through Cognitive AI

11.4.3.1 Hypothesis

AI frameworks furnished with the capacity to understand people on a profound level will assume a basic part in monitoring employee prosperity, suggesting interventions, and offering customized engagement procedures. These AI-fueled frameworks will become menial helpers that can follow an employee's psychological well-being, position fulfillment, and general prosperity, providing constant criticism and suggestions to the two, employees and management.

11.4.3.2 Model

11.4.3.2.1 AI-Controlled Remote Helpers

Menial helpers furnished with AI and the ability to appreciate people on a deeper level calculation will give customized input to employees. These collaborators will screen ongoing feeling through correspondence stages (e.g., email, internal talks) and suggest interventions, for example, psychological wellness support or extra training assuming an employee gives indications of stress or disengagement (Chen et al., 2021).

11.4.3.2.2 Opinion Examination and Predictive Interventions

Cognitive AI devices will perform feeling examination on employee correspondences and criticism to measure close to home states. In light of this examination, the framework can proactively suggest counseling meetings, changes in responsibility, or expert advancement projects to further develop employee engagement and prosperity (Dutta and Mishra, 2023) (Figure 11.3).

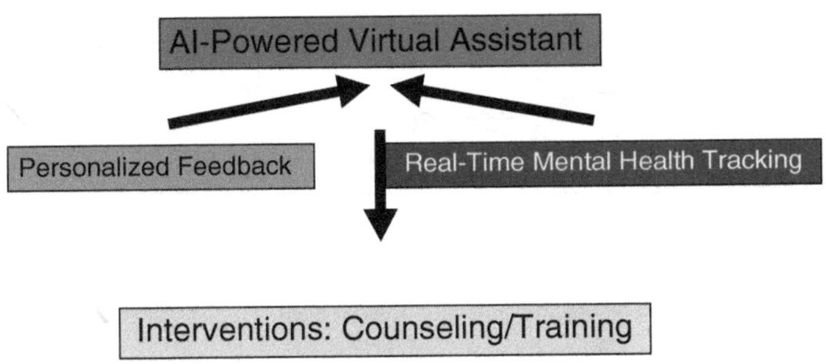

FIGURE 11.3 Employee engagement through the cognitive AI model.

11.4.3.3 Real-Life Scenario

An IT organization facing elevated degrees of burnout among employees could convey cognitive AI apparatuses to screen group interchanges for indications of stress, for example, negative language or strange work designs. At the point when the framework recognizes potential burnout, it can make HR aware of initiating prosperity programs like adaptable work hours, decreased jobs, or psychological wellness counseling, fundamentally improving employee fulfillment and retention.

11.4.4 Predictive Hiring and Cultural Fit Analysis

11.4.4.1 Hypothesis

Profound learning calculations will upset the hiring process by analyzing both express (e.g., capabilities) and implied (e.g., character traits) data during enlistment to survey a candidate's social fit within the association. These AI frameworks will assess different data sources to determine whether a candidate lines up with the organization's qualities, culture, and long haul goals.

11.4.4.2 Model

11.4.4.2.1 Far Reaching Data Investigation

AI frameworks will examine candidate interactions during interviews, their virtual entertainment movement, and even miniature articulations during video interviews to evaluate whether they fit the organization's way of life. Profound learning calculations will assess factors, for example, correspondence style, flexibility, and critical thinking way to deal with measure social fit (Chaudhuri et al., 2022).

11.4.4.2.2 Social Fit Forecast

The framework will utilize verifiable data from effective and ineffective recruits to make a predictive model. This model will rank candidates in light of their arrangement with the organization's way of life, values, and objectives. The examination may likewise include character appraisals and social analytics to guarantee a more all-encompassing assessment of every candidate (Triana et al., 2021) (Figure 11.4).

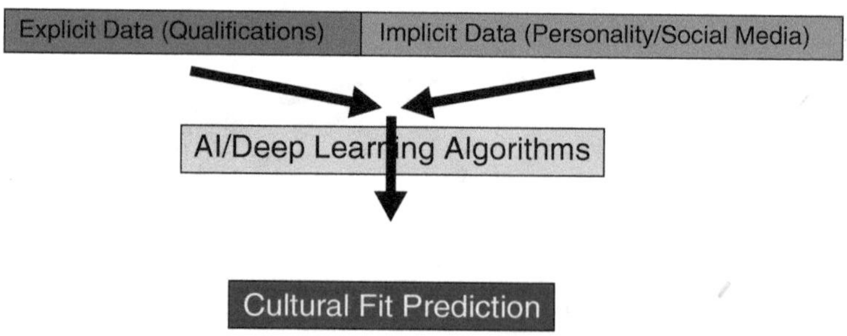

FIGURE 11.4 Predictive hiring and cultural fit analysis model.

11.4.4.2.3 Real-Life Scenario

A quickly developing startup is facing difficulties in reducing employee turnover, especially because of social misalignment. To resolve this issue, the startup chooses to use AI innovation to further develop its hiring process by assessing both the specialized capabilities of candidates and their social fit. Using AI devices during video interviews, the framework will examine candidates' non-verbal communication, discourse designs, looks, and even virtual entertainment action to foresee whether they will thrive in the organization's dynamic, cooperative climate.

11.5 METHODOLOGY

11.5.1 Study Design

This study incorporates a semi trial plan that partitions fresh recruits into two distinct gatherings: a benchmark group, following conventional hiring techniques, and an exploratory gathering, which integrates AI-driven evaluations to determine both specialized capabilities and social fit. The review centers around evaluating the viability of AI-based hiring processes by analyzing their effect on employee turnover rates contrasted with conventional hiring techniques. The independent variable in this study is the hiring technique, ordered into conventional hiring (continue screening and interviews dependent exclusively upon specialized capabilities) and AI-driven hiring (which includes social fit examination using AI apparatuses, for example, video interview evaluations and conduct profiling). The reliant variable is the employee turnover rate, which is estimated as the extent of fresh recruits leaving the organization within the initial year in the wake of being recruited. The review controls for factors, for example, work job, experience level, and group elements to guarantee that distinctions in these variables don't slant the outcomes. By minimizing outer variables that could influence turnover, the review aims to confine the effect of the hiring strategy on retention rates.

11.5.2 Sample

This study draws from an example of 100 employees recruited in more than a year time frame in different branches of a quickly developing startup. The example is parted into two gatherings, with 50 employees in the benchmark group (recruited through conventional techniques) and 50 in the trial bunch (employed through AI-driven strategies). Employees are chosen from a scope of occupation jobs and experience levels, ensuring variety within the example. The AI-based evaluations utilized for the trial bunch include video interview investigation, feeling examination, and character profiling, all of which produce a social fit score to foresee the candidate's arrangement with the organization's qualities and workplace.

11.5.3 Data Collection

For the benchmark group, data include customary resume surveys and interview notes, with employee turnover being followed over the initial year of work. The trial bunch includes data from AI-driven evaluations, for example, video examination of non-verbal communication, discourse designs, and social insights. The two gatherings are checked over the year time frame, with employee execution surveys gathered at the 6-year points to assess work execution and engagement. For employees who leave the organization, subjective data are assembled through post-employment surveys to gain further insight into their purposes behind flight.

11.5.4 Data Analysis

The study depends on both quantitative and subjective data investigation to think about turnover rates between the control and exploratory gatherings. Clear measurements, including mean and middle turnover rates, are determined for each gathering, while segment data, for example, work jobs and long periods of involvement are summed up to guarantee similarity. To test the speculations, a chi-square test is utilized to examine the connection between hiring technique and turnover rates, with an importance level set at $p < 0.05$. Furthermore, a relapse examination might be utilized to investigate the influence of AI-produced social fit scores on the probability of employee turnover, providing a more nuanced understanding of the AI-based hiring process.

11.5.5 Ethical Considerations

This study agrees with all applicable data privacy regulations, including GDPR, ensuring that all employee data, especially video interviews and computerized footprints, are handled safely and straightforwardly. Members are informed of the AI-based appraisals and agree to the assortment and investigation of their data. To address likely biases, the AI calculations utilized in this study are routinely evaluated to guarantee that they don't sustain or introduce biases connected with race, orientation, or other safeguarded qualities. Customary fairness checks are led to ensure evenhanded treatment, all things considered.

11.5.6 Hypotheses

This study tests the following hypotheses:

- H0 (Null Hypothesis): There is no significant difference in turnover rates between employees hired through traditional methods and those hired through AI-driven cultural fit analysis.
- H1 (Alternative Hypothesis): Employees hired through AI-driven cultural fit analysis exhibit a significantly lower turnover rate than those hired through traditional methods.

11.6 ANALYSIS

11.6.1 Analysis of Job Role, Experience, and Turnover Data

Table 11.1 presents a breakdown of the benchmark group by work job and normal experience. It gives an outline of the variety of work jobs within the benchmark

TABLE 11.1
Breakdown by Job Role and Experience (Control Group)

Job Role	Number of Employees	Average Experience (Years)
Engineer	15	2.5
Designer	8	3
Manager	10	5.5
Developer	9	1.5
Analyst	8	4

group and shows that experience shifts, with chiefs having the most long stretches of involvement overall and engineers the least. This table aides in contextualizing what customary hiring strategies could mean for various work types.

Table 11.2 presents the breakdown of the exploratory gathering by work job, including both the normal Social Fit Score and Experience. Supervisors, who have higher normal experience, additionally have the most noteworthy social fit scores, while investigators show moderately lower fit scores. This table offers insights into how AI-based hiring assesses employees across various work jobs as far as both social arrangement and experience levels.

Table 11.3 thinks about the turnover rates between the control and exploratory gatherings for each occupation job. The benchmark group encounters higher turnover rates across all occupation jobs, especially among architects and investigators.

TABLE 11.2
Breakdown by Job Role and Experience (Experimental Group)

Job Role	Number of Employees	Average Cultural Fit Score (Out of 10)	Average Experience (Years)
Engineer	15	8.5	2.5
Designer	8	7.5	3
Manager	10	9	5.5
Developer	9	8.5	1.5
Analyst	8	6.5	4

TABLE 11.3
Comparison of Turnover Rates by Job Role

Job Role	Control Group Turnover Rate (%)	Experimental Group Turnover Rate (%)
Engineer	33	0
Designer	50	0
Manager	20	0
Developer	33	0
Analyst	50	12.5

TABLE 11.4
Experience Levels and Turnover Comparison

Experience Level (Years)	Control Group Turnover Rate (%)	Experimental Group Turnover Rate (%)
0–2	40	10
3–5	20	0
6+	30	0

Interestingly, the trial bunch, which includes AI-driven social fit evaluations, shows fundamentally lower turnover rates, with no turnover among engineers, originators, designers, and directors.

Table 11.4 presents the turnover rates by experience level for both the control and trial gatherings. It uncovers that employees with less experience (0–2 years) have higher turnover rates in the benchmark group (40%) contrasted with the trial bunch (10%), indicating that AI-driven social fit examination might be especially powerful in retaining less experienced employees.

11.6.2 Hypothesis Testing

The *p*-worth of 0.143 is more noteworthy than the importance threshold of 0.05, meaning we fail to dismiss the invalid speculation. For this situation, the distinction in turnover rates between the benchmark group and the exploratory gathering isn't measurably huge. This indicates that, in light of the ongoing example, the AI-driven hiring process doesn't significantly affect reducing turnover contrasted with customary hiring strategies (Tables 11.5 and 11.6).

TABLE 11.5
Turnover Data by Group (Control vs. Experimental)

Group	Left	Stayed
Control group (traditional hiring)	5	5
Experimental group (AI-driven hiring)	1	9

TABLE 11.6
Chi-Square Test Results for Turnover Differences

Test Statistic	Value
Chi-square statistic	2.14
Degrees of freedom	1
P-value	0.143
Significance ($P < 0.05$)	Not significant (false)

11.7 DISCUSSION

The fast reception of automation advancements in HRM has changed how associations deal with their workforce, bringing critical upgrades in proficiency and direction. As verified by Fukuda (2020), the integration of RPA has streamlined redundant errands like finance processing and employee data management, freeing HR experts to zero in on strategic initiatives. This shift is critical for associations aiming to streamline tasks and lessen costs while enhancing employee engagement and generally speaking efficiency.

However, with administrative automation, one has been able to realize measurable benefits while talent management automation challenges are more complex. Enrollment and execution assessment have improved because of the advanced innovation that offers an intelligent approach to spot the candidates and decide on the employee's execution. Adekoya (2022) points out that AI-based tools such as LinkedIn talent arrangement have significantly cut the time and effort required in continue screening and candidate matching. Still, this is an issue of algorithmic bias, which undoubtedly remains a challenge. Triana et al. (2021) pointed out that concentrates by Triana et al., AI frameworks, although may not be closely scrutinized and audited, might perpetrate biases in hiring and progression, when the said frameworks are trained on contingents of authentic data that themselves contained biases. To alleviate these dangers, associations should perform solid fairness examines and improve the information sets used for preparing AI estimations.

Additionally, the eventual fate of HR process automation is probably going to be molded by emerging advancements like blockchain and cognitive AI, which vow to improve straightforwardness and dynamic abilities. Blockchain, for instance, gives a protected and changeless framework for managing finance and employee confirmation processes, addressing worries about extortion and data control (Fukuda, 2020). Blockchain's decentralized nature guarantees compliance with worldwide regulations, for example, the GDPR, a fundamental variable given the increasing scrutiny on data privacy (Harney and Collings, 2021). Simultaneously, cognitive AI frameworks furnished with the ability to appreciate individuals on a deeper level could reform employee engagement, offering customized prosperity procedures through continuous monitoring and opinion investigation (Dutta and Mishra, 2023).

In spite of these promising headways, associations face critical difficulties in the reception of strategic HR automation. Bennett and McWhorter (2021) recommend that while predictive analytics and cognitive AI offer useful assets for workforce planning and employee retention, they require significant initial investments and hierarchical change. Protection from change, especially from HR experts worried about the ramifications of AI for employer stability, remains a hindrance to execution (Graham and Colin, 2023). Furthermore, moral contemplations connected with AI-driven direction, particularly regarding straightforwardness and responsibility, should be addressed to guarantee that the advantages of automation are acknowledged without undermining trust and fairness in HR processes.

11.8 CONCLUSION

HR process automation has in a general sense changed the field of HRM, offering associations new roads to improve effectiveness, lessen expenses, and pursue data-driven choices. From administrative undertakings, like finance and leave management, to additional strategic regions like talent securing and workforce planning, the integration of innovations like AI, ML, and RPA has altogether diminished manual jobs and further developed HR tasks. The advancement of the strategic HR methodology with the help of automation, enabled by the undertaking of sophisticated, powerful solutions such as AI, big data, and blockchain, has showcased this capability's potential of providing core insights on workforce plans and controlling many of the retention processes and engagement methods. Nevertheless, as it will be seen, despite the many advantages, challenges such as data privacy, introducing algorithmic bias, and compliance with the administration remain formidable. Since associations rely progressively on the computerized systems for handling HR procedures, managing these moral and legitimate issues becomes essential to HRM to guarantee straightforward and reasonable procedures. However, safeguarding from change inside associations includes the respect of feasible communication on the role of AI in enhancing as opposed to eradicating human direction.

The future of HR automation is likely to seem as more elaborate frames which include the capacity to comprehend and appreciate people and dynamic capacities for integration into the HR functions. Blockchain assures to enhance the simplicity and clarity of HR transactions and, at the same time, AI goes on to evolve to provide a strategic decision-making enabler, aimed at real-time decision-making via data processing. Over time these innovations will develop and HR will stop being an administrative function and then turn into a crucial strategic partner in the organization's development and employee well-being.

In other words, a certain methodical approach is necessary for the associations to fully harness the benefits of HR automation, which at the same time considers the ethical and social implications of the mechanical innovations. Thusly, businesses can guarantee that automation improves their functional productivity as well as the general prosperity of their workforce, creating a more sustainable and inclusive future for HR management.

REFERENCES

Abbas, A., Ekowati, D., & Suhariadi, F. (2022). Social perspective: leadership in changing society. In M. I. Hassan, S. S. Roy, U. Chatterjee, S. Chakraborty, U. Singh (Eds.), *Social Morphology, Human Welfare, and Sustainability* (pp. 89–107). Cham: Springer International Publishing.

Adekoya, O. (2022). Responsible Management: Promoting Work-Life Balance through Social Sustainability and Green HRM (Doctoral dissertation, University of East London).

Aiginger, K., & Rodrik, D. (2020). Rebirth of industrial policy and an agenda for the twenty-first century. *Journal of Industry, Competition and Trade*, 20, 189–207.

Amey, M. J., & Eddy, P. L. (2023). *Creating Strategic Partnerships: A Guide for Educational Institutions and Their Partners*. New York: Taylor & Francis.

Benade, L. (2020). Is the classroom obsolete in the twenty-first century? In L. Benade, M. Jackson (Eds.), *Design, Education and Pedagogy* (pp. 6–17). London: Routledge.

Bennett, E. E., & McWhorter, R. R. (2021). Virtual HRD's role in crisis and the post Covid-19 professional lifeworld: accelerating skills for digital transformation. *Advances in Developing Human Resources*, 23(1), 5–25.

Biswas, K., Boyle, B., & Bhardwaj, S. (2021, February). Impacts of supportive HR practices and organisational climate on the attitudes of HR managers towards gender diversity–a mediated model approach. *EvidenceBased HRM: A Global Forum for Empirical Scholarship*, 9(1), 18–33. Emerald Publishing Limited.

Carroll, N., & Conboy, K. (2020). Normalising the "new normal": changing tech-driven work practices under pandemic time pressure. *International Journal of Information Management*, 55, 102186.

Chaudhuri, S., Park, S., & Johnson, K. R. (2022). Engagement, inclusion, knowledge sharing, and talent development: is reverse mentoring a panacea to all? Findings from literature review. *European Journal of Training and Development*, 46(5/6), 468–483

Chen, M., Ran, B., Gao, X., Yu, G., Wang, J., & Jagannathan, J. (2021). Evaluation of occupational stress management for improving performance and productivity at workplaces by monitoring the health, well-being of workers. *Aggression and Violent Behavior*, 60, 101713.

Dhanpat, N., Buthelezi, Z. P., Joe, M. R., Maphela, T. V., & Shongwe, N. (2020). Industry 4.0: the role of human resource professionals. *SA Journal of Human Resource Management*, 18(1), 1–11.

Dutta, D., & Mishra, S. K. (2023). Bots for mental health: the boundaries of human and technology agencies for enabling mental well-being within organizations. *Personnel Review*, 53, 1129.

El-Farr, H., & Hosseingholizadeh, R. (2019). Aligning human resource management with knowledge management for better organizational performance: how human resource practices support knowledge management strategies? In M. Wickham (Ed.), *Current Issues in Knowledge Management* (pp. 1–27). London: IntechOpen.

Fukuda, K. (2020). Science, technology and innovation ecosystem transformation toward society 5.0. *International Journal of Production Economics*, 220, 107460.

Graham, J., & Colin, C. (2023). Exploring the dynamics of education in Australia: policies, practices, and progressions in the 21st century. *Influence: International Journal of Science Review*, 5(3), 14–23.

Harney, B., & Collings, D. G. (2021). Navigating the shifting landscapes of HRM. *Human Resource Management Review*, 31(4), 100824.

He, B., An, R., & Berry, J. (2019). Psychological adjustment and social capital: A qualitative investigation of Chinese expatriates. *Cross Cultural & Strategic Management*, 26(1), 67–92.

Heizmann, H., & Fox, S. (2019). O Partner, Where Art Thou? A critical discursive analysis of HR managers' struggle for legitimacy. *The International Journal of Human Resource Management*, 30(13), 2026–2048.

Kuknor, S. C., & Bhattacharya, S. (2022). Inclusive leadership: new age leadership to foster organizational inclusion. *European Journal of Training and Development*, 46(9), 771–797.

Li, M. (2023). Adapting legal education for the changing landscape of regional emerging economies: a dynamic framework for law majors. *Journal of the Knowledge Economy*, 15, 1–30.

Miller, D. (2023). Embracing the technological metamorphosis: envisioning higher education for generation alpha in a shifting educational landscape. *International Journal Software Engineering and Computer Science (IJSECS)*, 3(2), 88–96.

Parry, E., & Battista, V. (2023). The impact of emerging technologies on work: a review of the evidence and implications for the human resource function. *Emerald Open Research*, 1(4). https://doi.org/10.1108/EOR-04-2023-0001

Peng, Y., & Lorenzo, L. C. (2023). Corporate sales in the digital era: the relationship between human resource technology integration and organizational performance. *Frontiers in Business, Economics and Management*, 10(2), 289–303.

Podgorodnichenko, N., Akmal, A., Edgar, F., & Everett, A. M. (2022). Sustainable HRM: toward addressing diverse employee roles. *Employee Relations: The International Journal*, 44(3), 576–608.

Triana, M. D. C., Gu, P., Chapa, O., Richard, O., & Colella, A. (2021). Sixty years of discrimination and diversity research in human resource management: a review with suggestions for future research directions. *Human Resource Management*, 60(1), 145–204.

Tschang, F. T., & Almirall, E. (2021). Artificial intelligence as augmenting automation: implications for employment. *Academy of Management Perspectives*, 35(4), 642–659.

12 The Intersection of Technology and Social Science

Transforming HR Functions and Shaping Futuristic Trends

Neha Aggarwal and Kriti Bhaswar Singh

12.1 INTRODUCTION

In today's rapidly evolving landscape, every facet of operations from the boardroom to factory floor, from managing our day-to-day tasks to making the optimum utilization of resources, from maintaining customer relationships to supply chain logistics, all is entwined with the technology within an organization. This pervasive integration of technology has left no room for complacency or resistance to change. It has become an indispensable driving force behind innovation, efficiency, and competitive advantage in the business world and the businesses that embrace and adapt to technology's impact will be the ones to thrive and can get first mover advantage.[1] They gain the ability to streamline processes, leverage data-driven insights, and deliver seamless customer experiences. On the other hand, those who fail to adapt risk being left behind in an increasingly interconnected and digitized marketplace.

The Human Resource (HR) department plays a pivotal role in ensuring the success and growth of organizations. Traditionally viewed as a cost centre where managers show little or no interest of an employee well-being, primarily focused on administrative tasks, but now HR functions have sparked a shift from a purely administrative role to that of a strategic contributor within organizations. Digitalization has cleared the path for HR professionals to play an important role in improving organizations' value chains, aligning human management with business objectives, and cultivating a more flexible and inventive workforce. Technological advancements such as automation and predictive analysis have transformed industries in several ways. From screening resumes to hiring talents, handling payroll, and assessing performance of an employee to providing required training, everything is revolutionized so that HR managers can now focus on strategic initiatives that can help the company to compete. One of the biggest technological advancements in HR is the introduction

DOI: 10.1201/9781032619651-12

of Internet of Things (IoT). Integrating IoT with HR leads to a more connected and responsive workplace.

The study explores the transformation held in the field of HR with the introduction of technology such as automation, predictive analysis, chatbots, and blockchain technology. It tries to emphasize on how HR professional can embrace the technology in reshaping the field of workforce management so that HR department can act as a strategic player to amplify the success of the organization.

12.2 HR PRACTICES THEN AND NOW

HR management is more than just hiring and maintaining the best talent for the organization. Earlier it was believed that a HR manager will screen the pool of candidatures and select the best suitable candidate for the organization. With time HR department evolved as one of the most crucial departments for the success of an organization. Humans were treated as the most valuable asset and maintaining suitable and competent workforce gained momentum and then form where HR was formed as a separate department. This was where it became quite clear that there was a need for an HR function that would focus on different facets of employee requirements and align them to the organizational goals. The HR department is mainly responsible for recruitment, employee development, performance management, employee relations, and creating a positive work environment. The HR department is becoming essential for development and career advancement, motivating employees, and creating a work culture. Basically, a compilation for HR department grew as an integral part in the new-age organization to systematically manage the prime asset of the organization, i.e., its employee.

The role of HR has changed significantly in relation to workforce management. HR was mostly responsible for administrative duties like as payroll processing, record keeping, and law compliance from the beginning of 1900s until 1940s. The phrase "personnel management" was first used during the Hawthorne Experiment, which took place between the 1950s and the 1970s, recognized "human" as the most valuable asset for an organization, and discussed its better treatment.

In the year 1980s and 1990s, the term "human resource management" was widely used. In this era, HR evolved as a strategic partner by aligning its goals with the organizational goals. In the areas of employee development, talent acquisition, and performance management, HR professionals began to play a more significant role. This period saw HR developing into a more essential capability. It further developed into a strategic function in the 2000s, with a strong emphasis on integrating HR strategies with overall business goals. Ability of the board, progression arranging, and representative engagement became basic areas of concentration. HR pioneers effectively took part in essential decision-production at the leader level. The rise of digital tools and technology in the 2010s changed HR practices completely. Cloud-based human resource information systems (HRIS), applicant tracking systems (ATS), and Human Resource analytics tools became commonplace, streamlining HR operations and providing data-driven insights for better decision-making. The present era is characterized by people analytics and artificial intelligence (AI)-driven, where HR embraces data analytics and artificial intelligence to optimize talent management, employee experience, and workforce planning. HR leverages people analytics to make evidence-based decisions and predict workforce trends. Moreover, it has shifted its focus towards creating positive employee experiences and promoting employee well-being. The future lies in its ability to play a strategic role in shaping organizational culture, driving innovation, and fostering a diverse and inclusive work environment. The COVID-19 pandemic has accelerated the adoption of remote and hybrid work models, prompting to adapt and support flexible work arrangements while addressing new challenges in managing virtual teams. As HR continues to evolve, staying agile, embracing emerging technologies, and anticipating the changing needs of the workforce will be essential for HR professionals to thrive and succeed in the dynamic business landscape.

A survey conducted by Oracle and Future Workplace AI (2019) showed that the rise of AI in the workplace is no longer a threat rather people are ready to adopt the technology and can see its possibilities.[2] 53% of respondents, who had practical expertise in AI and machine learning, were enthusiastic and upbeat about working with robots. Earlier, AI was frequently viewed as a danger to job loss, but today, leaders throughout the world are viewing it as a chance to enhance the workplace. As a result of having more free time to devote to training and development as well as expanding their present function to make it more strategic (28%), 36% of respondents to the poll indicated that AI will assist employees in learning new skills and 82% of poll participants responded that robots are capable of performing some tasks superior to managers. A staggering 64% of respondents claimed that they would trust a robot more than their manager. Yet managers are more effective than robots at tasks including counselling employees (33%), understanding their sentiments (45%), and assessing team performance (26%). However, robots do responsibilities such as giving objective information (36%) and upholding work schedules (34%) better than human bosses.

Also, in another study by PWC shows that by 2030, AI could contribute a staggering $15.7 trillion to the global economy.[3] Over 55% of all GDP gains from AI are anticipated to come from increases in labour productivity between 2017 and 2030.

12.3 ROLE OF TECHNOLOGY IN TRANSFORMING HR FUNCTIONS

As we are heading into the era of Industrial Revolution 4.0, organizations are increasingly embracing innovative technological solutions to optimize their operations and enhance decision-making processes. HR func ` tions, a critical component of any organization, are also not immune to this transformative wave. As organizations strive to stay competitive and thrive in this dynamic environment, they are increasingly turning to cutting-edge technological solutions, with a particular emphasis on AI, to revolutionize their HR functions.

This study explores the transformative role of AI in HRs management, highlighting its impact on strategic planning, decision-making, talent acquisition, and organizational performance.[4] For instance, AI-powered ATSs have significantly expedited the recruitment process by efficiently screening hundreds of resumes and identifying the most suitable candidates based on predefined criteria. Furthermore, customized learning platforms driven by technology have allowed employees to access tailored programs, fostering skill development, and boosting overall productivity. However, HR competencies play a significant role in adoption of such evolving technology that can result in overall growth and success of the organization (Penpokai et al., 2023).

12.3.1 Talent Acquisition and Screening

Being an HR, one has to deal with the abundance of resumes to not only fill the vacant position but also to deal with challenge of hiring the best candidates among the list of applicants. AI-based algorithm-fed tools can act as a saviour. The predefined set of skills needed for the job can help HR to eliminate non-eligible resumes in one go, which could save a lot of effort and time as AI uses text keywords, phrases, or patterns to separate the desirable candidates from the undesirable ones. One remarkable example of technology's impact on HR is the implementation of ATS. ATS utilizes AI algorithms to screen and analyse a vast pool of resumes, effectively identifying the most suitable candidates based on predefined criteria. This process expedites the hiring cycle, reduces administrative burden, and ensures a more data-driven approach to selection.[5] Also attitudes towards an organization also play an important role in the minds of job seekers who constantly visit websites frequently. The study Allen et al. (2007) showed that people's attitudes toward a company's website had a significant impact on their overall perception of the organization as a potential employer. A well-designed and professional website can give a positive impression of the company and make applicants more interested in working there. Moreover, the research highlighted that the information available on the website, such as details about the job and the organization, also influenced job seekers' intentions to pursue employment with that company. In other words, if a website provides the information job seekers are looking for and presents the company in a favourable light, it can increase their interest in applying for a job. The study also emphasized that the experience of interacting with a company's website can be just as crucial as having contact with actual company representatives like interviewers. Another survey (Chapman and Webster, 2003) collected data from HR professionals representing 125 organizations, all of which were members of the Society for Human Resource Management[6] and held corporate-level positions with 'Employment/Recruitment' as their primary function. Notably, none of the companies viewed technology use in HR as a passing trend; instead, they expressed firm intentions to increase reliance on technology-based recruitment and selection approaches. The companies believed that employing technology in the screening process could lead to reduced hiring cycles and costs, while optimizing HR resources to identify the most qualified candidates.[7] Lastly, diversity and inclusion initiatives have benefited from technology integration. AI-enabled software can mitigate bias in recruitment processes by anonymizing candidate information, ensuring fair and equitable selection based solely on qualifications and skills (Table 12.1).

12.3.2 Hiring and Onboardingw

AI is used by HR managers to acquire fresh talents by shortlisting qualified applications. AI is used to map desired skill sets, expertise, and competency from a big pool of data from many industries. Additionally, chatbots with AI capabilities are being

TABLE 12.1
Technology Transforming HR Practices

HR Function	Example of Technology Usage
Talent acquisition	Applicant Tracking System (ATS): Automatically screens resume to identify qualified candidates based on predefined criteria (predefined keywords)
Employee onboarding	Onboarding Software facilitates a digital onboarding process, streamlining paperwork, training, and HR tasks
Performance management	Performance Management Software enables continuous feedback, goal tracking, and data-driven performance evaluations
Employee engagement	Employee Engagement Surveys utilize digital surveys to gather employee feedback and gauge satisfaction levels
Training and development	Learning Management System offers online courses and personalized training programs for employee skill enhancement
Payroll and benefits	Automated Payroll System calculates and processes employee payments and benefits in an accurate and timely manner
HR analytics	People Analytics Software analyses HR data to gain about workforce trends and make informed strategic decisions
Talent management	Talent Relationship Management Software nurtures and maintains relationships with potential candidates for future hiring needs
Workforce planning	Predictive Analytics Tools use historical data to fore-cast future workforce needs and develop workforce planning strategies
Employee offboarding	Exit Management Software automates the offboarding process, ensuring a smooth transition for departing employees
Employee data security	HRIS with Encryption and Access Controls safeguards sensitive employee information with encryption and restricted access protocols

utilized to screen and shortlist qualified individuals. Companies such as Unilever hired the AI-enabled platform Hire Vue, reduced the time to hire by 90%, and enhance hiring diversity by 16% as these platforms are mainly devoted to gathering applications from multiple sources. These platforms are primarily used to collect applications from various sources. This has eliminated the gap between employers and job seekers. Among the few businesses employing Mya Systems, which facilitates hiring from applicant screening to employee onboarding, are L'Oréal and Deloitte. LeenaAI is another example, which is a US-based start-up that is engaged in providing HR-related expertise to its clients. Employers can simply improve the evaluation of candidates by placing them in virtual circumstances with the use of IoT technology and HRMS integration. This will make it easier to assess each candidate's behaviour individually.

12.3.3 Personalized Training and Development

The HR managers can be guided by machine learning and natural language processing (NLP) to identify the disparity between the abilities required by the organization for a specific work position and those of an employee already had and what kind of training is required for the employees. Employee training and development is equivalent to organizational development (Sakka et al., 2022). The employee could receive efficient training with the use of such tools and methods. As offline training classes have been replaced by online classes where professionals from many fields can participate and share their insights to train employees, the cost burden on businesses has also decreased. These technologically based applications have made on-the-job training more accessible. IoT will make it possible for newly hired staff within a corporation to learn in a simulated setting. Employees will then engage in embedding activities related to training, such as putting out fires and putting together product components. Using analytics and video sensors, the trainers will be able to obtain precise information on how employees are doing during the learning process and make the required adjustments.

12.3.4 Employee Engagement

With the increasing shift towards tech-driven HR functions, employee engagement platforms are one of the clear outcomes of such major transformations in an organization. By using AI-powered sentiment analysis and feedback tools, these platforms allow for real-time insights that give HR teams the ability to measure employee satisfaction and sentiment. With all this streaming data, action can be taken in real time to prevent employee flight. In addition, the use of machine learning algorithms in predictive analytics for talent management is also increasing. Advanced tools, such as those that study employee data and performance indicators, will uncover patterns and predict future success. These are the kinds of capabilities HR professionals can use to get ahead of employee needs and identify potential obstacles. This strategic insertion of technology is indicative of HR's commitment to making the workplace a more integrated and inclusive space for employment.[8]

12.3.5 Performance Appraisal

AI-embedded tools have smoothened and also expedited the process of monitoring and providing appropriate feedback to the employees (Hmoud and Laszlo, 2019). IoT devices can ease the workload of HR staff by collecting feedback. For example, cameras can capture an employee's expressions after a meeting to deliver real-time feedback. It can be used to compile data, keep a database for the same, and conduct evaluations by contrasting employee goals with those of the company's standard performance measure. Technology is greatly assisting in HR analytics, which is the process of collecting, storing, and analysing HR data in order to improve workforce performance in an organization. IoT has a positive impact in terms of enhancing the productivity of employees in an organization.

12.3.6 Competency Mapping

This will make it easier to create a competency model that will help to pinpoint the precise knowledge and abilities required for the job, enabling the individual to perform at his/her peak for the benefit of the company. Along with intellectual ability, this also emphasizes physical ability, which allows an employee to carry out the duty physically, as well as behavioural and social ability, which helps to keep peace and minimize conflict inside the organization. An employee's ability to grow personally will be aided by behavioural competency. An AI-based competence model will provide a roadmap by first identifying the competencies or abilities required for the specific job position, then it will direct how to make these talents accessible so that an employee can acquire them and apply them to perform better. Last but not least, the machine can assist in gathering comments and rating the employee so that he or she might be inspired to work more. Thus, an AI-based model will not only help in analysing the exact competency needed but also in retaining talents.

12.3.7 Employee Database and Contract Management

Blockchain technology is being used to encrypt and store employee data for payroll or managing contracts by certain organizations. The application of blockchain technology is low in the case of the HR domain as compared to the field of finance. Blockchain has emerged as a key technological tool for maintaining and sharing personnel repositories among parties for background and reference checks on experience and necessary skill sets in the IT sector, which has a high attrition rate.

Additionally, it assists in lowering the transaction costs associated with storing such a vast amount of data. As the data are virtually saved using blockchain technology, it can also lower the chances of a data breach. HR analytics—the process of gathering, storing, and evaluating HR data to enhance worker performance in an organization—benefits immensely from technology. Organizations always work to protect and preserve their internal talent in order to make the necessary adjustments to their HR management practices. IoT technology can assist in accomplishing this flawlessly. Employees will become frustrated if the proper modifications are not made. This significantly lowers worker engagement. Employees can, however, very quickly adapt to IoT.

The table below shows several instances of technology's role in optimizing HR practices, liberating HR professionals from tedious tasks like going through numerous job applications to gather and maintain each employee records. By leveraging these technological advancements, HR experts can focus on devising strategic HR approaches to enhance workforce efficiency (Table 12.2).

12.4 EMERGING TECHNOLOGY AND ITS POTENTIAL IN HR PRACTICES

The future of HR technology will be driven by a human-centric approach, where technology complements and enhances the employee experience. As organizations embrace these advancements, HR will continue to evolve into a strategic partner, fostering a dynamic and engaged workforce that drives business success in the digital age.

12.4.1 IoT Devices in HR

The advent of Industry 4.0 has brought new opportunities for HR professionals to embrace smart HR competences. It has led to an interpersonal relationship with the employees. With the introduction IoT gadgets such as wearables and smart devices, employers can constantly check on the well-being of employees and can motivate them to perform better. This can help in enhancing the overall productivity and efficiency of the organization.

TABLE 12.2
Role of Technology in Optimizing HR Practices

Software/ Application	Usage
IBM Watson Orchestrate	• Utilize Natural Language Processing (NLP) to automate HR tasks of acquiring and retaining fresh talents • Collecting and maintaining huge employee databases • Eliminates tedious and repetitive tasks so that HR professionals can focus on strategic decision-making
SAP Success Factors	• A human resource solution software • Provides a diverse range of applications from recruit to retire • One stop solution from recruitment and onboarding to employee engagement, payroll, and performance management
Trello Employees	• A project management tool • Can be used by HR teams to track and manage various HR projects, such as recruitment campaigns and training initiatives • Provide an inbuilt template for team workspace with calendar view to ensure timely completion of task and managers can keep a track of the same
Slack	• Communication platform that facilitates real-time messaging and collaboration, enabling HR teams to communicate efficiently and share important updates • Facilitates a rapid onboarding process • Maintaining data well-organized and easily accessible
Kazoo	• An employee recognition and rewards platform • Helps HR teams foster a positive and engaged workforce by recognizing and rewarding employee achievements • Has 99% of customer satisfaction score
Switch	• Mobile application for networking job search • Popular tool as easy to use by job seekers, swipe-based interface like Tinder where users can "swipe right" to indicate interest in a job or connection and "swipe left" to pass
Mya Systems	• Uses conversational AI and natural language processing to engage with candidates throughout the recruitment journey, from application to onboarding • Conducts automated screening of employees by integrating itself to various job or career websites • Schedules automated interviews, ensure smooth conduction of interview process • Collects and analyses data to provide insights to the recruiter for formulating hiring strategies

12.4.2 Blockchain Technology in HR

Blockchain technology is used by HR professionals in order to enhance security and transparency particularly in the area of verification of candidate credentials and the management of employee records as data once recorded on the blockchain cannot be altered. The information stored on the blockchain is secure, transparent, and trustworthy, as it provides a permanent and unalterable record of transactions or data entries.[9] Machine learning algorithms continuously evolve talent prediction models, aiding in talent retention and succession planning.

12.4.3 Social Media Integration

Social media platforms are used for employer branding, talent sourcing, and employee engagement initiatives, expanding the organization's reach and enhancing employer reputation.

12.4.4 AI and Machine Learning Advancements

AI will continue to play a central role in HR technology, with machine learning algorithms becoming more sophisticated. AI-driven chatbots will handle employee queries and provide personalized support. Machine learning will further enhance talent acquisition, enabling recruiters to identify the best-fit candidates with greater accuracy. AI-powered chatbots and virtual assistants streamline employee queries and support, enhancing the employee experience. AI-driven talent acquisition tools improve candidate screening and selection, saving time and resources. AI-driven analytics offer valuable insights into workforce trends, helping HR professionals make data-driven decisions (Jarrahi, 2018).

12.5 RECOMMENDATIONS

In the current business landscape, technology has taken centre stage, with a strong emphasis on terms and concepts like cloud computing, big data analytics, social media integration, gamification, IoT, robotic process automation, chatbots, virtual

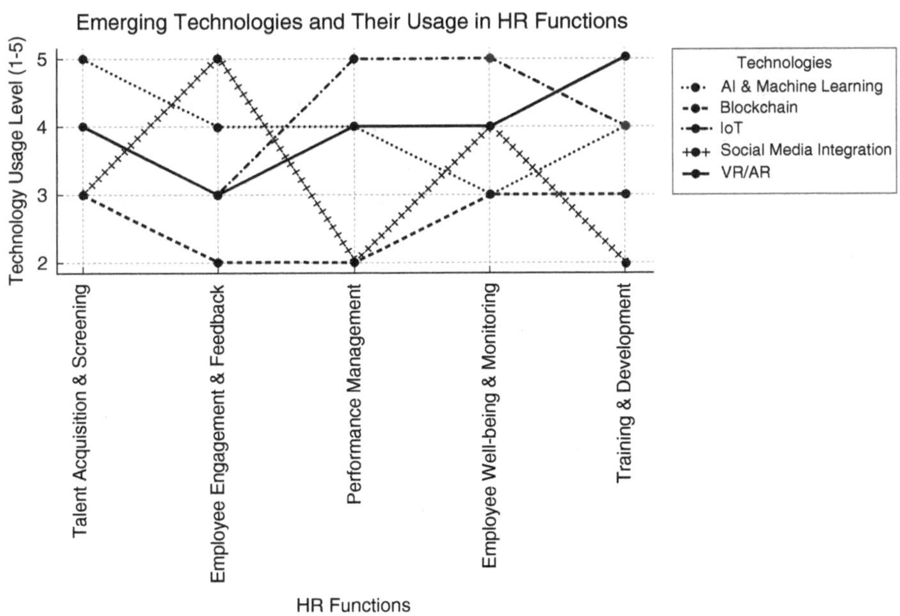

FIGURE 12.1 Depicting usage of various emerging technologies.

and augmented reality (VR/AR), blockchain, AI, machine learning, and more. HR professionals are leveraging advanced tech tools to revolutionize talent acquisition, employee engagement, and performance management. Organizations should invest in HR analytics tools to gather and analyse data on employee performance, engagement, and well-being (Figure 12.1). Data-driven insights can inform strategic decision-making, talent management, and workforce planning. Leveraging AI-based ATSs and chatbots can streamline candidate sourcing, screening, and communication. This will enhance the efficiency of the hiring process and improve the candidate experience. Achieving HR transformation through the implementation and adoption of HR technology goes beyond merely introducing the tools and systems.

The true success of this transformation lies in the correct optimization and strategic utilization of these technologies by HR experts and professionals (Jani et al., 2023). Through effective optimization, HR professionals can harness the full potential of HR technology, driving positive business outcomes and enhancing the overall success of the organization.

HR professionals need to establish strong data security protocols, including encryption, access controls, and routine data audits, to prevent unauthorized access and data breaches. Employees need to know how their data are used. Ethics are important in handling employee data. HR should get consent before using data. Data should only be used for HR reasons. Data privacy builds trust with employees. Technology and HR work together. HR uses tech for success. HR balances tech and human needs for a better future of the organization. By leveraging the power of these technological advancements in the field of human interaction, HR is now evolving into a strategic partner as routine task of an HR is simplified.[10]

12.6 CONCLUSION

The study concludes that the availability of technology with its intersection in social sciences not only creates but is embedding a new era for HR functions related to talent acquisition and workforce management. It showed that AI-driven tools and software are instrumental in changing HR practices for the better, providing substantial benefits to a multitude of organizations from almost all the sectors. AI-powered HR technologies will only develop further in the future, offering a set of new business opportunities and threats alike. The HR functions can adapt and ride the wave of an ever-evolving and competitive environment by tapping into the power of technologies and by being ethical and transparent. Access to continued research and innovation in the space of technology and social science is what will help us move forward and realize the full potential of AI in HR.

In addition, such progress may enable organizations to recognize the experts, anticipate the experience required, personalize development plans, transform a "culture of learning" into a reality, and even help establish a new benchmark in the workplace, thus fostering a new wave of progress and innovation in each Industry.

NOTES

1 Capgemini Invent. (2018). Now or never – HR's need to shape its own future.
2 https://www.oracle.com/a/ocom/docs/applications/hcm/oracle-ai-in-hr-wp.pdf

3 PWC. Artificial intelligence in HR: A no brainer.
4 Capgemini Invent. (2020). How automation and augmentation will change the future of HR.
5 https://www.managementstudyguide.com/case-of-amazon-ai-powered-recruitment-tool-means-for-other-corporates.htm
6 https://www.shrm.org/hr-today/trends-and-forecasting/special-reports-and-expert-views/documents/hr-technology.pdf
7 https://medium.com/tech-cult-heartbeat/5-companies-that-are-revolutionizing-recruiting-using-artificial-intelligence
8 https://www.qandle.com/blog/artificial-intelligence-the-future-of-employee-management/
9 Capgemini Invent. (2020). How automation and augmentation will change the future of HR.
10 Ashawathappa, K. (2017). *Human Resource Management Text and Cases* (8th Ed.) McGraw Hill Education India.

REFERENCES

Allen, D. G., Mahto, R. V., and Otondo, R. F. (2007). Web-based recruitment: Effects of information, organizational brand, and attitudes toward a web site on applicant attraction. *Journal of Applied Psychology*, 92(6):1696.

Chapman, D. S., and Webster, J. (2003). The use of technologies in the recruiting, screening, and selection processes for job candidates. *International Journal of Selection and Assessment*, 11(2–3):113–120.

Hmoud, B., and Laszlo, V. (2019). Will artificial intelligence take over human resources recruitment and selection? *Network Intelligence Studies*, 7(13):21–30.

Jani, A., Muduli, A., and Kishore, K. (2023). Human resource transformation in India: Examining the role digital human resource technology and human resource role. *International Journal of Organizational Analysis*, 31(4):959–972.

Jarrahi, M. H. (2018). Artificial intelligence and the future of work: Human-AI symbiosis in organizational decision making. *Business Horizons*, 61(4):577–586.

Penpokai, S., Vuthisopon, S., and Saengnoree, A. (2023). The relationships between technology adoption, HR competencies, and HR analytics of large-size enterprises. *International Journal of Professional Business Review*, 8(3): e 0971–e0971.

Sakka, F., El Maknouzi, M. E. H., and Sadok, H. (2022). Human resource management in the era of artificial intelligence: Future HR work practices, anticipated skill set, financial and legal implications. *Academy of Strategic Management Journal*, 21:1–14.

13 Building the HR Function of the Future

Technology and Beyond

Deepa Gupta, Mukul Gupta,
Rajesh Kumar Dhanaraj, and Parth Mukul Gupta

13.1 INTRODUCTION

13.1.1 Overview of Human Resources (HR) Evolution

The job of HR has gone through huge transformation throughout the long term, evolving from an essential administrative function to an essential accomplice in hierarchical achievement. All things considered, HR was predominantly centered around administrative undertakings like finance, recruitment, and consistence. These customary jobs were fundamental for managing employee records, handling complaints, and ensuring adherence to work regulations [5].

In the mid 20th century, HR offices were generally viewed as a help function, essentially worried about managing employee benefits, maintaining staff documents, and addressing employee relations issues [12]. The attention was on ensuring that the association's HR were very much overseen and agreeable with guidelines [6].

The late 20th century denoted the beginning of a more essential way to deal with HR. With the ascent of globalization and mechanical progressions, HR professionals started to assume a more essential part in hierarchical turn of events. Vital HR arose as an idea where HR professionals were administrators as well as essential accomplices involved in shaping the association's way of life, aligning HR rehearses with business objectives, and fostering employee commitment.

In the 21st century, the job of HR has expanded further with the approach of technology and data analytics. HR offices are presently leveraging progressed tools and systems to drive dynamic cycles, improve talent management, and add to general business procedures. The center has moved to creating a positive employee experience, fostering diversity and inclusion, and driving hierarchical change [6,12].

13.1.2 The Importance of Adapting

The HR function faces new and evolving challenges as we enter the 21st century, necessitating ongoing work development. The fast speed of creative types of progress, moving workforce/labour economics, and changing representative presumptions are driving the necessity for HR to change and change [1,4,15].

 DOI: 10.1201/9781032619651-13

1. Technology Developments: The incorporation of artificial intelligence (AI), machine learning, and automation into HR procedures is reshaping how businesses interact with their workforce. Innovation is making it feasible for HR to work all the more proficiently and successfully in each viewpoint, from enlistment and onboarding to execution of the board and representative responsibility. For HR experts to stay cutthroat and impact information-driven bits of knowledge for worked on free course, embracing these advancements is fundamental [6,12].
2. Economics of Work/Labour Forces: People of varying ages coexist in today's workforce, which is becoming increasingly diverse. Methods for age-related requirements, such as a variety of characteristics, assumptions, and work styles, must be developed by HR [15]. Traditional HR processes have been further complicated by the rise of remote work and flexible work schedules, requiring novel approaches to talent management and employee support [21].
3. Adjusting Worker Speculations: The ongoing agents are searching for something past intense compensation and advantages. They underscore a balance between fun and serious activities, professional success, and a productive progressive culture. Undertakings and drives that further develop representative experience, energize business improvement, and cultivate a positive workplace ought to be carried out by HR to oblige these moving presumptions [4,6,23].
4. Changes to Guidelines: The HR administrative landscape is constantly evolving because a variety of business functions are affected by new regulations and guidelines. For HR to lighten bets and avoid legal problems, it is essential to maintain consistency by following each of these steps [11].

HR's change from a routine regulatory capability to a fundamental accomplice mirrors the developing work environment. In order to meet future requirements, HR should continue to adapt by adopting novel methods, addressing a variety of workforce requirements, responding to shifting employee assumptions, and navigating administrative changes. As a result, HR can anticipate playing a crucial role in encouraging diverse levels of achievement and a flourishing work environment.

13.2 THE ROLE OF TECHNOLOGY IN HR

13.2.1 HR Technology Landscape

In today's rapidly changing business environment, technology has become the foundation of HR management, driving effectiveness, enhancing employee experiences, and aligning HR practices with hierarchical objectives [5,24]. There are a few important frameworks and tools in the continuous HR innovation scene that are designed to smooth out various HR capabilities.

- Human Resource Information System (HRIS) (Human Asset Data Frameworks): HRIS stages work like big databases when it comes to managing employee data. In addition to processing benefits and finances, they offer features like consistency tracking and performance management.

HRIS frameworks further enhance receptivity, accuracy, and capability in HR tasks by bringing information together [25].

- Applicant Tracking System (ATS), or Systems for Tracking Candidates: ATS are intended to deal with the enrolment cycle from work introducing to utilizing. They help HR departments track applications, streamline the screening process, and monitor candidate interactions. ATS devices accelerate the enrolment cycle and improve the competitor experience via mechanizing various advances [6].
- Learning the Executives Frameworks (LMS): By providing a structured environment for distributing and tracking educational content, LMS platforms aid in employee training and development. Online training, certificate projects, and ability development are all supported by these systems, allowing businesses to continuously upskill their workforce and guarantee compliance with industry standards [7].

13.2.2 Emerging Technologies

As technology keeps on progressing, new developments are reshaping HR works, offering incredible assets to upgrade enlistment, employee management, and generally speaking authoritative adequacy.

- Man-Made Brainpower (Computer-Based Intelligence) and AI (ML): Simulated intelligence and ML are reforming HR via mechanizing complex cycles and giving significant bits of knowledge. In enlistment, man-made intelligence-driven devices can computerize candidate obtaining, screening, and talking, diminishing predisposition and working on the effectiveness of the employing system. Predictive analytics controlled by ML calculations can conjecture employee execution, distinguish potential maintenance gambles, and illuminate talent management procedures, empowering more educated independent direction [6,12].
- Blockchain: Blockchain technology offers a protected and straightforward method for overseeing employee records and confirmation processes. By making unchanging records of business history, accreditations, and accomplishments, blockchain upgrades the honesty and dependability of HR information. This technology can smooth out historical verifications, diminish extortion, and improve on consistence with administrative necessities [17,25].
- Mechanical Cycle Automation (RPA): RPA is changing HR via computerizing redundant and rule-based undertakings, for example, information section, finance handling, and advantages organization. By sending programming robots to deal with these standard exercises, HR groups can zero in on additional essential drives, further develop precision, and decrease functional expenses [16].
- Virtual and Expanded Reality (VR/AR): VR and AR advancements are acquainting creative methodologies with training and onboarding. VR can make immersive reenactments for employee training, permitting staff to rehearse abilities in a virtual climate that imitates genuine situations.

AR improves onboarding by giving intuitive, hands-on direction, and backing. These advancements further develop learning results, speed up the onboarding system, and improve employee engagement [23].

The integration of trend-setting innovations into HR functions is changing the manner in which associations deal with their workforce/employees. By utilizing HRIS, ATS, LMS, and arising innovations like man-made intelligence, blockchain, RPA, and VR/AR, HR experts can improve productivity, decrease costs, and make a seriously captivating and strong workplace. As technology keeps on advancing, HR will progressively depend on these devices to drive advancement, further develop independent direction, and backing the essential objectives of the association [8,21].

13.3 DATA-DRIVEN HR: ENHANCING TALENT MANAGEMENT THROUGH ANALYTICS

In the developing scene of HR (HR), information-driven approaches are reshaping the way that associations deal with their talent. By utilizing enormous information and progressed analytics, HR divisions can acquire profound bits of knowledge into employee experience, gauge trends, and go with informed choices that drive hierarchical achievement. Nonetheless, the utilization of information in HR likewise requires a cautious harmony between utilizing bits of knowledge and regarding employee security.

13.3.1 Big Data and Analytics in HR

13.3.1.1 Employee Experience Insights: Enhancing Satisfaction and Engagement

The coming of large information has changed how associations comprehend and improve employee experience. By gathering and investigating an abundance of information from different touchpoints—, for example, employee studies, execution metrics, and engagement instruments—HR divisions can acquire significant bits of knowledge into the elements that impact employee fulfilment and engagement [15,18].

- Reviews and Feedback Devices: Normal overviews and feedback systems give information on employee opinions, work fulfilment, and regions for development. Examining this information permits HR to recognize normal problem areas and carry out designated intercessions to upgrade the general employee experience.
- Measurements for Execution: By examining execution information, HR can perceive high-performing agents, grasp their prospering factors, and duplicate those practices across the alliance. Additionally, these data assist in anticipating and anticipating proactive responses to potential issues.
- Responsibility Examination: Worker motivation and affiliation can be gleaned from devices that monitor representative commitment levels, such

as assistance in association events, preparation tasks, and social activities. Programs and consistency standards that foster a positive work environment are aided by these data.

13.3.1.2 Predictive Analysis

Foreseeing patterns and settling on informed choices prescient examination utilizes quantifiable estimations and information that can be confirmed to sort out what will occur from now on. This limit is useful in HR for determining basic choices and anticipating workforce requirements [7,15].

- Securing Abilities: Prescient models are able to evaluate the requirements for recruiting based on things like business growth, turnover rates, and skillset requirements. As a result, HR is better able to plan recruitment campaigns and ensure a consistent pipeline of talent [9].
- Care for Workers/Labourers: By separating plans for employee turnover and recognizing representatives in danger, HR can encourage assigned upkeep strategies. Understanding the motivations behind specialist exits and finishing allocations to reduce wear is made easier with farsighted assessment [9].
- Workforce Planning by Employers: Gauging future limit requirements, recognizing potential expertise openings, and shifting skill development drive genuine goals, farsighted assessment maintains key workforce planning.

13.3.2 Morals and Security

As HR departments increasingly rely on information to drive decisions, it is essential to address security and moral considerations in order to maintain trust and adhere to guidelines.

13.3.2.1 Balancing Data Use with Security Opportunities

- Straightforwardness: Affiliations should be immediate about the thing information is being collected, the norm utilized, and who approaches it. Clear correspondence with representatives about data rehearses encourages entrust and guarantees consistence with security rules [11,19].
- Information Minimization: By collecting only essential information for specific purposes, security risks are minimized. A best practice for keeping up with worker privacy is to try not to share unreasonable or unessential data.
- Keep Data of the Board Safe: Executing energetic information security tries, for example, encryption, access controls, and standard overviews safeguards delegate data from unapproved access and breaks [11,19].

13.3.2.2 Ethical Problems with Data Use

- Reasonable Consent: Representatives ought to be shown about data assortment activities and given the choice to acknowledge or dismiss explicit data utilizes. An ethical objective is freedom in data-related decision-making [11].

- Keeping Away from Tendency: Information-driven choices ought to be liberated from inclination to guarantee reasonableness and worth. It is easier to make fair decisions and avoid unfair practices when calculations and information hotspots are regularly evaluated for potential predispositions.
- Application of Experiences Consistently: Effective use of knowledge fragments should focus on improving employee happiness and hierarchical viability. It is fundamental with guarantee that data-driven choices comply to moral rules and regard for representative pride [11].

By giving significant bits of knowledge into the representative experience, enabling prescient investigation for an essential course, and empowering a workforce/employee that is more associated with and satisfied, data-driven HR is changing the ability of the board. To fully appreciate the advantages of information-driven strategies, organizations must, however, strike a balance between information use, security, and ethical considerations. By performing straightforward repairs, safeguarding information security, and taking care of preferences, HR departments can deal with the power of information while safeguarding employee freedoms [11].

13.4 ENHANCING EMPLOYEE EXPERIENCE: STRATEGIES AND TECHNOLOGICAL SOLUTIONS

In the present unique workplace, improving employee experience has turned into a vital component for hierarchical achievement. As organizations endeavour to draw in and hold top talent, zeroing in on personalization, employee wellbeing, and backing for remote work and adaptability is fundamental. This is the way associations can successfully address these regions to make a really captivating and strong working environment.

13.4.1 Personalization: Tailoring HR Services to Individual Employee Needs

Personalization in HR departments is about tailoring services and facilities to each worker's specific needs and preferences. Rather than the standard one-size-fits-all game plans, this system means to make a work environment that is more comprehensive and responsive [3,24]. Some important frameworks are:

- Changed Onboarding Activities: Onboarding experiences that align with individual positions and calling goals help new enrolees plan much more effectively and feel welcome from the start. Work express readiness, modified welcome packs, and one-on-one training can all be coordinated through changed onboarding.
- Improved Business Development: By providing them with valuable growth opportunities and individualized calling progress plans, representatives can pursue their individual calling objectives. This could include opportunities for individualized education, professional development projects, and mentoring opportunities that align with their professional goals.

- An Adaptable Methodology for Finding Support: Employers ensure that their employees will receive support that is generally relevant to them by providing a variety of benefits options that employees can choose according to their own requirements, such as medical services plans, health projects, and benefits that strike a balance between fun and serious activities.
- Man-Made Brainpower in View of Information: Using data examination and recreated knowledge to grasp representative inclinations and execution, HR offices can give more individualized encounters. Thinking machines made by humans are able to evaluate input, execution estimates, and work improvement in order to provide appropriate assistance and support.

13.4.2 Representative Prosperity and Health: Mechanical Responses for Profound Prosperity and Wellbeing Tasks

Specialist prosperity and achievement are fundamental bits of a positive delegate experience. By ensuring that employees take advantage of resources and support, innovative arrangements have the potential to significantly improve health and emotional wellbeing programs [22]. The most crucial areas of the center are:

- Emotional wellbeing Applications and Stages: Integrating emotional wellness applications and stages into employee health programs gives admittance to directing, care activities, and stress management apparatuses. These stages frequently offer private help and assets that employees can access whenever it might suit them [10].
- Prosperity Analytics: Utilizing information analytics to screen and evaluate employee prosperity distinguishes trends and regions where extra help might be required. This proactive methodology permits associations to execute designated health drives and measure their viability.
- Virtual Wellbeing Training: Offering virtual wellbeing instructing and health online classes permits employees to get customized direction on sustenance, wellness, and stress management. These assets can be custom-made to individual wellbeing objectives and inclinations.
- Employee Help Projects (EAPs): Present-day EAPs frequently incorporate computerized assets, for example, web-based directing, psychological wellbeing online classes, and self-improvement apparatuses. Guaranteeing that these projects are effectively open and very much advanced can build their usage and viability.

13.4.3 Remote Work and Flexibility: Tools and Strategies to Support a Hybrid Workforce

The shift towards remote and crossover work models has required the improvement of apparatuses and systems to help adaptable work courses of action [15,21]. Viable remote work and adaptability arrangements include:

- Cooperative Instruments and Stages: Executing strong joint effort apparatuses, for example, project management programming, video conferencing stages, and group informing applications guarantees that remote groups can convey actually and keep up with efficiency.
- Adaptable Work Strategies: Growing clear and adaptable work arrangements that frame assumptions for remote work, like accessibility, correspondence standards, and execution metrics, oversees remote groups really and encourages a feeling of trust and responsibility.
- Remote Work Framework: Giving employees the fundamental technology and assets for remote work, including secure Virtual Private Networks (VPNs), ergonomic workspace hardware, and solid web access, guarantees they can work effectively and serenely from any area.
- Virtual Group Building Exercises: Putting together virtual group building occasions and social exercises keeps up with group union and engagement in a remote setting. These exercises can incorporate virtual blissful hours, internet games, and cooperative activities.
- Balance between Fun and Serious Activities Backing: Empowering a solid balance between serious and fun activities through adaptable planning, time-off strategies, and advancing limits between work and individual life upholds employee prosperity and forestalls burnout.

Improving employee experience through personalization, health, and backing for remote work is fundamental for making a thriving and connected to workforce/employees. By embracing custom-made HR administrations, utilizing mechanical answers for emotional wellbeing, and carrying out powerful remote work methodologies, associations can encourage a more certain and strong workplace [15,21]. As organizations keep on advancing, zeroing in on these key regions will help draw in, hold, and engage top talent, driving general achievement and development [20].

13.5 FUTURE SKILLS FOR HR PROFESSIONALS

As the scene of HR keeps on developing quickly, HR experts should furnish themselves with a different arrangement of abilities to remain significant and successful. The future of HR will be formed by progressions in technology, changing authoritative requirements, and a rising spotlight on key and profound parts of human resources management. To explore these progressions effectively, HR experts need to foster capability in three key regions: specialized abilities, delicate abilities, and a promise to nonstop learning.

13.5.1 Technical Skills

Capability of HR Technology Instruments: The way that HR professionals manage selection, employee commitment, execution, and investigation is being transformed by the combination of cutting-edge HR tools. Experience with HR tech devices, for example, candidate overall arranging structures (ATS), human asset data systems (HRIS), and execution of the board composing PC programs is fundamental. The use of these instruments encourages HR professionals to streamline procedures, enhance capability, and make decisions based on data. To remain in front of the opposition, it is likewise fundamental to have a strong comprehension of forthcoming improvements, for example, computerization stages, worker self-administration gateways, and man-made reasoning driven enlistment frameworks [12].

Analysing the Data: Information-driven direction is getting more and more important in HR. Due to their ability to analyse information, HR professionals are able to decipher intricate datasets regarding employee performance, turnover rates, and workforce/employee socioeconomics. HR experts can recognize patterns, set informed assumptions, and do methodologies that improve progressive practicality with the help of abilities in the utilization of data portrayal gadgets and quantifiable assessment programming. Being able to measure the impact of HR drives and utilize information to assist in making crucial decisions is a huge advantage [15,19].

Security Online: Because HR departments handle sensitive employee data, such as personal and financial information, it is essential to understand network safety standards. Best practices for protecting information from breaches and unapproved access should be known by HR professionals. By having access to information on network protection protocols and conventions and staying up to date on potential threats, HR departments are guaranteed to adhere to legitimate requirements and meet individual information security expectations.

13.5.2 Soft Skills

Versatility/Adaptability: The capacity to adjust to quick changes in the work environment is a basic expertise for HR experts. As associations face advancing difficulties like remote work, computerized change, and moving workforce socioeconomics, HR experts should be adaptable and open to new methodologies. Being versatile assists HR experts with overseeing changes without a hitch, carry out creative arrangements, and address unanticipated issues really [5].

Vital Reasoning: HR experts are progressively expected to add to hierarchical methodology. Key reasoning includes understanding the more extensive business setting, adjusting HR practices to hierarchical objectives, and expecting future workforce/staff needs. By taking on an essential mentality, HR experts can uphold hierarchical development, drive change drives, and add to long-haul achievement.

The Capacity to Understand People at Their Core (Emotional Intelligence): The capacity to understand individuals on a deeper level (EI) is fundamental for overseeing connections and encouraging a positive workplace. HR experts with high EI can relate to employees, handle clashes delicately, and convey actually. Building solid relational connections and understanding the feelings of employees are critical to improving engagement, maintenance, and by and large work environment culture [14].

13.5.3 Continuous Learning

Significance of Progressing Learning: In a quickly developing field like HR, ceaseless learning is basic to remaining current with industry trends and best practices. HR experts ought to look for valuable open doors for proficient improvement through studios, certificates, and high-level courses. Taking part in continuous schooling assists experts with refining their abilities, gain new information, and remain cut-throat in the gig market [19].

Proficient Turn of Events: Putting resources into proficient improvement upgrades individual abilities as well as adds to the general viability of the HR capability inside an association. Taking part in industry meetings, joining proficient affiliations, and systems administration with peers are significant ways of acquiring bits of knowledge, share encounters, and investigate novel thoughts. By embracing deep rooted learning, HR experts can adjust to changing requests and drive advancement in their jobs.

The future of HR requests a mix of specialized mastery, delicate abilities, and a pledge to ceaseless learning. By creating capability in HR technology, information examination, and online protection, HR experts can explore the intricacies of current human asset management. In the meantime, developing versatility, vital reasoning, and the ability to understand people on a profound level guarantees that HR experts can really address the developing requirements of the workforce. Embracing continuous training and expert advancement will furnish HR experts with the devices they need to thrive in a steadily changing scene and make significant commitments to their associations [5,15,19].

13.6 REDESIGNING HR PROCESSES

13.6.1 Recruitment and Onboarding: Modern Approaches to Attracting and Integrating Talent

13.6.1.1 Recruitment

In the present serious work market, customary enrolment strategies are frequently lacking to draw in top talent. Present-day enlistment procedures influence trend-setting innovations and creative ways to deal with upgrading the employing system:

- AI Controlled Obtaining: Man-made consciousness (computer-based intelligence) has changed talent procurement via robotizing candidate obtaining and screening. Computer-based intelligence-driven instruments investigate huge measures of information to recognize possible candidates, match them to work necessities, and even foresee their fit inside the association. This approach speeds up the enlistment cycle as well as improves the precision of candidate determination [6,12].
- Business Marking and Virtual Entertainment: A solid manager brand is significant in drawing in top talent. Organizations are progressively utilizing virtual entertainment stages and advanced promoting to exhibit their way of life, values, and employee encounters [5,21]. Drawing in satisfied, employee tributes and intelligent missions assist with building a positive picture and draw in candidates who line up with the organization's ethos.
- Variety and Consideration: Present-day enrolment procedures stress variety and incorporation by carrying out fair-minded AI calculations and organized screenings. These strategies assist with moderating oblivious

inclinations and guarantee a different pool of candidates, adding to a more comprehensive working environment [6,11].

Onboarding

Compelling onboarding is fundamental for coordinating recently added team members and getting them in a good position. Contemporary onboarding rehearses center around making a consistent and connecting with experience:

- Computerized Onboarding Stages: Technology-driven onboarding stages smooth out managerial undertakings and give a concentrated area to fresh recruits to get to assets, complete desk work, and get accustomed to the organization [12,23]. These stages frequently incorporate intuitive components like virtual visits, onboarding agendas, and social gatherings to encourage associations among new employees.
- Customized Onboarding Encounters: Fitting the onboarding system to individual jobs and foundations improves the recently added team member's integration. Customized onboarding plans incorporate job explicit training, one-in one gatherings with key colleagues, and altered learning modules that line up with the recently added team member's profession objectives and range of abilities [20].
- Persistent Feedback and Backing: Compelling onboarding doesn't end after the initial few weeks. Progressing support through standard registrations, mentorship projects, and feedback meetings assists fresh recruits with changing, address any difficulties, and feel esteemed inside the association [12,23].

13.6.2 Performance Management: Innovative Methods for Evaluating and Enhancing Employee Performance

Conventional execution management systems frequently depend on yearly audits and unbending metrics, which can be incapable of driving nonstop improvement. Creative ways to deal with execution management center around ongoing feedback, nonstop turn of events, and employee engagement [12,16].

13.6.3 Learning and Development: E-Learning Platforms, Microlearning, and Personalized Learning Paths

The need for consistent capacity enhancement and imaginative movements is driving the rapid growth of the learning and development sector:

- E-Learning Stages: E-learning stages give adaptable and versatile preparation choices that can be gotten to from any area [1,6]. Representatives are provided the capacity to acquire new abilities and data at their own speed thanks to the various courses, modules, and assets presented by these stages. Exams, natural substances, and other components alter the growth opportunity and commitment [13].

- Little Knowledge: Little learning spins around conveying content in almost nothing, sensible fragments, permitting agents to learn in short impacts of time [5,23]. This tactic is effective for providing just-in-time training, supporting ideas, and filling in specific skill gaps. Smaller-than-expected learning modules are valuable for occupied experts since they can be conveyed promptly upon demand [2].
- Methods for Individualized Education/Training/Learning: Modified learning methods adapt preparation tasks to each worker's needs, preferences, and career objectives. By analysing employee performance data, ability evaluations, and career goals, associations can tailor learning experiences to meet specific developmental needs and support professional success [1,23].
- Blended Learning: Mixed learning, which combines e-learning and traditional classroom instruction, is an equitable approach that makes use of the strengths of both approaches. Employees benefit from the flexibility of online learning while still retaining the advantages of in-person interactions and active practice with this method [12,23].

Overhauling HR processes through current methodologies in enrolment, execution management, and learning and improvement is fundamental for making a dynamic and powerful workforce. Embracing technology, zeroing in on consistent improvement, and customizing employee encounters are vital to opening the maximum capacity of HR practices and driving authoritative achievement.

13.7 STRATEGIC HR LEADERSHIP

13.7.1 Change Management

1. Drawing in Partners: Viable change management includes connecting with key partners from the get-go all the while. HR pioneers ought to work intimately with chiefs, administrators, and employees to accumulate input, address concerns, and assemble purchases for the change drive. This cooperative methodology assists with limiting opposition and encourages a culture of help [5,11].
2. Executing Organized Change Cycles: To oversee change successfully, HR pioneers ought to utilize organized change management systems. This incorporates fostering a far-reaching change plan, setting clear achievements, and giving the important assets and training to help the progress [4,5].
3. Checking and Assessing Change: Nonstop observing and assessment are fundamental for fruitful change management. HR pioneers ought to follow progress, evaluate the effect of progress drives, and make changes on a case-by-case basis. Feedback systems, for example, reviews and center gatherings, can give significant bits of knowledge into the adequacy of progress endeavours [21].

13.7.2 Diversity, Equity, and Inclusion (DEI)

Advancing variety, value, and incorporation (DEI) is a critical need for vital HR initiatives, and utilizing technology can fundamentally improve these endeavours. Technology gives instruments and experiences to drive DEI drives and make a more comprehensive working environment [6,11].

1. Using Information Analytics for DEI Experiences: Technology empowers HR pioneers to examine workforce/employee information to distinguish holes and trends in variety and consideration. By utilizing information analytics, HR can follow a variety of metrics, survey the adequacy of DEI projects, and settle on information-driven choices to further develop portrayal and value.
2. Executing Comprehensive Enlistment and Talent Management Advancements: Simulated intelligence and AI apparatuses can assist with killing predisposition in enrolment and talent management processes. Technology can uphold blind enrolment rehearses, guarantee even-handed execution assessments, and advance fair professional improvement and opportunities.
3. Upgrading DEI Training and Schooling: Technology can work with DEI training and instruction through internet-based stages, virtual studios, and intuitive learning modules. These devices empower HR to convey predictable and versatile DEI training, encouraging a culture of inclusivity across the association.
4. Advancing Employee Asset Gatherings (ERGs) and Consideration Organizations: Computerized stages can uphold the creation and management of ERGs and incorporation organizations. These stages give space for employees to interface, share encounters, and drive DEI drives inside the association.
5. Estimating DEI Progress and Effect: Technology permits HR to track and gauge the advancement of DEI drives through dashboards and announcing apparatuses. Consistently surveying the effect of DEI endeavours assists with guaranteeing responsibility and driving constant improvement.

13.8 ETHICAL AND LEGAL CONSIDERATIONS IN AI-DRIVEN RECRUITMENT

Moral contemplations are essential for the cautious utilization of PC-based information in enlistment. This is how affiliations can drive moral practices:

1. **Avoidance of Separation and Predispositions:**
   - Evacuation of Inclination: Individual preferences should be identified and moderated by AI systems. This includes utilizing grouped preparation data, consistently testing computations for inclination, and carrying out parts to correct erroneous results.
   - Comprehensive Design: Guaranteeing that reproduced information contraptions are made considering inclusivity impedes the avoidance of express social gatherings and advances reasonableness in selection processes [6,11].

2. **Guarantee Straightforwardness and Responsibility:**
   - Explainability: PC-based knowledge decisions ought to be understandable to newcomers and partners. Giving clear clarifications of how man-made information structures seek after choices upholds trust and draws in competitors to understand and challenge choices if focal.
   - Accountability Systems: By distributing liability structures, associations are given a sense of responsibility for the results of PC-based insight-driven enrolment processes. This solidifies watching out for grumblings and executing accommodating activities when issues emerge [5,11].
3. **Keeping Applicants' Confidence Safe:**
   - Data Security: The personal information of applicants is shielded from unapproved access and breaches by undertaking extensive data security measures. The basics incorporate secure storing works, access controls, and encryption.
   - Informed Assent: Candidates ought to be educated about the utilization regarding computer-based intelligence in the enlistment cycle and agree to the assortment and handling of their information. Clear correspondence about information use and getting express assent keeps up with moral principles.
4. **Promoting Moral Simulated Intelligence Improvement:**
   - Ethical Rules: Taking on moral rules for simulated intelligence improvement and utilizing guarantees that technology is planned and conveyed with a promise of decency, straightforwardness, and regard for candidates' freedoms.
   - Ongoing Assessment: Constantly assessing and further developing man-made intelligence systems in light of moral contemplations assists associations with adjusting to arising difficulties and keeping up with moral principles.

Exploring the moral and legitimate scene of man-made intelligence-driven enlistment requires a proactive way to deal with consistence and capable technology use. By remaining informed about important regulations, executing powerful consistence gauges, and complying with moral standards, associations can saddle the advantages of computer-based intelligence while maintaining reasonableness, straightforwardness, and regard for candidates. Offsetting mechanical progressions with moral and lawful obligations guarantees that computer-based intelligence contributes decidedly to the enrolment cycle and lines up with more extensive cultural qualities [5,6,11].

13.9 LOOKING AHEAD: THE FUTURE OF HR

13.9.1 Trends and Predictions: Anticipated Developments in HR Technology and Practices

As we advance into a time of quick innovative development and moving working environment elements, the future of HR (HR) is ready for significant change.

A few vital trends and forecasts are arising, flagging massive changes in HR technology and practices:

1. **Artificial Insight and Automation:**
   - Enhanced Enrolment Cycles: AI will keep on refining enlistment processes via computerizing candidate obtaining, screening, and talking. Predictive analytics will further develop talent coordination and workforce/employee arranging.
   - Personalized Employee Encounters: Man-made intelligence-driven instruments will offer more customized learning and improvement open doors, professional way proposals, and execution feedback.
2. **Remote and Half-Breed Work Models:**
   - Flexible Work Plans: The shift towards remote and half-and-half work models will turn out to be more settled in, requiring new procedures for overseeing appropriate groups and keeping up with hierarchical culture.
   - Advanced Cooperation Apparatuses: Arising advances will improve virtual coordinated effort and correspondence, making remote work more consistent and useful.
3. **Employee Prosperity and Psychological Wellness:**
   - Holistic Prosperity Projects: There will be a developing spotlight on far-reaching prosperity programs that address physical, mental, and close-to-home wellbeing. Bosses will put resources into instruments and assets to help employee prosperity all the more actually.
   - Mental Wellbeing Backing: Simulated intelligence-fuelled psychological wellbeing arrangements and virtual directing administrations will turn out to be more pervasive, offering employees available help and assets.
4. **Data-Driven Direction:**
   - HR Analytics: High-level HR analytics will give further bits of knowledge into workforce/employee trends, employee engagement, and efficiency. Information-driven dynamic will turn into a foundation of vital HR management.
   - Predictive Analytics: Predictive analytics will be utilized to figure talent needs, turnover rates, and employee execution, considering proactive HR techniques.
5. **Diversity, Value, and Consideration (DEI):**
   - AI for Predisposition Alleviation: Man-made intelligence devices will help recognize and address inclinations in recruiting, advancements, and execution assessments, supporting more impartial and comprehensive working environments.
   - DEI Metrics: Associations will progressively track and measure DEI progress with modern metrics, intending to establish more different and comprehensive workplaces.
6. **Blockchain for HR:**
   - Secure and Straightforward Records: Blockchain technology will offer secure and straightforward systems for overseeing employee records, checking accreditations, and taking care of finances and advantages.

7. **Skill Turn of Events and Long-Lasting Learning:**
   - Continuous Learning Stages: The accentuation on constant ability advancement will develop, with computer-based intelligence-driven stages offering customized learning encounters and vocation improvement potential open doors.
   - Microlearning and On-Request Training: Microlearning and on-request training will turn out to be more normal, permitting employees to procure new abilities and information rapidly and effectively.

13.9.2 Anticipating What's to Come

Strategies for HR professionals to stay ahead of the curve experts need to actively plan for these changes if they want to succeed in the HR industry which is constantly changing. Significant systems for keeping steady over things are as per the following:

1. **Accept Change and Innovation:**
   - Stay Informed: Always keep up with the latest developments and HR advice. Attend studios, online classes, and industry events to keep up with the latest trends.
   - Put Automation and Simulated Intelligence into Practice: Put cash into computerization and reenacted insight devices that can make HR processes more proficient and smoother. Try out brand-new innovations and observe how they affect your company's HR functions.
2. **Establish a Culture That Is Flexible:**
   - Support Smoothness: Promote a culture of adaptability and openness to change within your company. Energize techniques for change the executives to assist workers with investigating headways effortlessly.
   - Encourage Work from Home: Implement effective remote work strategies and invest in devices that are compatible with effective cross- and remote work environments.
3. **Invest in Employees' Wealth:**
   - Put Success Projects into Action: Make and advance thriving undertakings that address physical, mental, and huge flourishing. Evaluate these tasks' sufficiency on a regular basis and adjust as necessary.
4. **Advance DEI Drives:**
   - Use Man-Made Intelligence for Decency: Use computer-based intelligence apparatuses to recognize and relieve predispositions in employing and advancements. Execute procedures to advance variety, value, and consideration inside your association.
   - Track DEI Progress: Consistently measure and report on DEI metrics to survey progress and distinguish regions for development.
5. **Prepare for Ability Advancement and Long-Lasting Learning:**
   - Promote Constant Learning: Urge employees to take part in persistent learning and expertise improvement. Give admittance to microlearning and on-request training assets.

- Support Vocation Improvement: Offer customized vocation advancement open doors and direction to assist employees with accomplishing their expert objectives.

By embracing these systems, HR experts can situate themselves and their associations to explore the future of HR with certainty and achievement. Embracing mechanical headways, cultivating flexibility, and focusing on employee prosperity will be essential in opening the maximum capacity of the advancing HR scene.

13.10 CONCLUSION

The fate of HR (HR) is being reshaped by innovative headways and advancing workforce/employee assumptions. The incorporation of AI, robotization, and information investigation is upgrading HR capabilities, from enlistment to ability of the board, while working on by and large hierarchical effectiveness. Employee wellbeing, diversity, and ethical considerations must be given top priority as HR professionals adjust to these changes by balancing technology with a human-centric approach. By embracing development, encouraging adaptability, and advancing ceaseless learning, HR can drive long-haul hierarchical accomplishment while keeping an emphasis on the representative experience.

REFERENCES

1. Agarwal, S., & Gupta, D. (2024). *Digital Analytics Applications for Sustainable Training and Education* (1st ed.). Apple Academic Press, Waretown, NJ.
2. Agarwal, S., Diwedi, S., & Ghai, R. (2020). Perception of trainees towards skill development program. *International Journal of Innovative Science and Research Technology*, 5(12), 11–15.
3. Agarwal, S., Gupta, D., & Gupta, M. (2023). Techno pedagogical concept with digital skills. In: Manpreet Singh Manna, Balamurugan Balusamy, Kiran Sood, Naveen Chilamkurti, and Ignisha Rajathi George (eds) *Edutech Enabled Teaching* (pp. 129–152). Chapman and Hall/CRC, New York.
4. Kumar, A., Gupta, D., Gupta, M., & Srivastava, G. (2021). India an emerging leader after pandemic: a strategy for the development of new India. *Global Journal of Enterprise Information System*, 13(1), 60–70. Retrieved from https://www.gjeis.com/index.php/GJEIS/article/view/629
5. Brown, M. (2019). The evolution of HR: from administrative to strategic. *Journal of Human Resource Management*, 45(2), 120–135.
6. Chen, Z., Wang, L., & Liu, Y. (2020). AI and automation in HR: revolutionizing recruitment and performance management. *Human Capital Review*, 38(4), 82–99.
7. Gupta, D., & Agarwal, S. (2018). Skill development initiative-literature review. *Inspira-Journal of Modern Management and Entrepreneurship (JMME)*, 8(2), 319–322.
8. Gupta, D., & Agarwal, S. (2018). Training prospects in power sector in India. *International Journal of Research in Engineering, IT and Social Sciences*, 8, 305–314.
9. Gupta, D., Gupta, M., & Rani, S. (2022). A study on training of workmen in a manufacturing organization—with reference to aluminium foundry. In: Dvivedi, A., Sachdeva, A., Sindhwani, R., Sahu, R. (eds) *Recent Trends in Industrial and Production Engineering*. Lecture Notes in Mechanical Engineering. Springer, Singapore. https://doi.org/10.1007/978-981-16-3330-0_19

10. Gupta, D., Gupta, M., Tiwari, S., & Singh, N. (2021). Motivation due to fear of failure is a key contributor in maximizing workers' productivity in today's competitive arena. *International Journal of Indian Culture and Business Management*, 23(2), 193–217. https://doi.org/10.1504/IJICBM.2021.115895
11. Johnson, S., & Harris, P. (2021). Ethical concerns and privacy issues in the AI-driven HR landscape. *Ethics and Privacy Journal*, 17(3), 45–60.
12. Jones, A. (2022). Transforming HR with technology: a focus on AI and automation. *International Journal of Technology in HR*, 52(1), 58–74.
13. Kumar, V., Gupta, M., & Gaur, S. (2023). Intrusion detection for the Internet of Things. In: Kaushik, K., Dahiya, S., Bhardwaj, A., Maleh, Y. (eds) *Internet of Things and Cyber Physical Systems Security and Forensics* (1st ed., pp. 183). CRC Press, Boca Raton, FL.
14. Mittal, S., Srivastava, P., & Gupta, D. (2022). Emotional Intelligence: Assessing Its Impact on Financial Productivity in an Organization. In: Rao, V. V., Kumaraswamy, A., Kalra, S., Saxena, A. (eds) *Computational and Experimental Methods in Mechanical Engineering*. Smart Innovation, Systems and Technologies, vol 239. Springer, Singapore. https://doi.org/10.1007/978-981-16-2857-3_22
15. Nguyen, T., & Patel, A. (2021). Data-driven talent management: how analytics is reshaping HR strategies. *Strategic Workforce Analytics Review*, 33(2), 100–112.
16. O'Connor, M. (2021). RPA in HR: streamlining repetitive tasks for increased efficiency. *HR Automation Quarterly*, 29(3), 30–45.
17. Rajvanshi, P.R., Singh, T., Gupta, D., & Gupta, M., (2022). Blockchain technology for pharmaceutical drug supply chain management. In: El-Metwally, R. Thakur, A. Khanna, V. M. García, & A. Joshi (eds) *Transformation in Healthcare with Emerging Technologies*. CRC Press, Boca Raton, FL.
18. Rani, S., Gupta, M., & Gupta, D. (2020). Artificial intelligence and personalized banking. In: Vikas Garg, Rohit Bansal, and Bhuvan Unhelkar (eds) *Transforming Management Using Artificial Intelligence Techniques* (1st ed., pp. 24). CRC Press, Boca Raton, FL. https://doi.org/10.4324/9781003032410
19. Singh, S., Gupta, D., & Gupta, M. (2022). Optimized task allocation technique using mathematical fuzzy logic in heterogeneous distributed computational system. *2022 International Conference on Computational Intelligence and Sustainable Engineering Solutions (CISES)*, Greater Noida, India, 2022, pp. 37–45. https://doi.org/10.1109/CISES54857.2022.9844410
20. Singh, S., & Gupta, D. (2023). Module allocation model in distributed computing system by implementing fuzzy C-means clustering technique. In: Agrawal, R., Mitra, P., Pal, A., Sharma Gaur, M. (eds) *International Conference on IoT, Intelligent Computing and Security*. Lecture Notes in Electrical Engineering, vol 982. Springer, Singapore. https://doi.org/10.1007/978-981-19-8136-4_14
21. Smith, J., & Lee, H. (2021). HR in the digital age: strategic alignment through technology. *Journal of Organizational Leadership*, 49(1), 65–78.
22. Agarwal, S., Gupta, D., & Gupta, M. (2023). Impact of training method on trainees learning and implementation on job – a study with special reference to power sector. *AIP Conference Proceedings*, 2427(1): 020020. https://doi.org/10.1063/5.0100893
23. Taylor, R. (2021). Virtual and augmented reality in employee training: the future of learning and development. *Learning Technologies Journal*, 36(4), 92–108.
24. Williams, K., & Davis, R. (2019). Leveraging cloud-based systems and analytics to enhance HR functions. *Cloud and Analytics Journal*, 24(3), 70–88.
25. Wilson, P. (2020). Blockchain in HR: enhancing transparency and security in employee records. *Emerging Technologies in HR*, 41(1), 22–34.

14 A Comprehensive Analysis of the Literature on HR Factors for Industry 4.0 Adoption Success

Sanjana Kaushik, Deepa Gupta, and Mukul Gupta

14.1 INTRODUCTION

The development of the Fourth Industrial Revolution brings autonomous forklifts, driverless autos, robot-talking screws, and smart manufacturing process management tools to life. With this, a modern company is trying hard to bridge the gap between the digital and physical worlds in order to provide fresh and effective policies, products, and services (World Economic Forum 2016), cyber-physical systems, the Internet of Things, robotics, big data analysis, artificial intelligence (AI), augmented reality (AR), virtual reality (VR), three-dimensional printers, cloud computing, etc. (Irudayaraj 2017; Kagermann et al., 2013; Lasi et al., 2014; Thoben et al., 2017). Characteristic exponents of such emerging technologies, based on extensive automation, digitalization, and real-time information exchange, are cyber-physical systems; the Internet of Things; robotics; big data analysis; AI; AR; VR; three-dimensional (3D) printing Accordingly, Industry 4.0 is expected to cause far-reaching changes both in the global economy and in the need to renew and replace a considerable number of procedures at industrial sites with new ones (Agarwal et al., 2023). In this change, developed nations like China, Japan, Germany, and the United States are the initiators; they produce strategies and set goals for national development. This is based on BRICS (2016), Dhanpat et al. (2020), and Kazancoglu and Ozkan-Ozen (2018). An increasing amount of developing countries, such as India and Indonesia, are getting more and more biased to Industry 4.0 and making significant organizational changes with an aim to have an edge to compete with the industrialized nations. As Irudayaraj (2017) notes, scientific publications on the topic have increased considerably in the last couple of years. Industry 4.0 has been covered in the literature, starting from sectors by Oesterreich and Teuteberg, 2016, companies by Bokrantz et al. (2020); Li et al. (2019), to geographical areas see Jerman et al. (2020); Liboni et al. (2019).

Though these existing contributions present some meaningful analyses, the primary aim of most of these is to investigate the technical and industrial aspects of

 DOI: 10.1201/9781032619651-14

Industry 4.0 and its complexity. The limited management literature, on the other hand, mentions that businesses have several kinds of managerial challenges during the adaptation period and are sometimes even resistant to the implementation of Industry 4.0. HR-related challenges, such as a lack of experts, internal knowledge gaps, skills shortages, and limited top management support, have been highlighted in research by Liboni et al. (2019) and Schneider (2018). Additionally, factors like organizational structure (Cimini et al., 2020; Li et al., 2020), leadership style, and the impact of change on human resource management (Bajpai et al., 2019; BRICS, 2016) are among the most critical concerns in Industry 4.0.. Emerging automation and development of digital technology would replace traditional labour-operated processes with robots, according to Liboni et al., 2019. It requires finding new talent and skills that are actually required to be found out in the coming years. The existing workforce has to re-develop through training and upskilling. The existing workforce has to re-develop through training and upskilling, necessary recruitment, retention, and incorporation of new employees within the organization Fareri et al. (2020). Thus, business leaders will need to focus on developing new ways of working mechanisms for managing HR effectively, training the future workforce, embedding lifelong learning culture within the organization, and thereby establishing an organizational climate. They also need to develop forward-looking plans that directly help business strategic objectives, including the practical implementation of Industry 4.0 (Lorenz et al., 2015; Verma et al., 2020). Various studies have been conducted which might investigate the various HR elements impacting adoption of Industry 4.0, and results from these studies clearly indicated the imperatives of HRM in Industry 4.0 adoption—Cimini et al. (2020), Fareri et al. (2020), Kazancoglu and Ozkan-Ozen (2018), Llinas and Abad (2019), Mohelska and Sokolova (2018). This study, therefore, has the purpose of depicting a holistic view of the variables that define HR success through a well-thought literary review. It also intends to provide an HR paradigm that will aid businesses and professionals in understanding better how Industry 4.0 will influence HRM and give a very robust foundation for further research (Figure 14.1).

Revolutionary stages of the Industrial Revolution: Since the beginning of the industrialization phenomenon, there have been four significant paradigm shifts that have occurred. The many technological advancements that are sometimes referred to as the "industrial revolutions" are responsible for defining and influencing these paradigm shifts (Miragliotta et al., 2018). Instead of using animals in the production process, mechanical methods and equipment were utilized during the first industrial revolution, which occurred in the latter half of the 18th century (Habanik et al., 2019; Thoben et al., 2017). Technology that was driven by steam and water helped to make it possible to create items in vast quantities. In the latter part of the 19th century, the second industrial revolution began with the intention of powering machinery with electrical energy. When compared to the tools that were utilized during the initial phase of the industrial revolution, these gadgets were more cost-effective, easier to operate, and required less maintenance. The manufacturing sector became entirely mechanized in the early 1970s and during the third industrial revolution as a result of improvements in electronics, computers, and information technology (Kagermann et al., 2013; Thoben et al., 2017). Transistors, integrated circuits, and software systems are examples of electrical technologies that have been developed to

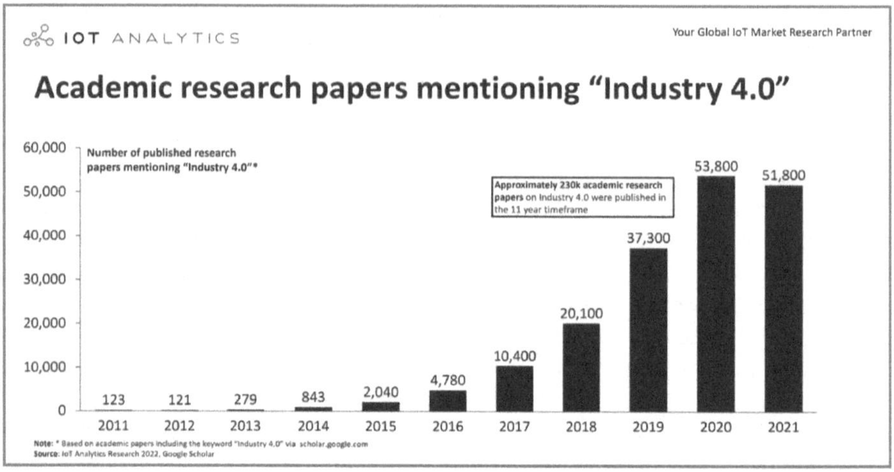

FIGURE 14.1 Academic research papers mentioning Industry 4.0.

reduce the amount of work that is required, as well as to increase speed and accuracy. The twenty-first century was marked by a surge in the development of Internet and telecommunications technologies, which therefore brought about a substantial shift in the paradigms of manufacturing processes. The boundaries between the physical and virtual worlds have become more hazy as a result of the fourth industrial revolution, often known as Industry 4.0.

14.2 INDUSTRY 4.0

Industry 4.0 first took center stage at the Hanover Fair in 2011. Later, in 2013, it was adopted by the German government as a strategic policy aimed at restructuring and reorganizing the manufacturing sector. Industry 4.0 has of late attracted more attention since it gives companies the following advantages. Although there are some writers who defined Industry 4.0 differently, most of them have taken a techno centric approach and centered their definitions mostly around the technical innovations Agarwal, S. et al., (2023). According to Kagermann et al. (2013), Industry 4.0 was defined as the integration of network resources, information, objects, and people by the industrial sector. Oesterreich and Teuteberg defined Industry 4.0 or the fourth industrial revolution as higher automation, digitization, and interactivity provided through the building of a digital value chain within a manufacturing environment. To Szalavetz, 2019, the fourth industrial revolution or Industry 4.0 is a generic term for a number of digital business technologies. As explained by Schwab (2016), Industry 4.0 is characterized by a spectrum of technologies that connects the physical, digital, and biological spheres. Economies are one of the aspects to take the impact of these technologies, amongst businesses, sectors, and spheres. On relative thought, as the components of the body are considered, the United Nations Industrial Development Organisation (2017) defined Industry 4.0 in terms of technologies. While cameras and other sensors are a need, data and connectivity make up the nervous system, AI is the brain, and for Industry 4.0, automation and robots are the limbs and legs.

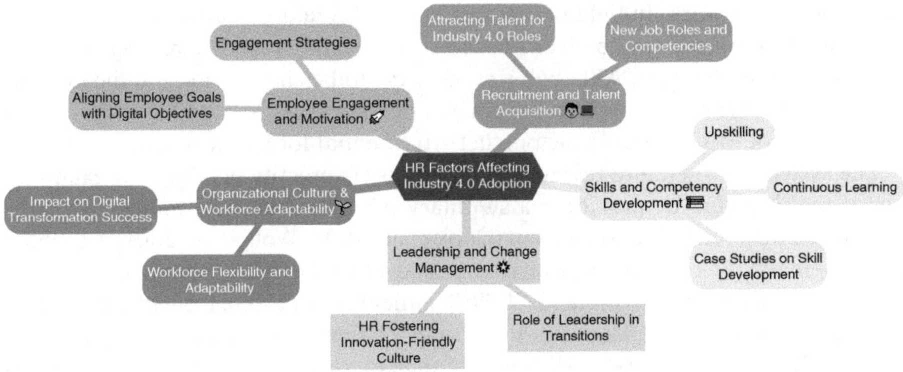

FIGURE 14.2 HR factors affecting Industry 4.0 adoption.

Industry 4.0 has aggregated people, equipment, processes, and infrastructure into one continuous loop, and manufacturing operations have become rather efficient to run (Miragliotta et al., 2018). It is in this way Smart processes, network architecture, logistics, and products enable organizations to digitally network with consumers, suppliers, and the outside world (Schneider, 2018). Industry 4.0's HRM. Business leaders from all countries and industries need to send in and contribute substantial proposals to address the challenges of the new era of rapid change and innovation, as only then can we fully maximize the revolutionary potential of the industry. Figure 14.2 depicts various HR factors affecting Industry 4.0 adoption.

The 4.0 CEOs are increasingly looking to HR professionals to drive innovation, embracing new technologies to acquire, develop, and retain the workforce of the future. The HR director is uniquely positioned to help organizations fully embrace and harness the new and evolving technologies by managing the workforce implications brought about by the so-called Industry 4.0. With more customary and administrative HR roles being automated, HR directors will have to be all the more innovative and strategic in supporting Industry 4.0. The major effects of change can be expected in the hiring, training, and development processes in HR. According to a 2018 estimation by the World Economic Forum, human work hours would decrease from 71% to 58% by 2025. By 2022, more than half of all workers will require retraining. The challenges are indeed big. HR professionals must therefore grow in this direction, as it is a necessity. Recent research corpus includes Li et al. (2020); Liboni et al. (2019); Cimini et al. (2020); Fareri et al. (2020); Kiatsuranon and Suwunnamek (2017).

14.3 RESEARCH METHODOLOGY

A number of the aspects of Industry 4.0 have reportedly already been studied, according to published works. The technical domains, above all, gain from a more in-depth analysis of the literature (Liao et al., 2017; Schneider, 2018; Shamim et al., 2017). An increasingly important issue that is being studied more and more is the implementation of Industry 4.0 (Calzavara et al., 2020; Kazancoglu and Ozkan-Ozen, 2018; Li et al., 2019). However, a great deal of clarification is still needed before practitioners, scientists, and the government can develop plans and regulations for Industry

4.0 adoption that work. In light of this, a thorough literature analysis offers the necessary toolbox by painting a clear picture of the common problems and solutions identified in the literature. Although a number of studies have employed the systematic literature review approach in the context of Industry 4.0, none have thoroughly investigated the HRM success factors that are essential for its execution.

The systematic literature review technique assists practitioners in their examination of the literature by providing a summary of comprehensive studies and highlighting the differences between them (Cook et al., 1997; Wolf et al., 2001). Recently, new systematic review approaches have been developed to select, compile, and present evidence (Denyer and Tranfield, 2009; Tranfield et al., 2003). It enables the analysis of earlier studies and identifies the corpus of literature relevant to a particular problem (Kitchenham, 2004). All stages of data extraction, including general information such as title, author, and publication details as well as research-specific characteristics like techniques, gaps, and future research prospects, must be documented as part of systematic reviews (Tranfield et al., 2003). These considerations led to the selection of the same methodology as the research approach for the current study. It maintains the same concepts but implements the three main phases of planning, execution, and reporting as stated by Tranfield et al. (2003).

14.3.1 Data Collection

Because of its importance for the contributions of numerous worldwide scientific publications that can be used to perform the systematic literature review, Scopus-Elsevier was selected for the first phase of data collecting.

Review the Situation: A rigid, predetermined scheme was followed in order to identify and extract the articles from the database. The search terms used to locate publications were Industry 4.0 and HR 4.0, Industry 4.0 and Smart HR Management, and Industry 4.0 and HRM.

14.3.2 Data Analysis

A search using the first keyword produced 349 publications. After that, papers that satisfied the enumerated inclusion and exclusion criteria were vetted, yielding 110 publications.

Inclusion standards.

1. Research reports released between 2010 and 2020.
2. English is the language of publication.
3. An article is a type of publication.
4. Journal publications only.
5. Research directly connected to HRM and Industry 4.0.

Exclusion standards.

1. Conference proceedings, monographs, book chapters, book reviews, theses, and project reports were excluded since refereed journal articles represent highly influential state-of-the-art research output (Chan and Ngai, 2011; Podsakoff et al., 2005).

2. Multiple search results were returned.
3. Books with only the abstracts offered.
4. Pieces that discuss Industry 4.0 without specifically mentioning HRM.

An essential component of a systematic literature review is the quality of the examined material as it depends just on a limited number of literary works (Yang et al., 2021). Originally chosen from the search, 110 full-text articles were therefore closely reviewed to ascertain their quality and eligibility. The review includes only first-rate journal papers from respectable publishers with usually referenced references. Five more studies that regularly featured in the references list of the chosen papers enlarged the set. The last sample produced 39 papers. Every article's goals and conclusions were developed and stored in an outline form within Microsoft Excel for review. The university totally sponsored the study. Derived from Moher et al. (2009), the flowchart outlining the many phases of the systematic literature review displays the suggested reporting items for meta-analysis methods and systematic reviews.

14.3.3 Descriptive Research

This section presents the articles' descriptive analysis. It focuses on the studied articles' chronological distribution. The figure illustrates how, following 2017, Industry 4.0 and HRM perspectives gained traction, with the bulk of research having been finished in the last 2 years. This indicates how interested the researchers are becoming in the topic. The statistics are still insufficient because this investigation was done in the middle of 2020.

14.3.4 Research Methodology

The study's methodology was reviewed in light of conceptual and empirical research. It shows that the bulk of investigations (72%) were empirical rather than conceptual (28%). This suggests further conceptual investigation in this area.

14.3.5 Research Approach

This category attempts to investigate the methodologies—qualitative or quantitative—applied in the articles that are being reviewed. With 51% of the research being quantitative and 49% being qualitative, it demonstrates a fairly similar distribution of techniques. This result may point to regions that both techniques should investigate in the future.

14.3.6 Approaches to Research

This category's goal is to verify the research techniques used in the papers under examination. It shows that over 33% of the papers used surveys as their main methodology, with literature reviews (26%) and interviews (23%) and case studies (18%) coming in second and third, respectively. It is imperative to underscore that no research was carried out that employed focus groups, simulation, programming, or other innovative approaches.

14.3.7 Information and Analysis

Several literature studies have identified that in the manufacturing ecosystem of Industry 4.0, staff needs to be trained along with strategic workforce planning considering organizational goals and policies, designing hiring plans for skilled candidates in new positions as well as updating existing positions with new techniques while monitoring compliance, regulation, and security related issues (Liboni et al., 2019). The formulation and implementation of HR strategy will significantly affect the deployment of Industry 4.0. This section gives, therefore, an in-depth analysis of the success factors of HR supported by a framework that may help ensure that Industry 4.0 is well implemented.

14.4 SUCCESS ELEMENTS IN HR

These come out as the most widely accepted HR success factors in the literature. Work plan. Some literature contributors argue that through new task executions of robots and mechanical arms, companies would be forced to design new employment and abolish old ones due to digitization and automation caused by the fourth industrial revolution. Various literature studies allude to the fact that low-skilled redundant professions are increasingly being replaced by more highly skilled complex jobs. Some of these include works by Benesova and Tupa (2017); Fareri et al. (2020); Grencikova and Vojtovic (2017); Kazancoglu and Ozkan-Ozen (2018); Liboni et al. (2019); Pejic-Bach et al. (2020); Schneider (2018); Shaw and Varghese (2018); Sony and Naik (2020). Various researche studies such as Kazancoglu and Ozkan-Ozen (2018), Kulyk and Parmova (2017), Gupta et al. (2024), Whysall et al. (2019) suggested that there will be a lot of DE jobbing, the emergence of several new professions, all of which will surely need to change the workforce to acquire new professional skills and competencies. Other authors also announced new positions and jobs that would arise due to digitalization and automation. The authors highlighted that professions should be structured in a manner to allow flexible allocation of tasks across different industries, significant job rotation, and distribution of power and responsibility. Clearly outlining criteria encompassing the information, abilities, behaviour, and attitude needed for the role is also essential as they motivate among colleagues' collaboration and teamwork (Cimini et al., 2020). Among the job duties and obligations are the amount of work to be done, the degree of autonomy, and control over tasks (Cimini et al., 2020; Wilkesmann and Wilkesmann, 2018). These elements have encouraged some authors—Llinas and Abad (2019); Sony and Naik (2020)—to suggest that companies make conscious new hires in accordance with the principles of Industry 4.0. According to Pejic-Bach et al. (2020), it is important to be "fully aware of the knowledge and skills needed to perform business tasks in rapidly changing times". According to the body of research, highly intelligent and skilled personnel will be required to understand the sophisticated and complicated technologies of Industry 4.0 (Bag and Pretorius, 2020; Grencikova and Vojtovic, 2017; Hasan et al., 2020; Johansson et al., 2020; Liboni et al., 2019; Nwaiwu et al., 2020). It is also underlined that in the case the need came to cover present roles in the fourth industrial revolution, the HR managers would need to use more strategic and inventive hiring techniques. The studies indeed have shown how critical it will be for educational institutions to provide the professional competencies necessary to facilitate the transition, and that organizations need to combine efforts and act rapidly with governments and educational institutions among others to develop curriculum for the 21st century that will better prepare those students entering the workforce to meet the demand of skills in the future.

Training: The best practice for solving historical problems concerning Industry 4.0, according to the literature review, is to train employees. Firms should guarantee that their working staff have the abilities and competencies that would enable them to go hand in hand with advanced technologies. A review of the literature suggests that development of any successful Industry 4.0 strategy will have to consider an assessment of any skills gap, employee retraining, and upskilling (Alba and Stucki, 2019; Benesova and Tupa, 2017; Nwaiwu et al., 2020; Shamim et al., 2017; Shaw and Varghese, 2018; Whysall et al., 2019). Furthermore, it was identified that for the shift towards training for change, as well as the exploitation of the advantages of Industry 4.0, training programs need to focus on teaching technical skills and soft skills including knowledge, social skills, attitude, adaptability, acceptance of technology, and teamwork.

Until now, Grencikova and Vojtovic (2017); Bokrantz et al. (2020); Fantini et al. (2020); Hasan et al. (2020); Johansson et al. (2020) and Liboni have done the same. That other authors came to the same conclusion is not surprising at all. Research from Bag and Pretorius (2020); Sony and Naik (2020), and Li et al. (2020) did further reveal the benefits that might occur for companies due to training programmes.

Other authors found this to be no surprise. For example, Li et al. (2020). The results of their study indicate that the application of competencies and capabilities can influence organizational structure to guarantee service excellence, as well as contribute to sustainable manufacturing. Several authors have established that the adoption of Industry 4.0 also demands certain skills and competencies (Cimini et al., 2020; Jerman et al., 2020; Li et al., 2020).

Development: Apart from training, which is the most important factor for success, several writers emphasized the vital significance of training plans and capable leadership. In the context of the Industry 4.0 paradigm, methodologies, opportunities for individual development, an efficient learning and innovation environment, and efficient communication are crucial (Alba and Stucki, 2019; Kulyk and Parmova, 2017; Shamim et al., 2017). The authors argued that a greater need exists for more varied personnel management strategies that prioritize internal development over external hiring in light of Industry 4.0's skills gap. The results of Whysall et al. (2019) indicate that if talent is scarce or if employees' expectations of rapid career advancement are not fulfilled, companies risk losing them. As a result, in order to encourage employees' loyalty and dedication to the firm, it is essential to evaluate them, help them grow in their knowledge, skills, and talents, give them opportunities, and create career routes for them.

Compensation: The ability of the business to offer incredibly competitive pay may play a role in drawing in suitable candidates. Shamim et al. (2017) argue that although this subject has not received enough attention in the literature, pay in Industry 4.0 must consider employees' contributions to the company. The author also discussed how profit-sharing, prizes, and performance-based pay can support the development of an atmosphere that is favourable to innovation, education, and the growth of knowledge.

Performance Evaluation: After reviewing the literature, a total of one study concluded that performance appraisal is a success factor in the Industry 4.0 paradigm. According to the authors of the report, the main focus of the performance evaluation system should be staff development. On the basis of regular feedback, this method will work properly. Management by the objective performance appraisal approach is the most suitable for Industry 4.0 to evaluate individual performance.

Conditions at Work and Safety: The welfare and security of workers may be significantly impacted by smart factories' self-organized multiagent work system, speedier decision-making, and innovative production procedures (Pejic-Bach et al., 2020). Therefore, it is essential to provide sufficient and appropriate working circumstances in order to guarantee the effectiveness and security of employees. As many writers have pointed out (Cocca et al., 2018; Tutak et al., 2020), safe working conditions are critical for volume production and reducing potential threats from swiftly moving machinery, trucks, and equipment. Fantini et al. (2020) and Park and Huh (2018) observed in their investigations that specific worker scenarios may involve the requirement for safety because of advanced age, a permanent or temporary handicap, stress, or tiredness.

HRM Best Practices: The welfare and security of workers may be significantly impacted by smart factories' self-organized multiagent work system, speedier decision-making, and innovative production procedures (Pejic-Bach et al., 2020) (Sivathanu and Pillai, 2018). Therefore, it is essential to provide sufficient and appropriate working circumstances in order to guarantee the effectiveness and security of employees. As numerous authors have noted (Cocca et al., 2018; Tutak et al., 2020), safe conditions are indispensable in cases of volume production, together with minimizing the potential risks related to fast-moving machinery, trucks, and equipment. Fantini et al. (2020) and Park and Huh (2018) noted during their studies that certain worker cases might include a need for safety due to advanced age, permanent or temporary handicap, stress, or fatigue.

14.5 THE HR FRAMEWORK FOR INDUSTRY 4.0

In the fourth industrial revolution, businesses need to reconsider how they produce value and how they handle employment. The HR department strives to broaden the purview of its mission. There are significant consequences for HR. New approaches to HR management must be developed. Based on the literature review, the ensuing Industry 4.0 HR framework has been developed for the successful application of Industry 4.0. Dhanpat et al. (2020); weariness, stress, or a permanent or temporary incapacity.

14.6 DISCUSSION, RAMIFICATIONS, AND A VERDICT

If the face of Industry 4.0 is at an ever-increasing pace, following how businesses have to adapt and deliver during the shift is important. Industry 4.0 has also cast tremendous managerial challenges. If HR workers want to succeed in the Industry 4.0 era, they need to whet their intellect. They will, therefore, need to innovatively alter continuously, grow, identify the barriers and talent shortages, and reshape outdated HR procedures to meet these radical changes that Industry 4.0 will come with.

The HRM strategies will be at response and shall change due to the effects of Industry 4.0 upon the workplace and tasks. The HR policies must be in line with the organization goals and policies. Generally speaking, jobs will be less physically demanding and more about process control and supervision. Workers will no longer be bound to a specific type of employment. They are supposed to share the space with intelligent robots. Data and information will be the commodities. Thus, training, upskilling, and continuous learning would be necessitated so that the skill sets pertinent to Industry 4.0 are created. The overall findings of the study support the notion of HR assuming a strategic role as Industry 4.0 progresses. In fact, good human resource practices will prove to be a game changer for organizations with so many opportunities availed to them. It would be able to offer customized products through agile, automated processes and a flexible, anticipatory supply chain. Increased productivity, profitability, and efficiency of the organization; lower labour costs; time, inventory, and maintenance; and new-value-added services created-for companies would provide a differentiator.

Businesses will compete for early-mover advantage in Industry 4.0 in order to be top of their rivals competing in the manufacturing industries of the globe due to the fast obsolescence of products and technology. Secondly, the rate at which changes are happening is increasing and this obligates further research to develop Industry 4.0 human resource strategies. This is because of the fact that the mission of Industry 4.0 has been funded by governments of many different nations.

14.7 LIMITATIONS

An exploratory strategy necessitating quantitative validation is one of the study's shortcomings. The review is only based on articles extracted from the Scopus scholarly database. Further research can make use of articles from other major databases, such as Science Direct and Web of Science, amongst others. The factors found in the future can also be further discussed and validated statistically through questionnaires and interviews across numerous sectors and countries.

14.8 FUTURE DIRECTIONS IN INDUSTRY 4.0 AND HR

HR departments are changing to fit fresh possibilities and challenges as Industry 4.0 technologies transform the corporate scene. In this environment, emerging HR trends point to a change towards data-driven decision-making, automation, and the integration of new technologies such AI and predictive analytics (Figure 14.3). These developments are altering how companies handle labour engagement, personnel management, and guarantees of ongoing education.

14.8.1 Emerging HR Patterns within Industry 4.0's Context

Several important HR developments are being driven by the acceptance of Industry 4.0 technologies like robots, the Internet of Things, and AI. Rising digital HR systems that use AI to simplify hiring, training, and staff engagement procedures represent one notable trend Kumar et al. (2023). These systems let HR managers make better decisions by giving real-time access to staff productivity.

In the age of digital change, personnel flexibility is also increasingly crucial. HR is more important in developing policies that accommodate a flexible, tech-enabled workforce as remote work and digital collaboration tools are growing more common. Organizations need constant learning to be competitive; hence, HR's involvement in reskilling and upskilling staff to match new technology needs is equally vital.

14.8.2 Forecasting HR Analytics

Predictive HR analytics is among the most important developments in HR for Industry 4.0. Using data analysis, this method forecasts future developments in organizational demands, employee performance, and talent management. Predictive analytics may assist HR managers project talent shortages, spot workers who could be departing, and evaluate the success of different training initiatives by examining past performance. This helps companies to proactively solve any problems before they develop, therefore guaranteeing a more adaptable workforce approach.

14.8.3 AI in Talent Management

By automating menial chores such applicant sourcing, interview scheduling, and resume screening, AI is transforming talent management. By rapidly evaluating candidate credentials and matching them to job criteria, AI-powered recruiting solutions help to minimize the time and prejudice inherent in hiring choices. Beyond hiring, AI is improving performance management by means of constant analysis of employee behaviour and real-time feedback. By means of tailored career development paths and high-potential employee identification, AI-driven solutions assist HR departments in increasing retention and employee happiness.

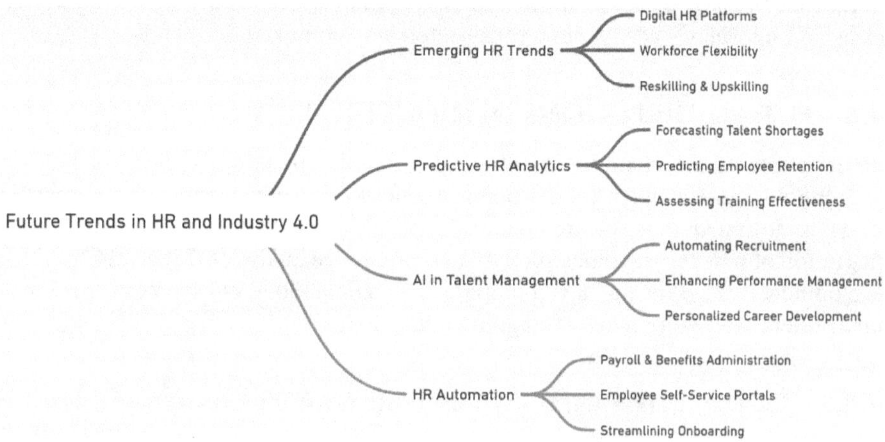

FIGURE 14.3 Future trends in HR & Industry 4.0.

14.8.4 Automation for HR

By enabling HR professionals to concentrate on more strategic projects, HR automation is changing the way basic administrative chores are completed. Automated processes for payroll management, benefits administration, and employee onboarding help to increase efficiency and lower human error. Employee self-service portals—where employees may handle their own responsibilities, like updating personal information or requesting leaves—also fall under automation. Reducing manual procedures helps HR automation to enable quicker and more accurate HR operations, therefore freeing HR staff to devote more time to important tasks such organizational planning and people development.

Ultimately, with predictive analytics, AI, and automation fundamental, the future of HR in Industry 4.0 is defined by a movement towards technologically driven initiatives. HR departments will be front and first in making sure companies not only embrace new technology but also create a workforce fit for the digital era as these trends develop.

REFERENCES

Agarwal, S., Gupta, D., and Gupta, M. (2023). Techno pedagogical concept with digital skills. In M. S. Manna, B. Balusamy, K. Sood, N. Chilamkurti, & I. R. George (Eds.), *Edutech Enabled Teaching*, Chapman and Hall/CRC, Chapman and Hall/CRC, Boca Raton, FL, pp. 129–152.

Alba, J.M.D., and Stucki, V. (2019). Enhancing youth employability: a public private development partnership model to acquire industrial skills. *International Journal of Economics and Business Research* 17(1): 1–17.

Bag, S., and Pretorius, J.H.C. (2020). Relationships between Industry 4.0, sustainable manufacturing and circular economy: proposal of a research framework. *International Journal of Organizational Analysis*. doi:10.1108/IJOA-04–2020–2120

Bajpai, H., Tandon, A., and Sinha, A. (2019). *The Future of Work in the Automotive Sector in India (White Paper)*. India: The Centre for Internet and Society.

Benesova, A., and Tupa, J. (2017). Requirements for education and qualification of people in Industry 4.0. *Procedia Manufacturing* 11: 2195–2202.

Bokrantz, J., Skoogh, A., Berlin, C., et al. (2020). Smart maintenance: an empirically grounded conceptualization. *International Journal of Production Economics* 223(107534): 1–17.

BRICS (2016) Skill Development for Industry 4.0. India: BRICS Business Council.

Calzavara, M., Battini, D., Bogataj, D., et al. (2020). Ageing workforce management in manufacturing systems: state of the art and future research agenda. *International Journal of Production Research* 58(3): 729–747.

Chan, Y.Y., and Ngai, E. (2011). Conceptualising electronic word of mouth activity an input-process-output perspective. *Marketing Intelligence & Planning* 29(5): 488–516.

Cimini, C., Boffelli, A., Lagorio, A., et al. (2020). How do Industry 4.0 technologies influence organisational change? An empirical analysis of. *Journal of Manufacturing Technology Management* 32: 1–27.

Cocca, P., Marciano, F., Rossi, D., et al. (2018). Business software offer for Industry 4.0: the SAP case. *IFAC PapersOnLine* 51(11): 1200–1205.

Cook, D.J., Mulrow, C.D., and Haynes, B. (1997). Systematic reviews: synthesis of best evidence for clinical decisions. *Academia and the Profession* 126(5): 376–380.

Denyer, D., and Tranfield, D. (2009). *Producing a Systematic Review. The Sage Handbook of Organizational Research Methods.*Thousand Oaks, CA: Sage Publications Ltd, pp. 671–689.

Dhanpat, N., Buthelezi, Z.P., Joe, M., et al. (2020). Industry 4.0: the role of human resource professionals. *SA Journal of Human Resource Management* 18: 1–11.

Hasan, M.Z., Mallik, A., and Tsou, J.-C. (2020). Learning method design for engineering students to be prepared for Industry 4.0: a Kaizen approach. *Higher Education, Skills and Work-Based Learning* 10: 2042–3896.

Fantini, P., Pinzone, M., and Taisch, M. (2020). Placing the operator at the centre of Industry 4.0 design: modelling and assessing human activities within cyber-physical systems. *Computers & Industrial Engineering* 139(105058): 1–11.

Fareri, S., Fantoni, G., Chiarello, F., et al. (2020). Estimating Industry 4.0 impact on job profiles and skills using text mining. *Computers in Industry* 118(103222): 1–19.

Grencikova, A., and Vojtovic, S. (2017). Relationship of generations X, Y, Z with new communication technologies. *Problems and Perspectives in Management* 15(2–3): 557–563.

Gupta, M., Gupta, D., & Rai, P. (2024). Exploring the impact of software as a service (SaaS) on human life. *EAI Endorsed Transactions on Internet of Things*, 10. https://doi.org/10.4108/eetiot.4821

Habanik, J., Grencikova, A., and Krajco, K. (2019). *The Impact of New Technology on Sustainable Development.* Inzinerine Ekonomika.

Irudayaraj, J. (2017). *Industry 4.0—A Talent Perspective (Whitepaper).* India: Rinalytics Advisors.

Jerman, A., Bach, M.P., and Aleksic, A. (2020). Transformation towards smart factory system: examining new job profiles and competencies. *Systems Research and Behavioral Science* 37: 388–402.

Johansson, S., Kullstrom, M., and Bjork, J. (2020). Digital productioninnovation projects—the applicability of managerial controls under high levels of complexity and uncertainty. *Journal of Manufacturing Technology Management* 32(3): 772–794.

Kagermann, H., Wahlster, W., and Helbig, J. (2013). Recommendations for implementing the strategic initiative INDUSTRIE 4.0: securing the future of German manufacturing industry. Final report of the Industrie 4.0 Working Group. Acatech – National Academy of Science and Engineering. https://www.acatech.de

Kazancoglu, Y., and Ozkan-Ozen, Y.D. (2018). Analyzing workforce 4.0 in the fourth industrial revolution and proposing a road map from operations management perspective with fuzzy DEMATEL. *Journal of Enterprise Information Management* 31(6): 891–907.

Kiatsuranon, K., and Suwunnamek, O. (2017). Determinants of Thai information and communication technology organization performance: a structural equation model analysis. *Kasetsart Journal of Social Sciences* 40: 1–8.

Kitchenham, B. (2004). Procedures for Performing Systematic Reviews. s.l.: Keele: University Technical Report TR/SE-0401.

Kulyk, V., and Parmova, D.S. (2017). E-business development: the comparative study of the Czech Republic and the Ukraine. *The Central European Journal of Regional Development and Tourism* 9(1): 80–110.

Kumar, V., Gupta, M., & Gaur, S. (2023). Intrusion detection for the internet of things. In: K. Kaushik, S. Dahiya, A. Bhardwaj, & Y. Maleh (Eds.), *Internet of Things and Cyber Physical Systems Security and Forensics* (1st ed., p. 183). CRC Press.

Lasi, H., Fettke, P., Feld, T., et al. (2014). Industry 4.0. *Business & Information Systems Engineering* 6: 239–242.

Li, A.Q., Rich, N., Found, P., et al. (2020). Exploring product–service systems in the digital era: a socio-technical systems perspective. *The TQM Journal* 32(4): 897–913.

Li, D., Berglund, A.F., and Paulin, D. (2019). Current and future Industry 4.0 capabilities for information and knowledge case of two Swedish SMEs. *The International Journal of Advanced Manufacturing Technology* 105: 3951–3963.

Liao, Y., Deschamps, F., Loures Ed, F.R., et al. (2017). Past, present and future of Industry 4.0 a systematic literature review and research agenda proposal. *International Journal of Production Research* 55(12): 3609–3629.

Liboni, L.B., Cezarino, L.O., Jabbour, C.J.C., et al. (2019). Smart industry and the pathways to HRM 4.0: implications for SCM. *Supply Chain Management: An International Journal* 24(1): 124–146.

Llinas, D., and Abad, J. (2019). The role of high-performance people management practices in Industry 4.0: the case of mediumsized Spanish firms. *Intangible Capital* 15(3): 190–207.

Lorenz, M., Rüßmann, M., Strack, R., et al. (2015). Man and Machine in Industry 4.0—How Will Technology Transform the Industrial Workforce Through 2025? https://www.bcg.com/publications/2015/technology-business-transformation-engineered-products-infrastructure-man-machine-industry-4

Miragliotta, G., Sianesi, A., Convertini, E., et al. (2018). Data driven management in Industry 4.0: a method to measure data productivity. *IFAC Papers OnLine* 51(11): 19–24.

Mohelska, H., and Sokolova, M. (2018). Management approaches for 4.0—the organizational culture perspective. *Technological and Economic Development of Economy* 24(6): 2225–2240.

Moher, D., Liberati, A., Tetzlaff, J., et al. (2009). Preferred reporting items for systematic reviews and meta-analyses: the PRISMA statement. *PLoS Medicine* 6(7): 1–6.

Nwaiwu, F., Duduci, M., Chromjakova, F., et al. (2020). Industry 4.0 concepts within the Czech SME manufacturing sector: an empirical assessment of critical success factors. *Business: Theory and Practice* 21(1): 58–70.

Park, S., and Huh, J.H. (2018). Effect of cooperation on manufacturing it project development and test bed for successful Industry 4.0 project: safety management for security. *Processes* 6(88): 1–31.

Pejic-Bach, M., Bertoncel, T., Mesko, M., et al. (2020). Text mining of Industry 4.0 job advertisements. *International Journal of Information Management* 50: 416–431.

Podsakoff, P.M., MacKenzie, S.B., Bachrach, D.G., et al. (2005). The influence of management journals in the 1980s and 1990s. *Strategic Management* 26(5): 473–488.

Schneider, P. (2018). Managerial challenges of Industry 4.0: an empirically backed research agenda for a nascent field. *Review of Managerial Science* 12: 803–848.

Schwab, K. (2016). *The Fourth Industrial Revolution: What It Means, How to Respond*, s.l. Cologny: World EconomicForum.

Shamim, S., Cang, S., Yu, H., et al. (2017). Examining the feasibilitiesof Industry 4.0 for the hospitality sector with the lens of management practice. *Energies* 10(499): 1–19.

Shaw, P., and Varghese, R.M. (2018). Industry 4.0 and future of HR. *Journal of Management* 5(6): 96–103.

Sivathanu, B., and Pillai, R. (2018). Smart HR 4.0—how Industry 4.0 is disrupting HR. *Human Resource Management International Digest* 26: 7–11.

Sony, M., and Naik, S. (2020). Key ingredients for evaluating Industry 4.0 readiness for organizations a literature review. *Benchmarking: An International Journal* 22(7): 2213–2232.

Thoben, K.-D., Wiesner, S., and Wuest, T. (2017). Industrie 4.0 and smart manufacturing—a review of research issues and application examples. *International Journal of Automation Technology* 11(1): 1–13.

Tranfield, D., Denyer, D., and Smart, P. (2003). Towards a methodology for developing evidence-informed management knowledge by means of systematic review. *British Journal of Management* 14: 207–222.

Tutak, M., Brodny, J., and Dobrowolska, M. (2020). Assessment of work conditions in a production enterprise—a case study. *Sustainability* 12(5390): 1–32.

United Nations Industrial Development Organization. (2017). *Industry 4.0: The Opportunities behind the Challenge*. Vienna: United Nations Industrial Development Organization.

Verma, A., Bansal, M., and Verma, J. (2020). Industry 4.0: reshaping the future of HR. *Strategic Direction* 36(5): 9–11.

Whysall, Z., Owtram, M., and Brittain, S. (2019). The new talent management challenges of Industry 4.0. *Journal of Management Development* 38(2): 118–129.

Wilkesmann, M., and Wilkesmann, U. (2018). Industry 4.0—organizing routines or innovations? *VINE Journal of Information and Knowledge Management Systems* 48(2): 238–254.

Wolf, F.M., Shea, J.A., and Albanese, M.A. (2001). Toward setting a research agenda for systematic reviews of evidence of the effects of medical education. *Teaching and Learning in Medicine* 13(1): 53–60.

Yang, L., Zhang, H., Shen, H., et al. (2021). Quality assessment in systematic literature reviews: a software engineering perspective. *Information and Software Technology* 130(1–24): 93–112.

Index

Abad, J. 193, 198
Abraham, M. 99
adaptive learning 33, 34
Adekoya, T. 148
Adeney, R. 97
Adhiatma, A. 7
Afuah, F. 99
Agarwal, S. 99, 193, 194
Aiginger, K. 149
algorithmic bias 98, 149, 150, 159
algorithmic fairness 17–18
  bias mitigation 17
  fairness constraints 18
  transparency and accountability 18
alternate realities 1–2
alternative similarity measures 130–131
applicant experience 10, 12, 14, 16, 19, 21
  candidate engagement 12, 14
  ethical concerns 18
  personalization 10, 16
applicant tracking system (ATS) 165, 166
  AI-powered screening 167
  role in recruitment 166–167
applications of blockchain in HRM 66, 70–71
artificial intelligence (AI) 90, 92, 94, 107, 109–110, 112–113, 147–152, 164–166, 168–169, 171
  adoption in HR 165
  advantages in HRM 111
  AI-powered assessments 112–113
  applications in talent acquisition 166–167
  attendance tracking 117
  automated HR processes 116–117
  automation 109, 110, 116–117
  bias 99
  bias mitigation 186
  and blockchain in HR 47, 49, 56
  candidate sourcing 183
  challenges in implementation 144
  cognitive AI 150
  -driven decision-making 151
    AI and ML models for prediction 151
    cognitive AI for strategic insights 152
  -driven learning 32, 34
  -driven performance assessment 143–144
  -driven PMS 141–145
  -driven recruitment 9, 12–15, 17, 19, 22–25, 100
    advantages: scalability, accuracy, speed 13
    candidate commitment 12
    challenges 9, 11, 17
    ethical considerations 17–19
    future trends 22–26
    human-AI partnership 22
    integration in recruitment strategies 19–21
  in employee training 97
  -enabled HR tools 104
  -enhanced performance metrics 143
  ethical concerns 186–187
  ethical considerations and biases 114
  ethics 101
  in hiring 155
    cultural fit analysis 154
    implicit data analysis 154
    and performance evaluation 102
    predictive hiring 154
  HR interventions 150
  in HRM 98–100, 147–149
    impact on employee engagement 153
    predictive analytics 150
    strategic HR automation 150
  in HR processes 175, 176, 178
  impact on engagement 113
  impact on HR 111
  impact on workforce management 168
  machine learning (ML) 147, 149
  payroll processing 117
  in performance management 141–144
  performance reviews 117
  in performance tracking 113
  -powered metaverse 1–7
    ethical considerations 4
    impact on HR 5–7
    real-world applications 4
  -powered recruiting solutions 202
  -powered recruitment 184
    HR analytics 178
    performance metrics 177
    predictive analytics 177–178
  -powered virtual assistant 154
  predictive analytics 150, 165, 170
  in recruitment 184
  in recruitment and talent acquisition 112
  regulatory compliance 102
  robotic process automation (RPA) 110
  role in
    bias detection 143
    compliance 144
    decision-making 143
    employee engagement 143
    predictive analytics 143
    real-time feedback 142

artificial intelligence (*Cont.*)
talent management 178
workflow automation 144
sentiment analysis 169
and smart contracts 76
in talent management 202–203
technologies in recruitment 12–14, 16–18
chatbots and virtual assistants 14–15
computer vision 14–15
machine learning 13, 16
natural language processing (NLP) 14
predictive analytics 13, 16
training applications 177
in workforce planning 151
ARTXV 72
auditability in blockchain 52, 55
augmented reality (AR) 1, 3, 192
in training 98
automated sourcing 15
AI-powered sourcing platforms 15
identifying passive candidates 15
automation 163, 164, 167
in hiring 49, 50
HR operations 99, 100, 175, 203
impact on
HR functions 89–90, 165
in PMS 140, 144
recruitment processes 184
reducing administrative burden 165
role in talent acquisition 92–93
in smart contracts 65, 68, 77
trends in HR 91–92

background checks, blockchain-based 47–48
badges and rewards 35
balanced scorecard 138
Bardoel, A. 97
Battista, V. 97
Bayerische Motoren Werke (BMW) 3
BCT (Blockchain Technology) and employee retention 72–73
candidate verification 68
cross-border hiring and blockchain 80
cryptographic security 65, 78
behavioral algorithms 4
behavioural anchored rating scale 138
Benade, M. 148
benefits of blockchain in various industries 46
benefits of robotics
cost savings 91–2
efficiency 90–91
error reduction 90
Bennett, M. 149, 159
bias
in AI 98, 99
in recruitment 9, 11, 17–18
AI-generated bias 17
human biases 11
mitigation strategies 18
big computing companies 5
big data
in HR 177
in HRM 99
in performance evaluation 140
big data analysis 192
big data analytics 109, 110
bias in AI hiring algorithms 114
blended workforce management 108
predictive analytics 110
blockchain
applications in HRM 47–56, 65–66
automation benefits 68
decentralization 67, 71
diversity & inclusion 69–71
employee engagement 72–73
industrial relations 74–75
privacy concerns 77–78
-based HR system 58
-based recruitment 67–68
benefits in industries 46–47
challenges in HR management 55–57
compliance with regulations 56–57
decentralized identity verification 47
employment verification 176
future trends 58–60
HR data security 176
in HR transactions 152
immutability and security 50–51
legal implications 56–57
payroll automation 52
performance tracking 53–54
role in HR processes 176
technology 165, 169
applications in HR 169–170
contract management 169–170
employee data security 170
transparency and trust 47, 50
Bokrantz, J. 193, 199
BRICS (2016) 193
business strategy and HR 181

Calzavara, M. 197
candidate assessment 12–13, 16–17
AI-driven interviews 16
AI-powered evaluation 13, 16
predictive hiring 13
resume screening 12
candidate screening 166, 167
AI-driven processes 166–167
candidate tracking systems 175
candidate verification 47, 48
Carroll, B. 150
challenges
in blockchain adoption 55–57
of robotics
adoption in HR 90

high maintenance costs 91
workforce displacement 92–3
chatbots 14–15
automated communication 14
candidate support 14
interview scheduling 14
Chug, J. 6
Cimini, C. 193, 198–199
cloud-based learning management systems (LMS) 32, 34
cloud computing 110, 115, 171, 192
benefits in HRM 111, 115–116
centralized employee data management 115
Compliance in HRM 123–124
Continuous learning 121–122
Cross-breed work models 108
Cybersecurity in HRM 124
data privacy and security 124
health and safety compliance 124
impact on HR practices 171
real-time access 115
whistleblowing and reporting 124
cognitive AI 150
emotional intelligence 154
HR engagement strategies 154
cognitive computing systems 4
collaborative workplace 6
metaverse impact on 6
commerce 2
compensation strategies 199
competency development 138
competency mapping 168
AI-based models 168
competition in gamification 33, 35
compliance
automation benefits 92
legal considerations 93
compliance with data protection laws 56
Constructive Solid Geometry (CSG) 3
continuous feedback systems 142
continuous learning 182, 195
Corporate Social Responsibility (CSR) in HR 103
cost-effectiveness of RPA 90, 92
cotangent similarity measure 131–132
cross-functional collaboration in AI ethics 101
cross-platform compatibility 2
cross-referencing methods 130
cryptographic security in blockchain 46, 50, 57
cultural fit analysis 154
Customer Relationship Management (CRM) 140
customization of training 36
cyber-physical systems 192
cybersecurity
in HR 182
in HRM 98
cybersecurity and HR blockchain applications 55
data accumulation and automation 149
data analytics 164, 165, 167
in HR 178
decision-making 165
data-driven decision-making 114–115, 140, 201
challenges in implementation 120
digital HR tools 119–120
digital transformation in HRM 108
for employee well-being 119–120
importance in workforce management 114
predicting employee turnover 115
skills gap and upskilling 108
workforce analytics 115
data-driven HR 177
data-driven insights 32, 34
data integrity 149
data privacy 18–19
concerns 150
GDPR compliance 19
handling candidate data 19
in HR 99, 101
and security 55–56
transparency in AI decisions 18
data protection laws 102
data security 170
in blockchain 77
in HR 99
data visualization tools 4
decentralization in HRM 67, 71
decentralized feedback systems 54
decentralized HR framework 152
decentralized identity verification 47
decision-making in the metaverse 6
deep learning algorithms 154
DEI (Diversity, Equity, and Inclusion) 186
Deloitte Leadership Academy 36
Deloitte report on robotics adoption 90
Denyer, D. 197
detectors in metaverse 3
Dhanpat, N. 148
digital assets 2
digital clones 4
digital contracts 67, 75
digital HR 163, 165, 166, 168
emerging trends 171
systems 202
transformation 147
digital identity management 47, 57
digital possessions 2
digital tools in PMS 139
digital transformation
in HR 175
in PMS 139–140
dispute resolution using smart contracts 75–76
distributed ledger technology 45
diversity and inclusion 11, 17, 19, 22, 167
in AI 100
AI-driven recruitment 167

diversity and inclusion (*Cont.*)
  fairness in hiring 19
  impact of AI on diversity 17
  recruitment bias 11
diversity, inclusion, and belonging 6
diversity in digital workplace 6
Domino's Pizza Maker Training Game 37
Dutta, S. 154, 159

education providers 2
e-learning
  microlearning 185
  platforms 185
electronic commerce 2
emerging HR trends 201
emotional intelligence 182
employee assistance programs (EAPs) 119, 180
employee authentication 65
employee credentials and verification 50–51
employee database management 169
employee data ethics 101
employee data management 65, 70
employee data security 124
employee engagement 32, 34, 35, 72–73, 113, 119, 153, 164, 165, 168–169, 178, 181
  AI-driven engagement 113
  AI-powered tools 169
  cognitive AI role 153
  digital well-being tools 119
  employee monitoring via IoT 111
  employee performance tracking 113
  ethical considerations in AI 114
  and motivation 195
  predictive interventions 153
  sentiment analysis 153
employee feedback 169
  AI-driven sentiment analysis 169
  systems 142
employee monitoring technology 99
employee motivation 32, 34, 35
employee offboarding 167
  automation in process management 167
employee onboarding 166
  AI-enabled platforms 166
  automation in 90
  RPA applications 90
employee performance
  assessment 98
  tracking 53, 72
employee productivity 6
employee retention 150, 151
employee rights in HR tech 98
employee training and development 31, 32, 34, 36
employment agreements, blockchain-based 75
employment impact
  need for upskilling 92–93
  workforce reduction concerns 92–93
energy consumption in blockchain 82
engagement strategies 195
enterprises in the metaverse 1
entertainment in metaverse 2
ethical AI in hiring 17–19
  AI governance 18
  compliance 19
  explainability 18
  transparency 18
ethical challenges in AI-based PMS 144
ethical considerations 4, 149, 150
ethical HRM practices 99, 101
ethical metaverse 4
ethics
  in AI-driven recruitment 186
  in AI/ML 101
  of automation 91
  of automation in HR 100
  in HRM and blockchain 71
evaluation methods in PMS 138
evolution
  of HR automation 147
  of PMS 138

Fachrunnisa, O. 7
fairness in AI 150
fake resumes prevention 48
Fantini, P. 199
Fareri, S. 193, 198–199
Fermatean Neutrosophic Set (FNS) 129–130
finance and employee verification 152
financial automation 148
fraud reduction in HR processes 47, 48
Fukuda, T. 148, 149, 159
future directions of HR automation 151
  AI-driven decision-making 151
  blockchain 152
  cognitive AI 153
  predictive hiring 154
future of HR in Industry 4.0 203
future trends
  AI-driven HR 93–94
  in AI recruitment 22–26
    AI-driven workforce planning 22
    emerging AI technologies 22
    global recruitment strategies 23
    integration with HR processes 25
  in blockchain and HR 58–60
  in digital HRM 125
    AI-driven recruitment 125
    automation and robotics 125
    remote work management 125
  robotics-human collaboration 94
Fuzzy Sets (FSs) 128
gamification
  application in training 32, 34
  benefits 35

implementation challenges 37
key features 35
serious games in training 35

gamified training methods 32, 34, 35
gaming in metaverse 2
GDPR compliance in HR 124
General Data Protection Regulation (GDPR) 102
governance in digital HRM 123
Grencikova, A. 199
G-Rep 3
Gupta, D. 99, 101

Halteh, J. 97
Hamilton, S. 6
haptic technology 3
Harney, B. 150, 159
Hasan, M. Z. 199
Hawthorne experiment 164
impact on HR management 164
healthcare and blockchain applications 46
healthcare in metaverse 2
Heizmann, K. 148
hiring automation with smart contracts 49–50
hiring in the metaverse 7
hiring process automation 67
Hitt, M. A. 99
Holland, P. 97
Horizon Workrooms 5
HRIS (Human Resource Information System) 175
HRM
best practices 200
challenges in digital adoption 124
Huh, J. H. 200
human-AI collaboration 22–23
AI in HR decision-making 23
balancing automation with human judgment 22
human aspects in metaverse 4
human capital development 138
Human-centric AI (HAI) 4
human decision-making in metaverse 4
human-in-the-loop systems 102
human privacy 4
human resource information system (HRIS) 175
human resources (HR)
analytics 164, 168, 170
role in workforce planning 170
automation 203
benefits 90–91
challenges 91
trends 92–93
and blockchain 47–60
blockchain applications 65–66
and compliance regulations 175
compliance using smart contracts 74
contract management 75
data privacy 77
data security 77, 150
framework for Industry 4.0 200
functions 163–169
transformation through technology 163
implications of metaverse 5
and industrial relations 74–75
interventions 150
leadership strategies 185
process automation 116–117
technology adoption 165, 170
AI integration 165
technology transformation 66
transformation 163, 165
digitalization impact 165
human resource transformation 138
human-robot collaboration 176
hybrid evaluation methods 138
hybrid workforce 181
hybrid work models 108

immersive simulations 35
immersive work environments 6
immutability
in blockchain 46, 50, 53
of blockchain records 65, 68, 77
impact
of digital transformation on HRM 106–108
of Industry 4.0 on HRM 193
of technology on PMS 139–140
inclusion
and diversity in HRM 69–71
in HR technology 100
inclusivity in the metaverse 6
industrial relations and blockchain 74–75
industrial revolution 4.0 165
impact on HR practices 165
Industry 4.0
adoption challenges 193
history and evolution 193
and HRM 106
key definitions 194
industry-specific PMS adaptation 138
information security in HRM 98
Infosys BPM case stusdy
automation impact 89–90
innovation
in HR 175
in HR practices 195
integration challenges of blockchain in HR 56
integration of AI in PMS 141–144
integration of gamification and VR 41
integration of robotics
ease of adoption 90–1
role in talent acquisition 92–93
intelligent automation 147
interactive learning 35

internal mobility strategies 179
Internet of Things (IoT) 164, 166–169, 192
HR applications 168
in HRM 111
tracking employee wellness 111
workplace safety 111
in supply chain management 140
workplace integration 168
interoperability challenges 82
interoperability of metaverse platforms 1
Intuitionistic Fuzzy Set (IFS) 128
Ivanov, S. 98

Jerman, A. 193, 198
job automation 99
Johansson, S. 199

Kagermann, H. 192, 194
Kazancoglu, Y. 193, 198–199
key drivers
of digital transformation 140–141
of HRM transformation 109–110
AI and ML 109
big data analytics 109
cloud computing 110
IoT 111
Key Performance Indicators (KPIs) 139, 143
Khan, R. 97
Kiatsuranon, K. 195
Kim, S. 97
Kitchenham, B. 197
Kostakos, V. 100
Kulyk, V. 199
Kumar, V. 202

labour law compliance 124
leadership and change management 195
learning management systems (LMS) 167
AI-driven training 168
learning needs and technology 32, 34
legal compliance in HR AI 102
legal considerations in AI hiring 186
legal implications of blockchain in HR 56–57
legislation on HR technology 102
liability in AI-driven HR decisions 102
Liao, Y. 197
Li, A. Q. 193, 198–199
Liboni, L. B. 193, 198–199
limitations of blockchain in HR adoption 56
LinkedIn Talent Arrangements 148
Llinas, D. 193, 198
LMS (Learning Management Systems) 175
Lorenz, M. 193
Lufthansa Aviation Training 38

machine learning (ML) 109–110
in HR 176
in HRM 101
in metaverse 4
in PMS 140
in recruitment 13, 16
automated screening 13
candidate ranking 16
performance prediction 16
Malik, A. 98
managing HR data security 55
manual HR processes
automation solutions 90
limitations 89
McKinsey poll on metaverse commerce 2
McKinsey reports on blockchain in HRM 66
measurement of training effectiveness 38
Melnychenko, Y. 98
mental health support tools 119
metaverse
components 1, 3
development activities 3, 4
economy 2
in hiring 7
in HR 5
technologies 4, 5
training and onboarding 7
workplace 6
metrics for performance evaluation 140
microlearning 33, 34, 185
Microsoft 5
Microsoft Language Quality Game 37
Microsoft Mesh 5
Miragliotta, G. 193, 195
mobile applications in HR 170
impact on job search 170
mobile-friendly HR platforms 115
mobile revolution and metaverse 2
model for strategic automation 149
cognitive AI decision support 150
data accumulation and automation layer 149
predictive analytics layer 149
modern methods of PMS 138
modern recruitment strategies 183
Mohelska, H. 193
Moher, D. 197
monetization models 2
monitoring robotics adoption 92–93
monitoring third-party vendors 54
motivation strategies in HR 195
Multiple Criteria Decision-Making (MCDM) 129, 132

Nankervis, A. 98
natural language processing (NLP) 14
job description automation 14
resume parsing 14
Neurosurgical Spine Center 2
Neutrosophic Fermatean Set (NFS) 129–130

Neutrosophic Sets (NS) 128–129
New job roles and competencies 195
non-discriminatory AI practices 98
Non-Fungible Tokens (NFTs) 2, 3
Nurhidayati 7
Nwaiwu, F. 199

objectives of HR robotics 89
Oesterreich and Teuteberg 193, 194
onboarding automation 90, 117
onboarding software 167
  automation in HR processes 167
onboarding strategies 184
online retail 2
operational workflows in metaverse 4
organizational change 185
organizational culture in Industry 4.0 195
Osso VR surgical training 38
Ozkan-Ozen, Y. D. 193, 198–199

Pandya, A. 98
Park, S. 200
Parmova, D. S. 199
Parry, E. 97, 151
payroll automation 52, 90, 117, 175
Pejic-Bach, M. 199, 200
performance analytics 112–113
performance appraisal 168
  AI-powered evaluation tools 168
  systems 138
  using AI 98
performance evaluation 133–134
  in HR 199
performance feedback automation 142
performance improvement strategies 138
performance management systems (PMS) 137–145
performance reviews with blockchain 53
personalized performance evaluation 143
practical learning and VR 35
predictive analytics 13, 16, 150
  AI-driven decision-making 13
  in HRM 110
  in PMS 143
  turnover risk prediction 16
predictive hiring 154
privacy concerns
  in HR blockchain 55
  in HR data 124
  in HR technology 99
  in metaverse 4
process automation 147–149
process optimization in PMS 140
productivity in digital workplaces 6
promotion decision process 133–135
proposition, similarity measure properties 131–132
prosperity analytics 180
protected characteristics and AI bias 98
protection against AI bias 150
psychological appraisal method 138
PwC Metaverse Survey 38
PwC Virtual Park 7

Quick Response (QR) codes 2

Rajvanshi, P. R. 100
real-time feedback 35
  in HRM 98
  and mentoring 142
real-time performance tracking 142
real-world case studies of blockchain in HR 58
recruitment and hiring with blockchain 47–49
recruitment automation 9, 12–15, 17, 92, 99, 148, 184
  AI-powered hiring tools 12
  efficiency improvements 12
  interview automation 14
recruitment process automation 67–68
recruitment strategies 19–21
  AI integration 19
  data-driven hiring 20
  HR technology selection 20
  in Industry 4.0 195
recruitment technology 166–167
  AI-driven screening 166
regulations and HR automation 150
regulatory challenges 81–82
  in blockchain adoption 57
regulatory compliance in HR AI 102
remote collaboration in metaverse 5
remote work and HRM 117–118
  benefits 118
  challenges 118
  reskilling workforce 121–122
  Robotic Process Automation (RPA) 110
remote work management using blockchain 78–80
remote work models 165, impact of COVID-19 165
remote work support 181
remote work technology 99
research methodology for blockchain in HRM 66
reskilling workforce 182
responsible AI implementation 101
retention strategies 170, 178, 195
  with blockchain 72
  HR technology applications 170
risk-free environment in VR training 35
risks in blockchain-based HR systems 55
robotic process automation (RPA) 147–149
  in PMS 140
robotics
  adoption in HR 90–91
  efficiency 90
  in HR 192, 202

role of leadership in HR transitions 195
RPA (Robotic Process Automation) 176

Sadok, H. 98
Samsung *see* Korean electronics company Samsung
scalability
  of blockchain in HR 56
  challenges in blockchain 82
  of cloud-based HRM 115
  of digital PMS 140
  of training methods 32, 34
Scherer, M. 98
Schneider, P. 193, 195, 197
Schwab, K. 194
self-sovereign identity 48, 51
semantic processing 2
similarity computation methods 128–130
Singh, S. 100
skill development 168, 182
  personalized training programs 168
  through PMS 138
skills gap and upskilling 108, 121
Smarandache, Neutrosophic Sets 128
smart contract applications 65–66
  for employment agreements 75
  implementation 66–67
  legal aspects 77
  smart contracts: deployment 66
smart contracts
  automating hiring 49–50
  for HR 152
  payroll processing 52
  performance incentives 54
  stakeholder trust in blockchain HR systems 50
  supply chain applications of blockchain 46, 54
  transparency and compliance 57
smart HR
  management 197
  systems 115
social connection tools in HRM 119
social impact of HR technology 100
social learning platforms 34
social media in metaverse 1
soft skills in HR 182
software programs for metaverse 3
Sokolova, M. 193
Stefano, L. 98
strategic HR automation 149
  cognitive AI and decision support 150
  implementation challenges 150
  machine learning and predictive analytics 150
strategic HR leadership 185
strategic HR management 164, 165
  technology-driven transformation 165
strategic HR transformation 92–93
strategic workforce planning 178, 198
success elements in HR 198–199
succession planning 171, 182
  AI-driven models 171
supply chain optimization through AI 140
survey and feedback tools 178
sustainability of gamification engagement 37
Suwunnamek, O. 195
synthetic equity tokens for employee engagement 73
Szalavetz 194

talent acquisition 166–167, 183
  AI and automation 92–93
  AI-powered tools 166
  for Industry 4.0 195
talent acquisition using AI 112
talent management 164, 165, 170, 178
  AI-driven analytics 170
talent management automation 148
  AI-driven recruitment 148
  bias mitigation 150
  cognitive AI in talent management 150
talent retention strategies 195
tangent similarity measure 130–131
team engagement strategies 181
technical considerations in metaverse 4
technological advancements in PMS 139
technological barriers in gamification and VR 37
technology adoption 163, 165, 171
  role in HR functions 165
technology-driven CSR 103
technology integration in HRM 106–108
technology in workforce management 97
technophobia *vs.* tech-savviness 6
text mining and analytics 4
training
  and learning platforms 121–122
  in metaverse 2, 7
  programs 167, 168
    AI-powered learning 168
  and upskilling 92
Tranfield, D. 197
transparency
  in AI hiring 186
  in blockchain 47, 50, 53
  in HR AI 101
trends in PMS digitalization 139
trust
  in AI-driven HR decisions 99
  in blockchain-based HR systems 50
turnover analysis 178
turnover rates and AI-driven hiring 157
  comparison between traditional and AI-driven hiring 157

United Nations Industrial Development
Organisation 194
upskilling HR professionals 182
upskilling workforce 121–122
importance in HR automation 92–93
upwork and blockchain integration 58
use of AI in HR 175
use of robotics in HR 90–91
user interaction in metaverse 3

value creation in metaverse 2
vendor accountability and blockchain 54
virtual and augmented reality in HR 177
virtual architecture 6
virtual collaboration tools 181
Virtual Money 2
virtual reality in HR training 98
virtual reality (VR) 1–3
application in training 32, 34
benefits 35
implementation challenges 38
integration with gamification 41
virtual show *see* Lil Nas X virtual show
Vojtovic, S. 199
VR headsets 7
Vrontis, D. 97

Walmart training simulations 41
Wang, similarity computation 128–129
Webster, C. 98
well-being in the metaverse 6
well-being programs 180
Whistleblowing policies in HR 124
Wilkesmann M. 199
Wilkesmann, U. 199
Winstanley, D. 99
Wolf, F. M. 197
Woodall, J. 99
workday PMS tools 140
workflow automation in PMS 144
workforce adaptability 195
workforce analytics 114–115, 170, 178
role in HR decision-making 170
workforce automation 109–110, 147
workforce displacement
concerns 92
mitigation through training 92–93
workforce diversity 183
workforce management 164–168
with blockchain 50
digital transformation 165
workforce planning 22, 151, 170, 178
AI-powered insights 170
AI role in future workforce management 22
predictive modeling 22
work–life balance initiatives 119
workplace digital transformation 106–108
workplace equity 6
workplace safety considerations 199–200
workplace safety in metaverse 6
workplace transparency with blockchain 71
World Economic Forum 192

Yang, L. 197

zero-bias AI recruitment 186
zero-error automation in PMS 144
Zielinski's study on blockchain in HR 68
Zvarikova, K. 6